D1296199

SURVIVAL

SURVIVAL

Ita Dimant

Translated by **Teresa Pollin**
and edited by **Martin Dean**

BOSTON
2023

Library of Congress Cataloging-in-Publication Data

Names: Dimant, Ita, author. | Pollin, Teresa, translator. | Dean, Martin, 1962- editor.
Title: Survival / Ita Dimant ; translated by Teresa Pollin and edited by Martin Dean.
Other titles: Moja cząstka życia. English
Description: Boston : Cherry Orchard Books, 2023. | Includes index.
Identifiers: LCCN 2023009326 (print) | LCCN 2023009327 (ebook) | ISBN 9798887192321 (hardback) | ISBN 9798887192338 (paperback) | ISBN 9798887192345 (adobe pdf) | ISBN 9798887192352 (epub)
Subjects: LCSH: Dimant, Ita--Diaries. | Jews--Poland--Diaries. | Holocaust, Jewish (1939-1945)--Poland--Personal narratives. | World War, 1939-1945--Jews--Poland--Sources. | Getto warszawskie (Warsaw, Poland) | Gordonyah--Makabi ha-tsaʻir (Association) | Holocaust survivors--Biography.
Classification: LCC DS135.P63 D5713 2023 (print) | LCC DS135.P63 (ebook) | DDC 940.53/1853841092 [B]--dc23/eng/20230309

LC record available at https://lccn.loc.gov/2023009326
LC ebook record available at https://lccn.loc.gov/2023009327

ISBN 9798887192321 (hardback)
ISBN 9798887192338 (paperback)
ISBN 9798887192345 (adobe pdf)
ISBN 9798887192352 (epub)

Copyright © 2023, Academic Studies Press
All rights reserved.

Book design by Kryon Publishing Services.
Cover design by Ivan Grave.

Published by Cherry Orchard Books, an imprint of Academic Studies Press
1577 Beacon Street
Brookline, MA 02446, USA
press@academicstudiespress.com
www.academicstudiespress.com

Contents

Preface

This manuscript is an edited version of a diary written by my mother, Ita Dimant née Rozencwajg, who also used the surname Miodownik. Her original diary was written (in Polish) from 1939 to 1942 in the Warsaw Ghetto. She had to destroy that diary upon leaving the ghetto for Częstochowa in August 1942. There, she tried to rewrite it in Polish from memory. That document remained in Częstochowa and was later copied by Henryk Brust. In July 1943, Ita was taken for slave labor in Kerstlingerode, Germany, and once there, she wrote a complete diary in Polish covering the events from September 1939 to July 1943. The diaries were translated by Teresa Pollin and edited by Martin Dean. The original diary from Germany and the copy made in handwriting by Henryk Brust are in the permanent collection of the United States Holocaust Memorial Museum (USHMM), Washington, DC. Ita wrote a summary of her diary in 1993, parts of which are included here as well. I added an introduction and an epilogue with an additional chapter on the survival of my father, Symcha Dymant.

The book is published in memory of my mother and father and their numerous family members (Rozencwajgs, Miodowniks, Fajgenbaums, Dymants, and Wislickis), many of whom are mentioned in this publication. I would like to thank Teresa Pollin and Martin Dean respectively for their excellent work translating and editing the diary and this book.

— Jacob Dimant

Introduction

A Story of Courage and Survival

Jacob Dimant

My mother Ita Lea's story starts as early as the eleventh century BCE. One of her ancestors on her father's side was Rabbi Meir ben Yitzchak Nehorai, Sheliach Tzibur (precentor) who was a cantor and the leader of the Jewish community of Worms, Germany and a contemporary or possibly a teacher of RASHI, who praised Rabbi Meir in his writings. Rabbi Meir composed various Piyyutim (religious poems), the best known of which is Akdamut Millin, a Piyyut recited to this day in Ashkenazi synagogues on the first day of the holiday of Shavuot. Tradition connects the Akdamut to the persecution of the Jews during the First Crusade, which started in 1095–1096. The Piyyut was composed in 1095 or 1096 and may have been Rabbi Meir's response to a forced debate he had to conduct with church officials, a debate that he had the courage to win. One of Rabbi Meir's sons was killed by the Crusaders. Tradition has it that Rabbi Meir moved to Lublin, Poland, in 1096, where he may have died shortly thereafter. This portended what was to come for his descendants hundreds of years later.

In 1720, more than six hundred years later, a descendent of Rabbi Meir named Rabbi Baruch ben Meir was born in Eastern Europe. Rabbi Baruch studied with the Baal Shem Tov, the founder of the Hasidim movement. Rabbi Baruch held an important place in the Hasidic world. He was known for his wisdom, and gossip had it that he performed miracles. He became known as the Maggid (an itinerant preacher) of Ryki (a town southeast of Warsaw, now in Poland). He became the first rabbi of Ryki when the Jewish congregation asked him to stay as their rabbi after listening to and being impressed by his sermons. During his service of more than thirty years in

Ryki, he initiated several Jewish welfare agencies, including a free loan fund and societies to care for the sick and provide free hospitality to indigent wayfarers. Rabbi Baruch initiated and supervised the construction of a synagogue that stood in Ryki until it burned down in 1925. Rabbi Baruch died in 1831, at the ripe age of 111. Rabbi Baruch had five daughters, one of whom was an ancestor of my grandfather, Rabbi Jakob Jehuda Rozencwajg, who was born in Ryki in 1887 to Lipa Rozencwajg and Frieda Mald. Rabbi Jakob had two sisters, one of whom remained in Ryki, while the other moved to Wołomin, a town northeast of Warsaw. Both sisters and their families eventually perished in the Holocaust with only a few survivors.

Rabbi Jakob became a Hasidic rabbi at a young age. Upon the death at a young age of the rebbe (grand rabbi) of Skierniewice, in whose court he was learning, he was appointed the Skierniewice Rebbe, being a grand rabbi to a small sect of Hasidim in Poland. Years later, when the young child of the original Rebbe matured and became a rabbi by himself, Rabbi Jakob resigned the position to allow the young son to take over, stating it was the right thing to do, and moved to Piaseczno, then a large center of Jewish life south of Warsaw. Rabbi Itzhak Gerstenkorn, the founder of the town of Bnei Brak in Israel, recalled him fondly in his writings about the house of Hasidim in Skierniewice.

Ita came from the Miodownik family on her mother's side. The Miodownik family roots were in Węgrów and Sokolów, two Polish towns some sixty miles east of Warsaw which had substantial Jewish populations. There, Moshe Reuven Miodownik had a son named Nachman, born in 1856. Nachman Miodownik married Malka Sokolow in 1873. Their children were Menachem-Mendel ("Uncle"), Feiga (Ita's mother), and Yitzchak. Nachman was a farming accountant. He died in 1909, and his grave remains intact in the central Jewish cemetery of Warsaw, which I visited in 2010, the first time a Kaddish was said over that grave in at least seventy years. Malka was also buried in that cemetery, but her grave was not found.

My mother, Ita Lea Rozencwajg was born on the seventh day of the Hebrew month of Iyyar (roughly corresponding to May), probably in 1918 in Piaseczno, Poland, then a small suburb south of Warsaw. She was the second daughter of Feiga Miodownik, Rabbi Jakob's second wife. When Ita was two years old, her mother Feiga and Feiga's two other daughters (then aged six years and six months) died of pneumonia, thought to be due to the final wave of the influenza pandemic of 1918–1920. Ita was Feiga's only survivor, along with her older half-sisters Chaja, Frieda, and Henia, daughters of

Jakob's first wife, also named Feiga Miodownik, who was also a descendent of Moshe Reuven Miodownik. This was her first test of survival.

In 1921, Rabbi Jakob married his third wife, Esther (née Vurshneitzer) and they had three additional children, Shifra-Menucha, Shimon, and the youngest, Yechezkel (b. 1928). Esther could not stand Ita and repeatedly abused her, thus earning the Hebrew nickname "Mechashefa" which means "witch." In the early 1920s, Rabbi Jakob again resigned his position because he felt that another rabbi, later known as the Piaseczno Rebbe, was more qualified for the position. Rabbi Jakob was truly a great man.

The family moved to Jeziorna, a small town a few miles east of Piaseczno, where Rabbi Jakob became the town's rabbi, and was also serving in an official Polish government capacity as the head and registrar of the Jewish community, then a substantial part of the town's population. Ita did have some pleasant memories from Jeziorna. She remembered walking in town behind her father, who was known as the "running rabbi" because he was known to walk briskly, and his family was always trailing far behind him, unable to keep up with his fast pace. She remembered that he was known to help poor families by making rabbinical rulings that helped them. Ita suffered at the hands of her stepmother. From a young age, she found support from her uncle (her mother's brother) Menachem-Mendel Miodownik. When at a young age Ita could no longer live at home with her stepmother, she left home to live with Menachem-Mendel and his wife Lea, who treated her like a daughter.

Menachem-Mendel was a warm and kind man, who integrated Ita into the family like one of his own children. She called him "uncle" and "father" at different times. He was a bookkeeper or accountant and made a modest living. Ita gave up her orthodox Jewish upbringing and went to a Polish school and also participated in Catholic activities at the church with her Polish friends. Ita soon became an integral part of Uncle Menachem-Mendel's family. She became very close with his children. His older son Moshe (Mojżesz) married Bella Rappaport in 1925, and they moved to Palestine but returned for a period thereafter before permanently moving to Palestine. The other children were Malka (also referred to as Dora and Mania), Fryda, Rachel (Rachelka), Sarah (Sarenka), and the youngest, Nachman (b. 1918). While living in Lublin and later Warsaw, Ita learned to speak Polish without a Yiddish accent and learned to recite Catholic prayers. This experience played an important role in her survival, as she was able to pass as a Polish Catholic woman during the German occupation. In the 1930s, Malka was married and moved to Sao Paulo, Brazil, with her husband, Sarah (Sarenka) married Kuba Wrocławski, and Fryda married Chaim Domb.

Ita Rozencwajg with her half-brother Shimon, Warsaw, April 1939. USHMM, Acc. Number: 1998.A.0258.2 (Series 3, Box 2.9, no. 44), courtesy of Jacob Dimant.

Ita Rozencwajg sits outside in the yard with her uncle Menachem-Mendel
Miodownik on a visit to Mińsk Mazowiecki in 1939. USHMMPA, no. 28505,
courtesy of Ita Rozencwajg Dimant.

In the late 1930s, a romance flourished between Nachman and Ita. It is not clear if they were engaged. In 1937, they planned to move to Palestine. However, at that point Uncle Menachem-Mendel needed someone to care for him, as his wife suffered from depression, and Ita decided to stay behind to take care of Uncle Menachem-Mendel and join Nachman, who left for Palestine, later. The two exchanged letters, but Nachman's last letter arrived on August 24, 1939. Mail contact was no longer possible thereafter as the war broke out.

Ita Rozencwajg with Nachman Miodownik walking down a street in Warsaw, 1938. USHMM Archives, Acc. Number: 1998.A.0258.2 (Series 3, Box 2.9, no. 6), courtesy of Jacob Dimant.

Ita was twenty-one years old and was living in Warsaw when the German army invaded. In November 1940, the Warsaw Ghetto was established. From then until August 1942, Ita remained in the ghetto and kept a diary of her daily life and the suffering of the ghetto population. She burned the diary upon leaving the ghetto for Częstochowa in August 1942. In Częstochowa, she received false documents as a Catholic Polish woman named Genowefa Zawatzka and was able to stay outside the ghetto, traveling in Poland for Gordonia (a socialist Jewish organization) and physically witnessing the slow annihilation of some of the Jewish communities around Poland. Back in Częstochowa, she interacted with the ghetto and later witnessed the annihilation of the Jewish community and the liquidation of the ghetto of Częstochowa. While in Częstochowa, she tried to rewrite the diary in the form of a letter to her cousin Malka (Mania), who was living in Brazil. By writing this document, she was risking her life. She later said that as she was witnessing the annihilation of the Warsaw and Częstochowa ghettos, as well as the actual murders and deportations to Treblinka in the other towns she visited, she started thinking that she may be the only Jewish person to survive, which apparently motivated her to persist writing. That diary remained hidden in Henryk (Heniek) Brust's home, where she was able to find shelter, after she was sent for slave labor in Germany. According to Henryk Brust's daughter Ala, he found the diary after the war and because of its poor condition he copied it by hand. His daughter Ala gave me that document in 2010, and it is now part of the permanent collection of the United States Holocaust Memorial Museum in Washington, DC. It was translated into English by Teresa Pollin. This version of the diary is rather disorganized, apparently reflecting her stress and state of mind during her desperate efforts to survive. (The "Brust Diary" is included below as appendix 1.)

While in the underground resistance in Częstochowa, Ita had a fake tooth containing cyanide installed in her mouth. This practice was common among some of the resistance members, who would rather take their own lives than be tortured and killed by the Germans in the effort to force them to disclose other members.[1] In July 1943, Ita was caught by the Gestapo. She was tortured and was close to swallowing her cyanide tooth when, with some help from Henryk Brust, the Gestapo concluded she was not Jewish

---

1   The tooth is now in the permanent collection of the United States Holocaust Memorial Museum.

and decided to send her to perform slave labor in Germany. (The German authorities deported numerous Polish, Ukrainian, and other nationals to Germany during the war to perform slave labor due to the shortage of manpower.) Ita was deported for slave work on the farm of Otto Sauerland in Kerstlingerode, Germany, a town close to Göttingen. She lived and worked on the farm for almost two years until her liberation by the United States Army on April 15, 1945. While on the farm, she secretly rewrote the diary for the third time, documenting the events in Warsaw and Częstochowa on wax paper used to pack butter or margarine. The diary survived the war, and thereafter she always carried it with her. Unfortunately, over the years, she chose to eliminate some paragraphs depicting personal experiences from her diary. Ita also provided ample oral testimony of the events during the Holocaust to Yad Vashem, in Jerusalem, Israel, Kean University in New Jersey, Steven Spielberg's USC Shoah Foundation, and the United States Holocaust Memorial Museum (USHMM) in Washington, DC. After her death, I donated the original diary, the copy of an older diary made by Mr. Brust, and additional documents to the USHMM in Washington, DC. The original diary is now part of the permanent collection of the USHMM. The diary was translated from Polish to English by Teresa Pollin, a curator who knew my mother and was familiar with her story from other sources, including my mother's multiple testimonies and those of other survivors who are mentioned in the diary.

Ita collaborated with Barbara Engelking of the University of Warsaw to write a book about her life in Polish (based on her diary), which was published in Poland, but she did not want to have it translated into English. In 1993, she wrote a short summary of the diary in English (later translated into Hebrew by Ofra Sarid, the daughter of another Holocaust survivor), but omitted many of the details vividly recalled in the original diary written so close to the actual events.

This book contains the diary as it was translated into English from the original with minor editing and an added introduction, prologue, and parts of the epilogue that Ita wrote in her published 1993 summary, to place the contents of the diary in their proper context. I also added chapters on Ita's life after the Holocaust. The manuscript was then edited by Martin Dean, a historian of the Holocaust, primarily to standardize the layout and adjust the Polish translation to a more idiomatic use of English. I attach a family tree kindly prepared by Marian Alster (the son of Rachelka Miodownik) to explain the relationships among the various family members. It should be noted that Uncle Menachem-Mendel is referred to as "father" or "uncle" in the diary and it is sometimes not clear if Ita is referring to him or to her biological father, Rabbi Jakob Jehuda Rozencwajg. Most of the photographs included in this publication are now in the Photo Archives of the United States Holocaust Memorial Museum.

Prologue

Ita Dimant
(from *A Diary of the Holocaust* published
originally in English and Hebrew in 1993)

My name is Ita Dimant (Rozencwajg). My father Jakob Yehuda Rozencwajg
was the rabbi of Jeziorna, a village next to Warsaw, the capital of Poland.
A few hundred Jewish families lived in this village for many generations. I lived
there with my father, stepmother, four sisters, and two brothers. My mother
died when I was two years old. At the age of seventeen, I left my father's
home and went to live with my uncle (my mother's brother) and his family
in Warsaw. My mother had one more brother, who, like my mother, died
very young. His widow, two daughters and a son lived in Minsk-Mazovieck
(Mińsk Mazowiecki). Uncle Mendel Miodownik was the only uncle left on
my mother's side of the family.

Through all the years I lived in my uncle's home he was like a father to me,
whom I loved and adored enormously. His wife was also a very dear person.
They had four daughters and two sons with whom my relationship became in
time close like sisters and brothers. At that time, only three of his daughters and
one son, my age, were living with my uncle at home. The oldest son, Moshe,
moved to Palestine, and one daughter, Malka, lived in Brazil. In September
of 1939, when the Nazi war began in Poland, my uncle's three daughters—
Fryda, Rachel, and Sara—were already married and lived with their husbands
in different parts of Warsaw. The youngest son, Nachman, went to Palestine
in 1937, and I was then the only person left living at home with my aunt and
uncle. My own three sisters, Chaja, Frieda, and Henia, were then also married.
Chaja was married to Leibel Erdman, and they had a girl, Fajgele. Two of them
lived with their families in Jeziorna, and the other sister (Henia) lived in Lublin.
My fourth sister, Shifra-Menucha, and my two brothers, Yeheskel and Shimon,
lived with my father and their mother. My father had two sisters. One lived with
her husband and seven children in the town of Ryki, and the other sister lived
with her four children in a small town named Wołomin.

Ita Rozencwajg with her half-sister Henia walking down a street in Warsaw, 1938.
USHMMPA, no. 28507, courtesy of Ita Rozencwajg Dimant.

The Diary

The Warsaw Ghetto Years[1]

Early Days

As the German troops were approaching Warsaw, many people left heading east. Rachelka (Miodownik) and her husband Leon, with their family left for the east. But my uncle, Menachem-Mendel did not want to move because he was convinced that he was no more in danger than everyone else who stayed in place; so, Fryda stayed as well. Sara (Sarenka) didn't intend to go, because her husband Kuba was stationed (with the Polish army) in Warsaw and from time to time he was able to phone or even drop by for a few minutes. And as for me? It was natural that I would be wherever Uncle was.

August 24 [1939]—Kuba was mobilized. Sarenka was desperate and shaken. I went to spend the night with her, and she cried long into the night. They've been together just a few months. So, after all—it is really war. What would this war bring us; I had no idea. But I knew one thing—this is the end to correspondence and who knows for how long. In the meantime, it was necessary to fulfill the daily responsibilities. I wanted to be with Sarenka all the time, but I had to go to the bank, and she had to go to the hospital. For her it was better; she was able to control herself among strangers. I acted as if I was a robot; on the 30th I lay in bed. I was done. My heart was beating like crazy. I spent a whole day in bed, looking at the ceiling without a thought in my head.

---

1   The chapter headings were added by Jacob Dimant and were not in the original, which is one continuous text.

Sara (Sarenka) Miodownik and her husband Kuba Wrocławski. USHMM,
Acc. Number: 1998.A.0258.2 (Series 3, Box 2.9, no. 50), courtesy of Jacob Dimant.

Sarenka came in the evening— "let's go to the doctor." "What for? I don't
care about anything ... I feel that everything is over." She started to cry: "Isn't
it enough that they took Kuba away from me? Now you want to get sick? Ita,
let's go to the doctor." We went out. We looked up a few specialists, but everyone was mobilized. The streets were crowded, crushed; excitement filled the
streets. The streetlights were very weak according to the blackout orders. I
returned home. I stopped at the post office, just in case—there was a letter
from Nachman— the last one. Friday, September 1—the first air raids. On
my way to the PKO (Powszczechna Kasa Oszczednosci) Bank I had to take
cover because of the alarms. Many people claimed that these were just trial
alarms. But German bazookas [bombs] were already falling on the ground.
I was very excited. At the train station, I had to run and hide in the trenches;
from there I observed the first air battle. I didn't go. After a few days, people
talked about the rapid advance of the Germans toward Warsaw, and on the
7th hundreds of people started to leave the city to go eastward. Among many
others was our Leon with Rachelka and his sister and the brother of her
husband, Wacek. A group of their friends left with them. Apart from Wacek,
there were a few Poles in this group. (Wacek's brother—Reginka's husband

was in prison as a political prisoner; later he was released and followed her—they reached Nowogródek.) Regina had an injured leg and she was supposed to stay with us, but when she started to say goodbye to Leon, she put her coat on and without any additional luggage she left with him—none of us left because father (Uncle Menachem-Mendel Miodownik) didn't want to move. Chaim (Fryda's husband) was not engaged politically. He volunteered for social causes and he was convinced that he was not more in danger than everyone else who stayed in place, so Fryda stayed as well. Sarenka didn't intend to go, because Kuba was stationed in Warsaw and from time to time he was able to phone or even drop by for a few minutes. And me? It was natural that I would be wherever Uncle would be. Rachelka's leaving was a difficult experience for father. (When one of the children was leaving for an unspecified time—it was a tragedy for father, but he never said "don't go" since this child saw a chance for happiness wherever he/she was going.) On the 8th, Chaim's brother left Warsaw. Is he alive? Did he survive? He lost so many years of life in prison . . . later on the Soviet side he was some kind of regional Commissar—did he manage to escape? Did he go into the Red Army? In the first days in Warsaw, he wanted to volunteer; did he die a cruel death with other Jews?

As the war came closer, buildings were burning and falling like houses of cards, corpses in the streets covered with paper, lack of food. I didn't undress for many long days and nights, sneaking close to walls and then the flashes of explosions, standing as close to the wall as possible. Trying to find something to eat, and later, when the phone didn't function anymore—trying to find out if Sarenka was well. My biological father with the whole family fled to Warsaw in the first days of the war; it was completely unnecessary because over there in the country it was much safer. So, all of them were at Grzybowski Square, staying at the in-laws of my oldest sister. Almost every other day I had to go all this way to bring them something to eat from what I had managed to buy.

We were all so discouraged that one day I couldn't take it anymore and I asked father where his deep faith in God is, without whose volition nothing happens? Where was his faith in a future better life, which should give him courage to face death peacefully? It is me who is supposed to be unsettled and distressed not having the spiritual support as they do. What did he answer—I cannot remember. In any case it was not a satisfactory answer. On the other hand, Uncle was calm and composed and he didn't surrender to panic.

If we had some bread in the first few weeks, it was because my sister Fryda's father-in-law owned a bakery. They baked bread from flour they had in stock, and they distributed it among family and neighbors. Naturally, I had to stand in line for hours like others, but at least I knew that I would not leave empty-handed. But later they stopped baking. Their daughter and grandson were killed, and soon after their bakery was burned down as well as my sister's apartment, which was next door.

The 25th of September [1939] was a tragic day when the bombing lasted from eight in the morning till eight in the evening. The worst was the shrapnel flying all around, and we couldn't know from where it was coming. Chaim (Fryda's husband) was a nuisance—it was impossible to keep him at home; he was constantly on the move. Either he was digging people out from under the rubble or he would go to food distribution points to get bread for refugees from Łódź and other localities or to take the wounded to nursing stations. We were dying of worry, and we couldn't rest until he returned. I remember the evening when one side of our street was on fire; our building gate was full of people and furniture; at the small square opposite there were a few dead, killed by shrapnel. Over one of the dead, knelt a mother with her hair undone and she howled like an animal. I will never forget this. There were other wounded in the street crying for help, but no one paid attention.

Fryda, Chaim, and I slept at the gate and a moment later Chaim wasn't there anymore. He took one of the wounded to the nursing station, but it was overcrowded there so he had to take the wounded someplace else. He walked through empty streets. Shrapnel flew over his head. But he succeeded in placing the wounded man in the next nursing station. He returned when I was already too tired to calm Fryda down. I just held her back from running out into the street when she wanted to go to look for him. She constantly yelled his name—I thought she had lost her mind. He returned and after five minutes he disappeared again with a wounded child in his arms.

By September 29th the Germans had occupied Warsaw. No one from the family was killed, but we knew from the very first day the kind of life that awaited us. What we didn't know was what kind of death awaited us. They entered with music (the loudspeakers were on the trucks). On the first day, they distributed bread on Bonifraterska Street and on Krasiński Square; people were gathering around, and everyone was trying to get some bread. Among the waiting people there were some Jews, but not too many. The Jews were scared of those who were distributing the bread. But when a Jew was recognized by a Pole standing next to him and shown to the German keeping order, he immediately threw the Jew out of the line. The Jews who went to get bread from the Germans either didn't have too much pride or maybe they had children at home who were dying of hunger. We didn't have bread either, but we didn't go. In the first days, Fryda, Chaim, a few others, and I went to Żolibórz (one of the districts of Warsaw) because we heard that we would be able to buy some potatoes. On the way, our boys were caught and forced to bury dead horses. They were tortured. They had to dig the earth with their bare hands while they were being beaten. We left home at 5 a.m. and we returned home late in the evening. We returned with sacks on our backs with some potatoes, which we gathered in the field shown to us by a gendarme only because he didn't think we were Jewish women. We bought some vegetables, and again some teenagers chased us pointing us out to a German and yelling "Jude, Jude" (how did they learn this German word so quickly?). The German stopped us and ordered us to join a group of Poles standing on the road. He proceeded to take away from us all we had and distributed it among the Poles. (I know that these were the bottom-feeders that the rest of society are not responsible for, but still . . .) I stood at the side and waited my turn to open my sack for inspection. I was boiling with anger and fury (in addition, I was very hungry because we had nothing at home to take with us, so the whole day we just ate a few carrots) as well as disdain. When he finally approached me and I opened my sack with contempt, he looked at me and left it all intact. He probably assumed I didn't belong to the group of Jews and that I was a Polish woman. Only because of this we were able to bring home some food—a few pounds of potatoes. But not much good came out of it when you had to divide it between eight people.

My (biological) father with his wife and children (already grown up—my sister was seventeen years old and of the brothers, one was fifteen years old and the other thirteen years old) returned to his village of Jeziorna. On the way, they were caught, and father and my brothers were ordered to clean outhouses. They had to remove feces with their bare hands. Father was ill for some time after that, throwing up constantly.

We were in pursuit of food all the time. Fryda and I went to my father's village, and we bought some potatoes and vegetables from peasants I knew. "Wow, wow, wow—look what happened to the rabbi's daughter," they shook their heads. "Looks just like her mother, but not as pretty; but doesn't look like a Jewess at all. Oy, the mother was some woman, the Rebetzin—she was able to dance and to pray" (It's a peasant proverb—good for dances and rosary. The comparison was a bit strange for a Jewish woman.) "Oh, well, we have to sell her something." From Rachelka, we had just this piece of news that they had reached Mińsk Mazowiecki on September 7th. They spent a night with cousins, changed bandages on her leg, and continued on. Kuba returned home.

The Typhus Epidemic

I went with Sarenka to work in a hospital. Most nurses went east, so there was a tremendous lack of workers in the hospitals (I don't know what the situation was in the Polish hospitals). During the period when there was a shortage of water, we took it from buildings where the sewage system was not damaged, but no matter what, we had to stand in line for hours. The same incidents of throwing Jews out of the line and yelling "Jude, Jude" happened over and over again. People started to take water from the Vistula River, where there were many dead animals. Epidemics of typhoid fever broke out, and there were more and more victims.

The hospitals were full of people sick with typhus. An order was issued to take the sick to the hospital, even though two patients occupied one bed as well as the floor. We didn't want Fryda to be in such a hell, where there was one nurse for fifty patients. We sent our parents to our relatives. We emptied the room of all furniture except the bed and separated the room from the rest of the apartment with white sheets. If the patients in hospitals had such care and such conditions of cleanliness, the death rate would fall to a minimum. We took turns every few hours taking care of her, and when the sanitary commission came to check the conditions, they left Fryda at home. The same day they took a neighbor and five other people from the building. After four weeks, our parents could return home, even though Fryda was still in bed.

I went to the hospital. There wasn't even one empty bed. In some beds, two children lay together. The typhus ward was on two floors. The second floor was dedicated to internal diseases and surgery with the operating room, and the first floor was for infectious diseases. The job in the hospital at Sliska Street gave me great satisfaction, despite being a great deal of work. Here one deals with real life and not with material issues. The sense that I am needed and that the patients need your care bring good feelings, especially since these were children (this was the children's hospital), who were so touchingly helpless and in need of warmth during their illness. Sometimes I had a whole floor, almost a hundred children, some of them very sick, just with the help of two other nurses, or one nurse on call on another ward. My on-call duty lasted twelve hours; during the day there were more student nurses. After such a night, I was so tired, but at the same time so satisfied that all was done properly, nothing was forgotten, and the nurse taking over from me wouldn't find anything wrong with the ward. No doubt all this happened because of Sarenka; she was in charge of the ward and when working under her supervision it was easy to show how excellent you were. She taught me how to give injections, and I was pretty good at that. Not once was there any vein atrophy, which happens often with typhus. After a few weeks, the supervisor put me on the list of paid student nurses. I was aware that I knew very little, so in my free time I took out my anatomy book and Sarenka's notebooks and I studied as much as I could. I know that I could've become a good nurse, because I really liked this work, but because of reasons beyond my control—it did not happen.

In early January 1940, two guides arrived from Bielsko to take Fryda and Chaim. This time they left. By that time, the border was well guarded, so their journey was very difficult, and Fryda almost died. In the end, they happily reached his parents, and soon after Chaim had a job in his profession. Fryda got a job as well. Father again lived through the tragedy of losing a child. On the eve of their departure, he sat dejected and cried . . . And as for me—if I could tear out my heart from my chest while it was still vibrating and give it as a sacrifice, just to save his tears, I would do it with joy . . . but what could I do? I could only stay, even though I received letters from Bilok to come, that they would open their home for me. Even though David wrote and asked me to come to him (he had enrolled at the Lvov Polytechnic, after the Russians captured Lvov; he wanted to do it right after graduation from high school, but the anti-Semitic events at Polish universities didn't allow it; only now was his dream fulfilled and he was happy. He studied agronomy.) Fryda and her husband's departure was for their own good, and we had to accept it. It was just me who remained at home, because Sarenka, after her apartment on Marianska Street burned down, moved in with her in-laws at Nowolipki 44.

Fryda's illness and the daily rise in prices depleted Uncle's savings. Uncle didn't have a job (what could he do?) so only Sarenka's pay helped our finances. Sarenka's pay was small, just two hundred zloty a month, and we had to take into consideration the rising prices and the fact that as time went by, they paid her salary less regularly. Our life here in Warsaw was more or less quiet; even if a gendarme could enter any time he wanted and take the men for forced labor. But the nights were quiet. The news that reached us from small cities and towns was not encouraging. Torture and deportations, confiscations of shops and goods—all these were just rumors. We were so busy trying to overcome daily difficulties that we didn't pay too much attention to this news. At the end of winter Aunt (Lea Miodownik) slipped and broke a leg close to her groin. It was a nasty break, and she was already more than fifty years old. We didn't want to place her in a hospital, and for a large sum of money a surgeon came home to set her leg. Our food supplies were dwindling. Sarenka left her hospital job and started to accept private night duty. She was an excellent nurse, and she was well-known among doctors, so she was recommended a lot. Typhoid fever and typhus were everywhere, so she had plenty of work. I have no idea how it happened that Sarenka and I did not catch typhus. I had to leave the hospital as well, because in order not to spread the epidemics the hospital was "quarantined," which meant that the doctors and the nurses had to live on the premises of the hospital and not go out until the epidemic had ended. I couldn't do it because I had to take care of my aunt, who was incapacitated with her broken leg. Sarenka had to work. Aunt had to be taken care of and I had to take care of the household. So, I took care of Aunt and of everything else, and, in addition, I went to give injections when Sarenka couldn't do it. From time to time, I made some money, which we could use. Money disappeared at an amazing pace, but we managed somehow. Sarenka earned a good salary, and it was OK. We had letters from Dora and news from Palestine through Fryda. Nachman wrote to her, but she was unable to send us his letters; I didn't receive even one. I started to think that he had forgotten me . . . even though they didn't send any letters for his parents from beyond the Bug River either. This fact made me sad, but I was so busy with daily life that I had no time for private feelings. It took three months till Aunt got up from her bed.

During her illness, my sister from Lublin came for a visit. She came because she had received no news from (my biological) father and her grandparents in Piaseczno. At that time, they didn't control so strictly if Jews were traveling by train. They were not questioned in the overcrowded train cars, especially people who didn't look very Semitic. She came to discover that her grandfather had died. Early one morning, he went to fetch water, and a few German soldiers attacked him and beat him up. He fell to the ground and had a stroke. She told us that horrible things were happening in Lublin. Jews were thrown out of their houses; the confiscation of shops and goods, just like everywhere; roundups for forced labor; the cutting of beards— often beards were torn out with the skin—and torturing. My father was left in peace for now and he managed somehow. In the country, everything was cheaper, and it was easier to buy everything.

In the middle of the summer, the typhus epidemic diminished or rather lurked for the time being, and Sarenka had no work. Sarenka and I started to think together what I could do to earn some money. We knew that Uncle suffered because of lack of employment; he wasn't used to this kind of life. He was not very healthy (lungs), but he never allowed himself to stay idle for long periods of time. Rest was necessary for his health, and it was advised by his doctors (he suffered from lung disease before; he was healed, but he still coughed in a frightening manner). Before the war, he had so many responsibilities that he would give up his vacation time to get double pay and now he just sat here idly, and it was difficult for him to accept. He didn't know how to smuggle or trade; he didn't have a shop (I don't think he would be able to keep a shop in these times, when it was necessary to lie and cheat), so what would a man of his stature do in such times? It was difficult to find something that would bring some income. A profession was unimportant because there were no jobs. It happened that I had a private patient, but after two weeks the patient thankfully got better. A few injections every now and then brought a pittance, even if I took from three up to five zloty per injection.

Children in the Ghetto

Destitution started to show in the streets. In every building, a so-called "house committee" was formed to take care of the very poor. The committee imposed a weekly tax on the more affluent residents, and from these funds a weekly stipend was paid to the poorest families. We didn't have as much as other residents in the building; most were wealthy merchant families, but we added our share to the budget for the poor. They wanted father to join this committee, but he wouldn't agree for many reasons: first of all, because we didn't contribute enough to make decisions and in addition, he didn't like such honors. There were no schools for children. People who could afford it would send their small children to nursery school and older children to illegal private lessons. Nursery school meant that a young woman would accept a few children and took care of them for a few hours a day. In some buildings, residents organized a "children's corner" for the poor. The building provided a space, and youth in the building took care of the children while the adults went to work. The young people would take the children for a walk, teach them songs, etc. They would take turns in taking care of the children. The more affluent mothers preferred to send their children to paid nursery schools, but those who did not feel that their children were better than others, sent their children to "children's corner." The youths who took care of the children in these corners did it without pay; these young people were incredible. The parents of these children didn't have any means and had to find some way to earn money for food for their family.

At the end of the summer of 1940, there was a plan to establish a "children's corner" in our building as well. It meant that I went to the building committee and to the "ladies association" with the proposal. They agreed on certain conditions that the five children from our building will attend and the young woman, a refugee from Łódź, who until now took care of the five, would continue working in the "children's corner" as a paid employee. They demanded that I supply the space for which they would pay. Sarenka and I deliberated for a long time and finally we decided that the sum we would receive for using the apartment for the "children's corner" would be small, but in our situation, it would be significant, and we would have to live with this. Uncle was difficult to convince, but we had to win him over because we saw how he lost strength and weight daily. He claimed that he had no appetite while he was not eating, and he thought that we believed him. We knew that he stopped eating, because he believed that he had no right to eat when he did not earn it. We had to find any trick, within reason, to increase our budget, and since the apartment belonged to Uncle, this would be the way for him to have a feeling that he contributed to the family income. He finally gave in, and on September 1, on the first anniversary of the outbreak of the war, the day when millions of Jews and non-Jews were given their death sentence, we opened the "children's corner." The day before, I went to visit my father because he was ill. I knew that after the opening of the nursery I wouldn't have time to see him. It was difficult to get a permit, so I travelled as a "Pole."

For about two weeks the nursery somehow functioned, but then the caretakers gradually stopped coming. They got tired of wiping children's noses and behinds. There were thirteen children under the care of Miss Roza and me. At that time, I finally expressed my opinion. Usually, when I wanted to undertake something for someone dear and close to me, I was able to overcome my natural bashfulness. I notified the building committee and the ladies association that if I were to continue to take care of the children by myself, I would no longer treat it as volunteer work. From this point on this would be a private nursery and each mother who wishes to leave her child under my care would have to pay for it. The seven poor children in the group would continue to be subsidized by the committee—they would pay for their meals only. It was important that all the children would be able to eat the same during the day. The building committee agreed and most of the mothers agreed as well, so almost all the children stayed in my care. (Roza with her five charges stayed as well, and the cleaning woman at first took care just of the five. Later, I had a talk with her that I pay half of her salary, and she needed to work with all the children.)

From that day on I couldn't complain about lack of work. Just the opposite; I was so happy that my work helped in the upkeep of my beloved uncle and aunt and even grandmother; the thought that I was able to sustain myself gave me so much satisfaction and joy that I became tireless. In the morning, I cleaned the room and the hall for the children—it had to be spotless (it was a time of many epidemics, and I was entrusted with more than twenty children for the whole day, so it could never be too clean). The rest of the apartment I cleaned thoroughly every Friday afternoon. Everyday cleaning was left to my aunt, but if I could, I would do it as well. They had time to do it, because I cleaned up, polished the floors in the room and the hall, and cleaned the windows every morning, and this took me a lot of time. At eight o'clock, I walked down to pick up some of the children (if their parents had to go to work). Roza would bring some of the children. Most of the children were from our building or from the neighboring buildings and later from close-by streets. Later, I had to turn down children, as our place was too small. I prepared a program for younger and older children. Later, I even hired a teacher for the older kids. I taught gymnastics, singing, stories, reading, cutting, and free games. Roza helped out, but she had this system of educating children by beating, which I firmly opposed. She wouldn't listen to me, and we had many clashes about this and the ways of educating children. At 2 p.m. the children went home, usually directly from the walk outside, as long as it didn't rain, and they returned at 4 p.m. They stayed till 6:30 p.m. During the lunch break I was cleaning again, but not as thoroughly—just the main room—and shopping for aunt, since I didn't want her to go up and down the stairs; we quickly ate lunch, and again I had to go to fetch some children.

I made many mistakes and often faced difficulties (unfortunately I hadn't studied pedagogy), but I found answers intuitively. I loved this small group of children and some even a lot. Somehow the seven poor children were most likable, even if their clothing was poor and they looked so different from the squeaky-clean children of the merchants. The children were young enough that they could be easily "formed" to develop a spirit of friendship —in those who were seven or eight years old. Others were too young. I formed a cooperative among the older ones, so all the children would have notebooks, pencils, and colored pencils, play dough, etc.; the children from more affluent families brought more supplies and the seven poor children didn't feel that they didn't have what the others had. I always remembered what I felt and what my desires were as a child and what was of interest to me at that time. I was able to become a child during the games with the children and appreciated these charming moments when they could just be children and they didn't have to feel the age difference between us. I can proudly claim that this small group really loved me.

Group portrait of Jewish preschoolers in the kindergarten established by Ita Rozencwajg in the Warsaw Ghetto. USHMMPA, no. 28513, courtesy of Ita Rozencwajg Dimant.

There were difficult moments as well—we didn't have suitable equipment and our room was much too small, and most of all we lacked knowledge about education. I found books about educating children, but it is always different in practice. I read all the stories and fairy tales known to me to better understand how children hear it. All this required time, and I didn't have any. Our domestic issues were of great importance to me, so I slept less. Once a month during a few nights, I washed our sheets and underwear. In the morning a quick wash at the water pump and back to work. The next night the same and again the whole day working with the children. I was tired, of course, but I was able to do it without harming my health, and today . . . at first Kuba and Sarenka would come to help with such big washes. Sarenka and I washed, and Kuba would operate the wringer as well as looking after father. I liked these nights. They passed quickly. Later, I saw that Sarenka started to lose weight, and I started to lie about the date of the wash. I always told her that I would do it a few days later, and when she came, the wash was already on the lines drying. Each time she would stop talking to me for a week and later she would not let me help her when she had washing in her house.

Life in the Ghetto

My days were so filled with activities that I had no time to think about myself, which was a blessing. Sometimes a thought occurred to me—what is happening with Nachman? Does he still remember me? But I had little time to think, even about that. So many things were happening. We already lived in the newly established ghetto. We had to wear armbands. Parts of the walls surrounding the ghetto were completed and the rest were being erected. In our section the ghetto ended at the corner of Franciszkańska and Freta. Bonifraterska up to Muranowska Street was inside as well. The tramways from downtown to Żolibórz crossed the ghetto. The ghetto became more overcrowded and close-together. Jews from small towns and villages in the vicinity of Warsaw were deported into the ghetto; half were murdered on the way. The Germans established a Jewish authority in the ghetto—it consisted of ten members of the Jewish community . . . and the Jewish police. This was comprised of the scum with no moral values—who else would decide to take such a shameful position? It is possible that many of these policemen came from so-called good homes. After they bought a policeman's cap for a few thousand zloty they were protected from roundups for forced labor and deportations to forced-labor camps. The fact that at the same time he became a henchman of his own people's executioners didn't bother him because of his low moral values. As far as I was concerned, he could be a son of kings (if such a thing exists among the Jews), he was scum, worse than criminals. Most of them were coachmen. Someone could say that every nation had such scum in these times. The Polish police might not be any better, and I don't know how the police of other nations under the German occupation behaved, but no matter what—this shame will not be erased by generations. When I think about it, the shame boggles my head and heart. I don't know, but this is how

I think about it, and I knew many who felt and thought the same way, but many of them are gone . . .

These policemen stood guard at the entrances to the ghetto together with German gendarmes; they conducted roundups in the streets for forced labor; they arrested people; they entered people's apartments to search and take those who did not report for forced labor. Men who had a family to support wouldn't report, because he would earn such a pittance that it would not be enough to feed just him. The Jewish Council had to supply a certain number of workers for labor outside the ghetto and the Jewish Council paid them. There were enough young people to release Uncle from this burden, but he had to show a doctor's certificate that he was unable to work physically. If he hadn't had such a certificate, we would have had to pay someone to go in his place. Those who were brought into the ghetto were dropped in so-called "stations," where they slowly died of hunger. People who had some family in Warsaw or were able to bring some money with them, they were able to find a place to live. The streets were filled with beggars—misery, misery, and misery.

The famous artist Michal Znicz was forced into the ghetto—he responded by creating a Cameral Theater and performed himself in theater productions on the same level as the ones shown before the war or now outside the ghetto. In these difficult conditions, the theater was always crowded. The situation was the same in the other theater, in which comedies and operettas were performed. Beforehand there were two Yiddish theaters, and they were always full. "Youth circles" were formed next to the building committees, in which youths from the age of fourteen up could engage in cultural activities. The sanitary committee made sure that the apartments and toilets were clean; they were responsible for the cleanliness of staircases and in cases of infectious disease or an accident—the committee took care of the basic needs of poor families. The most important duties were to make sure that the cashbox of the committee was full and provide help for the deportees [those deported from small towns into the Warsaw Ghetto]. Each of the residents paid their dues weekly, but when there was the need for a larger sum, no one complained. From time to time a building party was organized in one of the apartments. We sold tickets; there was first-class music, and the party lasted the whole night. We made sure that the guests went home with empty pockets. I didn't want to belong to the youth circle because of the workload. I had a lot of work as it was. Whenever a poor person needed an injection, right away they sent for "Miss Miodownik." It didn't even occur to anyone that I wasn't a birth daughter of Uncle. Everyone knew that Miss Miodownik would always do it, either at lunchtime or in the evening. From time to time, I had a paying patient and in such a case someone from the patient's family would come to take me there. (Even my father's family noticed and appreciated the previous "black sheep of that family.")

They didn't want to let me be and said that in such times I couldn't avoid activities for the good of society. They didn't remember that they lived at the cost of their parents, and I had to earn a living all day long, and I had to support my dear ones. Finally, I told myself, yes, I can do it all and I started to work in the Youth Circle. I was honored with the position as a member of the committee for culture and education. It's some joke, when you think about my constantly interrupted education and that my hunger for knowledge was never realized. I always treated people who were studying and people of science with a great deal of respect and I thought of them as better than me. The anti-Semitic events at the university taught me that the value of man is not directly related to his level of education. At the same time, I didn't start to dismiss knowledge itself. Now I was busy arranging new themes for literary evenings—I lost many hours doing it. Since we didn't want to spend any money for a professional attraction, at the end I had to be the one to sing. My days became shorter and shorter, and even my nights didn't give me the time I needed. My daily life was so intensive; I had so many issues to attend to; I had so many obligations to fulfill, but somehow, I did it. I passed the test. This was a real-life exam. Typhus was still in the ghetto. Sarenka slowly returned to work, and everything she earned she brought home.

Our cousins in Milosko sent us food sometimes; it was much cheaper there. We sent them money by postal order—they never wanted this money, but Uncle wouldn't have it any other way; even though these were the children of his only brother, Yitzchak, and he loved them, and they loved him and regarded him as their advisor, since their father was not among the living. Uncle hated to take anything from anyone, even from someone so close to him. He didn't know how to handle money himself; money didn't like him. I had to convince him from the beginning that it was natural that now I work for him and together with Sarenka we do it, because he is unable, for reasons not depending on him, to find work. After all, he worked for all his children for tens of years and later, for me too, so now, he could with a clear conscience live off the work of one of these children. (It took a long time until he accepted this idea.) After all, he loves me like all his children and regards me as one of his children. Together with what I earned, and the packages Fryda sent, we supported the household, eating simply, but not staying hungry. An additional plague we had to suffer was the "steamers." If in one of the buildings there was a case of typhus—not only the apartment in which the sick person lived was disinfected, but also all the residents from the building had to be "steamed." All the bedding from the building was taken to be gassed. One can only imagine in what state it was returned. [In addition, . . .] the gate to the building was locked and guarded by a Jewish or Polish policeman. For a few zloty they pretended not to see if someone came in or out. If they guarded the gate for a few days, a rate was worked out for entrance and exit. To avoid damage from gas to bedding and clothing, a larger sum was paid, and the gate remained open. After the payment, typhus could easily move from one building to another. When the orderly came to check the bedding, he couldn't care less if it was just washed or never washed. They started to pack, basically waiting for the bribe. These "pleasures" returned every few weeks. That's how 1940 passed and 1941 started in the same dark manner. The only breaths of fresh air were the letters from Fryda and Rachelka and their husbands. Our sweet Rachelka gave birth to a son out east in Kołki. My sister from Lublin had a son as well. We received letters from Dora (Malka) from Brazil. On the other side—they received letters from her as well.

At the end of February 1941, my biological father's village was resettled. He managed to go to Pokrówka, to a rich peasant, and in this way, he avoided a two-week quarantine in the St. Zofia hospital at the corner of Żelazna and Nowolipie [before eventually arriving in the Warsaw Ghetto]. All those resettled, before they were allowed into the Warsaw Ghetto, had to undergo "steam" and quarantine (so God forbid they wouldn't bring with them the germs—laughable). [Arriving at the ghetto,] they were eight people: father, stepmother, sister, two brothers, and my oldest sister with her husband and daughter little Fela. Four of them slept in our place and the rest in my sister in-law's place. They came without anything; they had just a few shirts. Luckily Sarenka had more work, so there was more money, and they needed it. Strange how in a moment I forgot all about old injuries from father and I even talked to stepmother. As for the boys—one was seventeen and the other fifteen years old, and sister was twenty years old. The older one had, like his mother, pulmonary illness. He was thin like a stick and dark like a Gypsy, but both boys were very handsome with large, black eyes and eyelashes reaching their cheeks. Many women would be glad to have such attributes. My father was quite well known in his milieu and even famous, so within a month he got an apartment at Nalewki 23—two rooms and a hall—in a building with two courtyards. My sister and her husband went to live with her in-laws at Grzybowska Street, and I took little Fela to live with us. It was an additional duty, but where four people could eat, there will be enough for five as well. Here she could be among children, she could play with them, and she could learn (she was in second grade and very talented), and she would develop properly. When the weather turned warm, we started to take the children to the little garden, created at a square next to the jail at Gęsia Street. I don't know what else was there. It wasn't exactly a square because there were a few trees and a few bushes. Policemen took care of this—they planted grass; made small lanes, a children's playground, and benches. It was called the "police garden," and there was a fee to enter. For my seven poor children I received a discounted rate for entrance, and the rest was paid by the building committee. I just couldn't leave the children at home. There was so much discussion about these seven children until they finally gave some sponsorship, but in reality, I gave the most because if I accepted seven paying children, my income would be much larger. The children presented a show: "The Parade of Fairy Tales" by Julian Tuwim (a Polish Jewish poet and writer of children's literature)—they staged it, sang, and danced. The children did it marvelously—all of them, including the youngest. It was admirable how they performed with intelligence and assurance, before a sizable audience. They all looked so cute . . . such sweet youngsters and later murdered in such an inhumane way.

The Seven Children

I had a reserve budget from which I could take money and use for these seven children. I worked hard to teach the children their parts in the play, and I made all the costumes myself from paper, not knowing what would fit each part. It was supposed to be sort of a demonstration of what I can do, for the mothers of the children, but seeing that the effect was so wonderful. I organized a real show, with tickets—and this way I got funds for my seven kids. I had immense satisfaction from this work. I didn't want the children to repeat the words without understanding, and, indeed, they got into their roles and each one felt the story they were portraying. "Little Red Riding Hood," "Cinderella," the "Seven Dwarfs," etc., will stay in the children's memories forever. The applause and the gifts thrown on the stage for the children were the reward. Whatever there is to say about life in the ghetto, one thing is certain: what was done for the children was incredible. The poorest mother preferred not to eat but sent her children to kindergarten, for which she had to pay, sometimes more and sometimes less.

There were buildings in which "Children's Corners" existed all the time, where small children, who were unable to attend kindergarten, were taken care of. During the summer days, we spent the whole day with the children outside, in the small garden. Mothers would bring lunch there because there wasn't enough time to go home for lunch. At the end of the summer, I finally parted ways with my co-worker. We had to divide the children, naturally; I gave back the children, which were hers from the beginning, and I added a few, so she would have the same income as when she worked with me. She supported her father, with whom she had fled from Łódź in 1939. There is no need to mention that in her view I was a heartless person, and we parted ways in an unfriendly way. Later she changed her mind when I was coming to her apartment to give her father injections. That's how the second year of war ended.

Caring for Family

I had fewer children under my care, but I had the freedom to make my own decisions. I hired our cousin Fela Fajgenbaum. She was a sweet, seventeen-year-old girl, and we worked well together. After the German-Soviet war broke out, we had no news from Bielsko or Rachelka for a long time. A month before this war started, Rachelka went to Fryda with her child for her vacation. After having a baby, she continued to work, and a woman used to come to take care of the baby. When the [German-Soviet] war started she left to reunite with Leon (her husband), who at that time was in Brześć for his ear surgery. Anyway, Rachelka didn't write about it all, and it was unknown whether they met and evacuated deeper into Russia or if they were killed immediately after the German invasion, when Jewish blood flowed in the streets, or if they were deported later to Treblinka—a burial place of almost a million Jews. Fryda, who was with her husband in Bielsko, we never heard from again. The mood at home was awful. Uncle walked around the house like a shadow. He would get up at dawn, then he would sit near the window with a holy book, which he hadn't done for years. He did read books, but secular Yiddish literature, and after the outbreak of the war he read more than me, in Polish, regular books, which I would take out from the library. He kept up with the times and he was young at heart. One could talk to him about any subject, and after the start of the war he treated me as an adult. We often had very personal talks, more than he would with any other of his "children." I told him once that I couldn't believe that after four years of separation, and after two years totally without contact, that Nachman would wait for me; that someone else is with him. He kissed me and said: "Don't worry about it; if that's the way it is, I will have two more children—he will give me a daughter and you will give me a son." He laughed and later he talked it over with me seriously, and I saw how much he understood and felt. And he cried. Every day before I got up, I heard his crying; and it was as if someone would clamp my heart and squeeze.

Life brought new problems all the time. Rumors started that the ghetto borders were again to be moved, and our area would be outside the new limits. After the fall holidays [in 1941] the rumor became a fact. Bonifraterska Street was supposed to be the border, and work started on erecting a wall. From the Twarda Street side, part of the ghetto was cut out as well, so finding an apartment became a very difficult problem. We still had time till December. I needed an apartment, which would enable me to take care of children and that should be in such a place where most of these children lived. In the meantime, my (biological) father contracted typhus. Because of his weak state and a year of poor nutrition, his prospects looked bad. In the first days and weeks of his illness, I visited him every morning before work and in the evening after work. I washed him, changed his sheets, and gave him an injection. I tried to bring them a vegetable. They suffered such misery that my heart went out to them. Sarenka and I had to do something, which we hadn't done up to that time, out of idiocy. We had to sell something. We had all of Fryda and Rachela's possessions and some of the things were quite valuable. Fryda constantly wrote that we should sell all her things, not to keep *shmattes* [rags], while we go hungry. Her father and mother would have nothing of this. I wanted to sell my watch, but Sarenka wouldn't let me. She sold her set of silver spoons and a few other things and from this money I purchased some necessities for my father. Somehow it was understood that of all his children, I was the only one who could take care of him during his illness. My father didn't let anyone get close to him; he behaved like a child in his illness. He wouldn't accept food from anyone, and I was the only one who could talk him into eating a little. I couldn't sit with him all the time. I had other obligations. After each visit I had to change clothes and disinfect my hands—after all I had children under my care. I knew that I shouldn't do it and I should not have contact with people sick with typhus and then go back to the children. But what choice did I have? Not one of the mothers would allow her child to stay home, not even for a day. For the money they paid they could find many places for their children, and if I let the children go for a few days, I would stay without work and without bread. After all we were four (little Fela now lived with her parents at Zamenhof Street). When father's crisis approached, I had to spend more and more time taking care of him. We started to fear for his life. My stepmother got on my nerves by constantly crying and breaking down—action was needed. Sarenka was on-call and only she could give him intravenous injections, but no matter what, we did everything in our power and more to bring him back to life. For seven nights in a row, I didn't even take my clothes off and I returned home during the day just for a few hours, to take care of basics. Fela took care of the children. I battled death for the life of the patient. There wasn't a thing I wouldn't be able to get if the doctor prescribed it. And I tore him away from death. How much I wish I hadn't done it! He would have died in peace, in his own bed, surrounded by his family. If I only knew then what kind of death awaited him—I don't know how he perished—from a bullet without suffering; in Treblinka, tortured, taken there in a cattle car, crammed with two hundred other victims. Whatever death was his share—it was horrible. If I had known then, I would have had enough will to leave him to a blessed death.

Typhus was raging again. There was a sick person in almost every home; no one was taken to the hospital—there was no space. Fela's brother got sick as well. They couldn't pay for a doctor or a nurse. So Sarenka was the doctor and I, after work, ran from Franciszkańska to 76 Leszno Street to give an injection and to be back home by 9 p.m. I had just an hour for it all, and sometimes even less. (We liked this family very much. This cousin—Fela's father—was a very nice and pedantically clean man. They lived in poverty, but their two rooms and kitchen sparkled. Fela's brother supported his whole family after the outbreak of the war: parents, two sisters and a brother—and he was just twenty-six years old.) I had just caught my breath after father's illness, I had to search for an apartment, because it was time to move ... and the oldest sister fell ill with typhus—little Fela's mother. In the first days of her illness, I could come to see her for just a few minutes, because we were moving.

We finally decided to rent a room with a kitchen at 12 Nalewki Street. No one wanted to rent us an apartment and allow me to bring in children during the day. To rent an apartment directly from a landlord would cost a few thousand zloty and we didn't have it. Some of our and Fryda's furniture went to Sarenka and the rest to Aunt's family at Karmelicka Street. In the large room I placed just the daybed and the wardrobe. At night we set up the beds, but in the morning, we had to take them out. I needed to have some space for the children. I showed this space to the mothers of the children, and I left the decision to them. Sometimes I didn't even care if the children would stay or not. The thought that I would have to work with fifteen children in such a small space wasn't attractive. All these mothers lived alone now, as roommates with strangers and their expectations were not too high. All the children continued with me except a few who lived too far away. Now I had to clean the apartment more often, vacuum, and polish. The thought that the conditions for taking care of children were totally inadequate bothered me all the time, regardless of what the parents of the children thought. When I talked to them, they would say: "what can be done, Ms. Ida (that's how they called me) we live in such conditions, and you cannot change it. But we know very well that our children are well taken care of." Yes, they didn't have to worry about that. Despite everything that preoccupied me outside of the work with the children, they were never neglected. My cousin Fela was very helpful to me in this respect. I couldn't decide to pay her a certain amount, which I very well knew wouldn't be enough for her basic needs, so she ate with us, and for other expenses she received a small salary. I always felt that I didn't treat her fairly, and she always told me that I gave her too much and that I should be her "boss." "You work for four people" she used to say, but I didn't tell her everything. I had to take care of my seriously sick sister. Again, I watched over her day and night, without a break, because her state was very serious. Her struggle with death was serious, but this time my effort didn't help—complications in the form of encephalitis made the situation helpless. At the end of the third week of her illness, she died while I held her. She was just thirty-five years old, and she was the gentlest of all the sisters. Her Jewish orthodoxy distanced me from her, but she was my sister and during her illness all such differences were forgotten. She always had a tremendous desire for life, but she wasn't aware that she was dying. A week before her death, she lost consciousness. I cried hard next to her bed—I didn't know at the time how lucky she was to die in her bed. She had her husband with her, her child, her siblings, and her father—and she didn't know what awaited them . . . She didn't see her child dragged to a cattle car, pressed between two hundred others, taken to a death camp, and savagely murdered there. Even her father would not have been able to hold her small hand at that moment because men were murdered separately from women with children.

I cried, not knowing that I should envy her. When my father came, he cried at her bed (unlike Uncle, my father cried very rarely). Little Fela remained, orphaned. I knew very well from my experience what a child's life was like without a mother. After the funeral, I went to Sarenka, and I stayed in bed for eight days. I just couldn't return to the happy-go-lucky atmosphere I would have to share with my small charges and play with them. Fela and Aunt had to take care of them without me. My other sister, living with her father-in-law, the baker, at Muranowska Street, took little Fela with her. Later they had to move as well, when their side of Muranowska was excluded from the ghetto.[2]

Back to Life in the Ghetto

I returned to work and daily life took over. My income grew constantly, but the prices grew faster, and I couldn't keep up. So, what if I earned up to six hundred zloty a month, when one kilo of bread cost fifteen to twenty zloty and one kilo of potatoes cost five zloty. Ration cards supplied us with one hundred grams daily—what was one to do when you were not able to buy more at the official price. Uncle lost a lot of weight and he coughed horribly. He needed milk, butter, sugar, and fruit. He needed good nutrition, but there were weeks when all we could cook was turnip, because my salary couldn't buy more. It was a short period of time, but I just couldn't stand it. Oh, how stupid one could be. If we sold just some of our things, Fryda and Rachelka's things—we could feed Uncle like a king; Aunt could return to health; we could disregard the fact that grandma became senile and maniacal—she wasn't able to eat and became convinced that we won't have enough food— so she carried bread in a small bag hanging on her neck. We all believed that we would survive the war together with our dear ones, so we saved for worse times. When Sarenka and I finally decided to sell all we could, without Uncle's knowledge, we had to wait quite a long time to get a good price.

I had to heat the room—the room in which we slept; every morning we removed the beds, cleaned the room, and opened the window for ventilation. I kept the windows open, so it got very cold, and we had to heat it properly. Coal was very expensive, if one could find it at all. Because of the cold and

---

2 According to Barbara Engelking and Jacek Leociak, *The Warsaw Ghetto: A Guide to the Perished City* (New Haven, CT: Yale University Press, 2009), 93, Muranowska Street was excluded from the ghetto in June 1942.

the blackout order, the children came only for half a day during the winter months. In the afternoon I took care of a child, whose mother worked in a waffle factory. I loved this child very much. She was a six-year-old, very intelligent, little girl, who had a golden heart. Most importantly she wasn't spoiled. Her mother was among the few who upheld the values I instilled in the children during the day. With pleasure, I agreed to give her a few extra hours. The mother offered breakfast and dinner and I accepted, since this way Uncle and Aunt could eat my bread, and I could avoid the constant clashes with Uncle during meals. He was afraid that I wouldn't eat enough, so in the mornings he pretended not to be hungry. All my tricks to make sure that he would eat—lack of appetite, pretending to have stomach ailment, etc., didn't work.

Sarenka had no work. Many nurses returned from the previously Soviet territories. We didn't want her to be constantly with typhus patients. But typhus bypassed her for what was eventually to be a death one hundred times crueler. As for myself, who was constantly in touch with people sick with typhus, and when my father was ill, I was with him all the time, day and night and the same with my sister—no germ got to me. My childhood sickliness was all gone, my strength was inexhaustible—I worked for people I loved.

After returning home at 7 p.m. from my afternoon work with the little girl—often I would go shopping or I would have to go to give an injection or to my father's place. This time it was my brother who had typhus. Or I would have to wash sheets through the night. In small quarters everything got dirty fast. Uncle or Aunt used to say: "Child—for God's sake—the sheets are totally clean." Or, "this tablecloth could last a little longer—you don't have to torture yourself with constant washing." I asked them: "give me some pleasure; when there is so little to put on the table, at least the tablecloth and the silverware should sparkle. This helps me to feel full and when I change bedding often, I need less sleep." The best argument I had was: "do you want typhus to come to us too?" Sometimes I joked that if I wouldn't have work with children, I would be able to earn a living washing bedding. I already had such good qualifications in this area. Work with children required preparation—reading material, stories, talking to the mother of a child about some issue, etc. With time I had more experience, but I still worried about filling every day, every week. My only dream was to keep Uncle and Aunt healthy through this cruel period, and later, when peace would come, to face Nachman and the rest of the children and tell them: "You see, with my own hard work and labor I paid for my place among you. I filled your place taking care of these two dearest people and here they are, healthy and happy that they lived long enough to see you all." This thought injected so much strength and energy into my veins, that no labor was hard enough for me. In addition, I had Sarenka, and Kuba—this silent, but so warm-hearted guy, was becoming more and more dear to them. He was so devoted to Uncle, and he took care of our home. He worked in a metal factory—to avoid roundups for forced labor camps[3]—and his whole salary he used to bring to me or used to buy something and brought it home. He remembered about cigarettes for father, wherever he could, he always thought about us. My heart swelled with joy seeing how these two loved each other.

Aba (Abe) Fajgenbaum, Parczew, c. 1940. Photograph courtesy of Sarah Halabe-Levine, his niece.

---

3   From the summer of 1940 large numbers of Jews from Warsaw were sent away to forced labor camps. Some of these camps continued to exist even after the mass deportations from the Warsaw Ghetto in the summer of 1942.

Pinhas (Piniek) Fajgenbaum, Parczew, c. 1940. Photograph
courtesy of Sarah Halabe-Levine, his niece.

Piniek and Abe

One Saturday at the end of February 1942, I was, as usual, still in bed, when
a young man, Piniek Fajgenbaum, ran in asking about Uncle. He was a relative who lived in Parczew. He was telling his story to Uncle, about how he
had escaped together with his younger brother Abe, from the Gestapo, who
caught their father, Mr. Fajgenbaum. They had a soda water and kvass factory

in Parczew, and they were suppliers to the German military. Recently they had a partnership with a Pole; the factory was actually registered in the Pole's name, but he had no knowledge of how to produce anything. When Jews were not allowed to own businesses anymore, they took this Pole, whom they knew quite well, as a fictitious partner and they paid him off very well. In the second year of the war, this Pole built a house and he in turn made arrangements for the family when they were unable to get a pass to go to Warsaw or Lublin. He (the Pole) worked together with one of the daughters of the owner of the store. The Jewish owners did everything else. Later this Polish man got married, and his new wife opened a restaurant next to the store and made a lot of money. This man visited us once when we still lived at Franciszkańska Street. Soon after that he was arrested for allegedly being a member of the "Green Ribbon" organization before the war.[4] His wife concluded that she could take advantage of "these Jews"—she demanded full partnership and later she removed them from the store completely. She could do it because they didn't have any rights. She started to interfere in the factory—this led to quarrels, and she decided to remove the owners altogether. She claimed that it was their doing that her husband was arrested. She went to Radzyń Podlaski to the Gestapo and denounced the Fajgenbaum father and his two sons for trading in forbidden merchandise, and their fate was sealed. One day the Gestapo came with a few Jewish policemen (these Jewish policemen were deported from Germany and since coming to Parczew, they had eaten at Fajgenbaum's. Now they came to "repay" the good deed) to take them away. The boys (Piniek and Abe) fought with the policemen and managed to escape, but the father—they caught him before he reached the end of the backyard, and they took him to jail in Radzyń. The boys, after many difficulties, reached Łuków, where Abe, the younger one, stayed in the meantime, and the older one, Piniek, came to Warsaw. What was he supposed to do, where was he to stay? He didn't know. He came to us, to ask for advice from Uncle, a relative and an old friend of his parents. Uncle had only one piece of advice (as usual in such cases)—"stay with me. You are used to better conditions, but we will do our best." This was easier said than done. In our conditions, to accommodate two more people, because his brother was to arrive soon, and men in addition, was not so easy. We had divided the kitchen for us before, and to fit two more people in it wasn't such an easy thing to do.

---

4   This is apparently a reference to the "Green Ribbon League" (Liga Zielonej Wstążki), a Polish nationalist organization that boycotted Jewish businesses before World War II.

The two additional people were used to luxuries in life. The whole issue wasn't so simple, but Sarenka and I would never protest in such a case. Whatever Uncle said—he could not do any other way. Now we had to, or rather I had to, (because Sarenka after all didn't live with us), deal with the new problem. A week later Abe, the younger brother, arrived. After long deliberations it was decided that the two brothers would pay one third into our shared household money. We were now six people, so they were one third of the total. We would live our lives just like before, since we cannot afford more, and we would not use more of their money—they would have to adjust to us. If they wanted to use their own money when they are in the city—this would not bother us. As a result, there were now two more people for whom I had to wash sheets, repair clothes, and iron shirts. Aunt had more work in the kitchen, which meant more help from me, and, in addition, every night we had to put up one more bed.

Meanwhile after typhus, my brother contracted tuberculosis. He stayed in bed all the time. Each time I came to visit; my heart broke seeing him. The few cookies, candy, or even fruit, which I brought with me, meant nothing, because what he needed was sun, good air, and better nutrition.

A week before Passover—there were deportations of Jews from Lublin. This is only what resounded off the walls of the Warsaw Ghetto or showed itself as refugees from other ghettos kept coming. The first escapees from Lublin told tales, which made our hair stand on end. One huge massacre, murder, sealed cattle cars with human beings taken into the unknown (later people already knew). My sister with her husband and one-year-old son marched with others from the same street. On the way, my brother-in-law, who loved this child, for whom he had yearned for such a long time, proposed to my sister that they should leave the child with his parents. The parents lived on Szeroka Street, and they were supposed to report for deportation the next day. There were rumors that this was to be the last day of deportations. So, he tried to convince her that maybe the child could be saved. My brother-in-law said: "My poor Henia cried agonizingly, not wanting to part from her child. Please let me have him with me—she begged—whatever will happen to me, the same will happen to him. But I convinced her." On the way, they left the child with his parents, and they, together with his sister and her husband went to the assembly point. That's where they were separated. He, as an able-bodied young man left behind for labor at Lipowa Street, and she went to the cattle cars. The next day his parents had to report to the assembly point and at the last moment they left the child with a neighbor, who was "released" to "Majdanek."[5] They left two thousand young laborers in place and a few women with children, most probably wives and children of the Jewish policemen. This woman, together with my sister's child was deported after a few days from "Majdanek," to the same place where all the rest were taken . . .

In the Warsaw Ghetto, we continued to live. Each had his own daily problems and somehow no one believed that here as well, in the Warsaw Ghetto, where six hundred thousand people were inside,[6] that this tragedy could happen as well. Since nobody believed that this could be the total annihilation of the Jews, that there are no better and worse, those deserving to die and not; it was enough that one was born a Jew, or that his parents were Jews. Those priests, who in cassocks, with armbands showed up in the ghetto, going to church—all for nothing; they were condemned as well. But in the meantime, during this last Passover holiday for hundreds of thousands of Jews, no one knew what awaits us all.

Ita Rozencwajg with her half-sister, Henia, at Henia's wedding in March 1939. USHMM, Acc. Number: 1998.A.0258.2 (Series 3, Box 2.9, no. 52), courtesy of Jacob Dimant.

---

5   Not the infamous Majdanek concentration camp for Poles and Jews. This reference is probably to Majdan Tartarski, a remnant ghetto established in Lublin in April 1942. Some Jews were deported from here to Majdanek.

6   The actual number was four hundred and sixty thousand at its highest point in April 1941, see Engelking and Leociak, *The Warsaw Ghetto: A Guide to the Perished City*, 49.

We prepared the holiday quite nicely. Cousins from Mińsk Mazowiecki sent meat. The Fajgenbaum boys' sister got a pass and came. She brought a lot of food. (Over there the food prices were five times lower than in Warsaw—for example cereal or beans cost thirty-two zloty per kilo and they paid six zloty.) She brought underwear and outer clothing for the boys as well as half of all they owned in gold. The boys asked that during the holiday we should stop the calculations for the festivities and later we could go back to our arrangements. So, it was like it had always been: wine, fish and meat, and traditional eggs—we had enough for everyone. Sarenka and Kuba spent half the holiday with us, and the second half with his parents. I had eight days free of work and except for cleaning up and helping Aunt in the kitchen, I had time to rest. I performed this rest most of the time in bed or stretched out on a daybed with Sarenka, in her place.

Grandmother died just before Passover, no one knew exactly when. She just fell asleep. I was sick and after the children went home, I didn't go as usual to little Fredzia, but I went to bed.

Abe entered to take something from the kitchen and said that grandma looked strange. All was peaceful, so we kept quiet. When Aunt returned from shopping and came to the kitchen, grandmother was already dead. Her death

Ita Rozencwajg with her niece, Fajgele Erdman, Warsaw Ghetto, 1942. USHMM, Acc. Number: 1998.A.0258.2 (Series 3, Box 2.9, no. 42), courtesy of Jacob Dimant.

liberated Aunt and it seems to me that the few months after her mother's death were the best months of her life. Her whole life she was psychologically mistreated and abused by her mother.

New problem: Piniek. About a week after his arrival, his behavior toward me changed, and he stopped behaving like just an indifferent acquaintance. After two weeks, he proposed marriage. It was very unpleasant for me. These issues were far from my mind. I was so completely absorbed with daily work and taking care of parents that even Nachman seemed to be in the fog, so far away, and I tried to imagine someone else next to him. In the moments, when I managed to be objective, I was telling myself that it wouldn't be right to hold it against him. Five years of being apart and more than two years without any contact and . . . But I couldn't decide about my life until I was absolutely certain that he would be the first to part our ways. It's possible that there were moments when my twenty-four years became dominant, but these were just moments, and these disappeared quickly next to my daily obligations. Only in the letters from David (a friend from before the war), who wrote to me constantly, there were elements that—if a stranger read them—he could think that I permitted him to go beyond just friendship. (This had lasted five years already, and I would tell Sarenka: If I'll remain a spinster, it will not be because no one wanted me. Sarenka always answered: "You should reward him for his constant feelings; you will not find a better man and if my brother doesn't wait for you—that would be his loss.") Anyway, his letters reminded me that something called love still existed. But the Piniek issue was becoming difficult and complicated because we were together all the time. I tried to explain calmly that this is impossible, but he was like a volcano, which cannot be stopped. I told him that someone else was in my life and I have not forgotten him yet. I didn't tell him who this person was, because knowing his explosive nature; I didn't want his respectful attitude toward Uncle to change to become more subjective. When he once found a note from David, this reassured him that it was David I meant. He harassed me with his jealousy. His views were totally alien to me and he didn't fit my ideal of a human being at all and not that of a man either (even though he was not ugly). The fact that he had so much money and that he had so much wealth and assets back home didn't make any impression on me. During all the months of his stay in Warsaw, I never allowed even the smallest of gifts from him. He argued with me about it all the time. Even when I let him ask me out to a coffee shop for cake and tea, I always paid for myself, and he was angry for days, but I didn't care. His presence brought disarray into my somewhat structured life.

I couldn't order him to leave, because it was Uncle's business and something I wasn't able to define didn't let me talk to him about it openly. Uncle never interfered in our private issues, even though he probably saw what was going on, but he never let it show. When Piniek and I would sit and talk it over again and again, Uncle would always knock before entering. It was nice of him, but it made me feel guilty, as if I had something to feel ashamed of. I wanted to tell him that he was mistaken, that he can enter the room without knocking on the door, but somehow, I couldn't say it. I befriended his brother easily. He was two years younger than Piniek and two years older than me. He was less impulsive than Piniek. He belonged to the Zionist organization Gordonia. It was a leftist organization, which wanted to rebuild Palestine according to their party line. I didn't know the details. Abe was a good and cordial boy, very talented and helpful too. He often went shopping with me, carrying my basket; at home he helped me with cleaning the house. They were not registered with us, but just in case, they were registered at Nowolipki 24, where their cousins lived (it came in handy later).

Summer 1942 was around the corner. I would spend the whole day in the garden with the children—it was a beautiful June. I found a drawing teacher for the children; I took them to a puppet theater, which was near the

Ita Rozencwajg performs exercises with the children in the kindergarten she established in the Warsaw Ghetto. USHMMPA, no. 26802, courtesy of Ita Rozencwajg Dimant.

garden. Frequently they would make a stage out of a few planks and children from the dance school would show us what they had just learned. In the "Znicz" (torch) theater, they often put on children's plays—and so cultural life, despite everything, flourished in the ghetto. Right next to it—there was misery that could not be described—masses of beggars; hungry children in tattered clothes and every morning there was a corpse of someone lying there, who had died of hunger. In our house conditions improved at that time. There was no need to heat the room and keeping a household for six people was easier from my salary and the money contributed by the boys than one for four people from just my income. The boys didn't disturb me that much anymore. I used the room only when it rained. This was one of the reasons I didn't tell Piniek to move out. It wasn't about me—I wanted Uncle and Aunt to continue eating better, without taking any handouts, so to speak. Even if a shadow of such a thought could come up, my washing and fixing their clothing and giving them a roof over their heads, would settle the score. But such a thought didn't occur to anyone, only Sarenka had a sense of why I didn't cut out this tension between Piniek and myself. She was very angry with me about it. "You think that I wouldn't notice? We managed till now; we will manage from now on as well. We have plenty of things to sell; Kuba still works, etc."

One day Abe started to feel a pain in his side and before we understood what was going on, his appendix burst. He was operated on immediately and just by a miracle he survived. His first word, still half under anesthesia, was: "Ita?" He thought that Sarenka, who took care of him, since she was a nurse, was me. [Oh, Abe, why did we save you? So later you would use cyanide to take your own life, not to let them murder you. You suffered so much before . . .][7]

I had an additional obligation to cook special meals for the recovering Abe and during lunch break I had to run from Nalewki Street to Leszno Street, to the hospital, to visit him and to bring him food. Piniek could have done it as well, but it was easier for me to go up to Abe, without a doctor's pass. Later their mother came. They loved her as much as we loved our father (Uncle). When they talked about her, they had this warm sparkle in their eyes, which each one of us had, talking about our father. This nice attitude warmed me toward them and in addition she replaced me. Abe returned

---

7   This comment was apparently inserted when the diary was reconstructed in 1943.

home in early July. Their father was executed in Radzyń. Their mother told us about it, but she asked that we wouldn't tell the boys due to Abe's illness and because Piniek wouldn't be able to control himself. Their mother said to me: "I am leaving a bit calmer, knowing that our boys are in good hands."

A new plague started: the confiscation of wardrobes with sheets and clothes for unpaid taxes owed from before the war. When people let the wardrobes be taken out, because they had no money, or didn't want to pay—they would seal the apartments and people had no place to live but in the street. The tax office from the Aryan side would do many things just to extract money from the ghetto, before it was too late . . . The landlord of the apartment we lived in was a former merchant, but during the war he was starving. He sent his wife and four children to relatives, and he remained with one son and one daughter in the last room. Of course, he owed taxes and when the tax officials came and couldn't find him or there was nothing to take . . . They overturned everything in our apartment and on these occasions, something always went missing. The people who came to get these things done didn't have high moral values, and by chance these were Poles. At a certain time, our landlord was somehow warned that his case was transferred from the tax office to others and any day they could come to get him (how he found out was beyond me), so one day he disappeared. They couldn't do anything to us, and his daughter pretended that she knew nothing. I was sick in bed when two Polish agents came to pick him up—probably these were Volksdeutsche [ethnic Germans]. Since they didn't find him, they started to bother Uncle with questions about his whereabouts. I have no idea whether Uncle knew or not, but anyway he claimed that he didn't know and that he wasn't responsible for the landlord. But the agents didn't believe him and ordered him to dress up and come downstairs—they arrested him. I tried talking them out of it, but they wouldn't listen. When they were taking Uncle downstairs, I jumped out of bed, put on a coat, and ran after them. One of them stopped me and ordered me to go back. I refused. I wanted to see where they were going to take Uncle. One of them returned and beat me up. I just pressed myself into a corner and let him beat me without uttering a word. I almost didn't feel these blows, all the time hoping that the other one wouldn't disappear with Uncle. When this one finally stopped hitting me, I ran after him. Evidently, they had no right to arrest Uncle, they just wanted to frighten him, so Uncle would reveal where the landlord was hiding. They let him go in the middle of the street. A few days later they came again and this time they took Piniek—again terrible fear, because the boys were in our apartment illegally and they weren't even [registered as] refugees. They lived in fear that they were still wanted. Each one of them was registered under a different name (who would check real personal data?) and not as brothers. The same scenario was repeated with Piniek as before with Father. They let him go at the next street corner. I couldn't get better. A week later—a new event. Our apartment was sealed for some unpaid, pre-war city tax. We were locked out in the street, and dinner, which Aunt was cooking, was completely burnt. After we paid half the debt—one hundred zloty—they let us back into the apartment. These were side "amusements."

The Beginning of the End

It was already the middle of July 1942—an anxious wind blew through the ghetto. People started to say that everybody had to work in so-called "shops" [these were workshops or improvised factories]—in this case it meant workshops: sewing, shoemaking, and any other profession, which were in the ghetto and worked for the German Army. The two biggest companies were Többens and Schultz, which at that time employed many Jewish laborers. Everybody, no exceptions, had to work—those who would not work would be deported. It sounded like "just talk." Somehow it didn't sink in, but sometimes at home they started to say that maybe I should start looking for a position in some "shop," but I just couldn't think about it. All one could earn in a "shop" was less than twenty zloty a week and a bowl of soup a day. I needed eight hundred to one thousand zloty a month and this was just for food, without fat and sugar. How could I think about working in a "shop?" Daily problems totally absorbed me. My father's family suffered great misery; my brother was still in bed looking like a skeleton with eyes huge like the moon—so young, only eighteen years old and he wants to live so much. Each time when I came, he asked me if he would get better. I ran away not to show tears in my eyes. My sister on Muranowska Street—the same misery; there were more than twenty mouths to feed there, which meant a few thousand zloty to satisfy all the stomachs. All their savings were gone, there was nothing left. One of my sister's sons was five years old—he was so thin and pale; she looked awful too. Even though we were on two opposite sides of the world, she had no bitterness in her. She was a very good woman, who always helped others. Now she is the only one of my three older sisters. Little Fela has been sick for weeks, all alone in the apartment at Zamenhof Street.

My brother-in-law spent whole days looking for ways to make some money. I could drop in only for a few minutes and bring her something to eat or fruit—"bring me books, auntie," she asked, "I am so sad here, all alone."

At home things were OK, except those never-ending problems with Piniek. Every few days he promised that he would try to keep his feelings in check and that he would try to live next to me like a friend. This lasted a day or two and he started all over again—begging, reproaches for no one knew what, again explaining and all over again. Finally, I told him to move out, for his and for my benefit—this could not go on. I became a nervous wreck.

Some terrible things started to happen—everyday several dozen people were shot and killed. No one slept quietly at night, one never knew who would be taken that night. During the day a taxi would stop at the entrance to a building and one or two gendarmes would come out and one man behind them—a Jew. They ordered him to walk ahead and killed him with a shot from a revolver. Such events were replicated in many places at the same time. It was dark, terrible, and frightening. It was getting closer to us.

July 20, 1942—At the corner of Nalewki and Franciszkańska a play garden for children from a community school (these had existed for a year) was inaugurated. Grass, a few trees, benches, a swing and even flowers; the occasion was attended by community representatives, teachers—each with his/her class; social workers and police—there was music and singing. Suddenly two uniformed Germans arrived on a motorcycle. They stopped and looked; then they looked at each other and laughed contemptuously— they already knew.

The next day the boys were supposed to move to their cousins at Nowolipki 24. "Will you come to visit us there?" asked Piniek—"if you'll be reasonable, I will" was my answer.

July 21, 1942—the whole ghetto was engulfed in anxiety—there was something in the air, but no one knew exactly what it was. I sent the children home; it was better they should be with their families now; Fela ran quickly to Leszno Street. The evening hours were tense; we couldn't do anything. What is awaiting us? In the evening announcements were pasted on the walls: "On the order of the German authorities, resettlement of the Jewish population to the East commences. They will be safely located; remaining in the ghetto are employees of the Shultz and Többens factories including their wives and children; employees of all workshops performing labor for the German authorities; those employed by the Judenrat with their wives and children up to the age of fourteen, as well as Jewish police with their wives and children. Remaining youths will be gathered and later employed in German workshops. The rest of the population was to report at the given time at the assembly square near the school: at the corner of Dzika and Niska Streets (the so-called *Umschlagplatz*). Deportees are allowed to take twenty-five kilos of luggage and food. Everyone is asked to keep calm and not to disturb the resettlement action. Signed: members of the Jewish Council." What a disgrace.

Wednesday, July 22, 1942—The Chairman of the Jewish Council, Czerniaków, committed suicide. He refused to sign his name on the announcement about the deportations. He knew what it meant. He asked for a few minutes delay, went to his office, and swallowed potassium cyanide. There was one good man among them. But why didn't he tell people what he knew; why did he keep it to himself? We shouldn't judge—maybe he couldn't.

In the early morning hours, the first buildings were blockaded. It was the Jewish police performing this action. At first, they took all the beggars and those who looked like beggars and forced them to the Umschlagplatz. In a few buildings the gates were locked, and trucks were parked out front. Policemen were forcing people onto the trucks—people who were dragged, screaming; trying to get away. Other residents had documents stating that they are employed in workshops or proving that the woman has a husband working in one of the workshops—it didn't work in reverse—if the woman worked it didn't cover the husband. Sarenka and I desperately searched for a placement for Uncle, which would ensure that Aunt is covered. We didn't think about us—they promised that young people would be placed in barracks and employed in workshops. So, the most important thing was to place Uncle. We wanted to find a place for him in one of the workshops but for this it was necessary to own a sewing machine. Only the sewing workshops accepted people, but on condition that they had a sewing machine, or if you knew somebody, or if you bribed with a hefty sum of money. We didn't have either. We lent our sewing machine to one of Aunt's relatives and it was never returned. We started to look frantically for a sewing machine. My father, as a rabbi, was registered as an employee of the Jewish Council. Three buildings were already blocked on Muranowska Street. It wasn't done systematically, and we couldn't know when they would come to a specific building. We were all candidates for deportation. We spent the nights at Sarenka's. We wanted to be all together. Piniek and Abe wanted to go to Nowolipki 24. They were completely lost. Today they tried to get out of Warsaw; they wanted to go to Mińsk or to Otwock. Yesterday it was still possible to get a pass to leave the ghetto, for a few thousand zloty, but today it's impossible. When it still looked possible to arrange, Piniek had asked if I would leave with them. It was enough for me just to give him a look—he knew my answer without asking. I think my answer was the reason for him not trying hard to get the pass. So, they went to Nowolipki 24, and we will be at Nowolipki 44.

Thursday, July 23, 1942—Starting at 5 a.m., we heard the police trucks going to blockade the buildings. Apparently, they have a daily quota of ten thousand people; in the meantime, they were blocking Niska, Wołyńska, and Stawki Streets; the poorest areas of the ghetto and the paupers were deported first.

Today again Sarenka and I spent the whole day searching for a sewing machine and a "shop"; Kuba's father needs a safe place as well. What are possibly available are the private workshops, which try to become suppliers for the German firms, so the workers might be exempted from deportation. In our building, at Nalewki, a branch of the Többens workshop is being organized. We managed to get a sewing machine from the in-laws of Kuba's brother. This brother is on the Aryan side and his wife, a nurse, works at the Umschlagplatz. There are thousands of people there and a few paramedics and nurses were designated to give first aid to those who were injured, fainted, or sick, and take them to the train cars. Others go by themselves to these cattle cars, which will take them to their deaths, but none of them knew about that yet.

We obtained the sewing machine and at that point we had to wait for the approval of the laborers' list—a list on which Uncle was placed. At the same time, we sent a telegram to Mińsk, asking them to try and take Uncle, Aunt, and me from here. But I was undecided what to do in case they would send for us from Mińsk. Many people manage to flee, bribing the sentries at the exit posts from Warsaw. Two days of deportations had passed already.

Friday, July 24, 1942—Sarenka was finally covered by Kuba; he obtained an *Ausweiss* (ID card) for himself and a wife. This gave us an idea to obtain coverage for me in the same way. I have to acquire a fictitious husband. A son of our landlord from Nalewki worked at the Schultz workshop—the best place. He was seventeen years old, but he could be a "husband" and he agreed right away. My father issued a wedding certificate in the morning; he didn't hesitate for a moment after I told him what it was about. Now he was just a father who wanted to save his child. We both forgot all our differences, the emotional abyss, which divided us. All the issues, so important in the past, were shattered in view of the present situation. I had to run to the regional rabbinate with the new wedding certificate to confirm it. My brand new "husband" had to go to his workshop with this piece of paper for them to issue an Ausweiss for a married man.

We had been up since dawn and the streets were filled with people running and trying to find rescue; workshops were besieged by people trying to get employment. Rickshaws hurried in the streets carrying sewing machines and knitting machines. Suddenly a few police trucks appeared and in the blink of an eye the street emptied. No one could guess where the trucks were headed. After an hour or two the trucks returned, but this time they were filled with people. In a moment they would block a street from both sides, and everyone had to show their ID. Those without the Ausweiss were taken away.

That night Uncle spent in a store locked from the outside—at Nowolipki and the corner of Zamenhof. Starting at 5 a.m. people were allowed in the streets, but the blockades started earlier and then any escape was impossible. Uncle and Aunt, with the landlord and a few more people, spent the night in the store and they were still there. We brought them food. We cooked for everyone at Sarenka's. After a few bites for breakfast, Sarenka and I went out and we each went in different directions. She tried to find a work placement for Uncle and her father-in-law, and I went to check if everything was all right with my father and my sister at Muranowska Street. At Muranowska everyone was a candidate for deportation—no one worked there, not the old parents of my brother-in-law, not him, not my sister, and the rest were children below the age of eighteen, grandchildren left as orphans. A young son of my sister said to me when I picked him up for a moment: "Auntie, you need to hide, because the police are catching people and Mommy is crying." But I had to go on. At my father's there was no round-up. My brother-in-law with little Fela was there as well. He was very upset—his parents and siblings were taken from Grzybowska on an early transport. Once again, I asked my father how to take care of my "wedding" issue with the district rabbi and I had to go on. I wanted to go to the store, where we had our ration cards; maybe I would be able to get some bread. On the way I wanted to drop in on our place on Nalewki. After the store on Wałowa Street I returned to Franciszkańska, it was already impossible to reach our side of Nalewki. The buildings numbers 17 to 29 were blocked off and number 23 was where my father lived. I stood at the corner shivering, trying to see if I could notice my father and his family in the passing trucks. But the trucks left in the other direction, toward Nowolipki. I ran to Muranowska, to my sister—impossible to get across, all the streets were blocked. When I returned, the roundup on Nalewki was over. I entered the building at number 23—the apartment was empty, everyone was taken. The rest of the residents of the building were very upset. When they recognized that I was a member of the family, they told me to go to the Umschlagplatz and try to get them out. They told me that many people return, when they were reclaimed as workers for one of the "shops," or for a few thousand zloty, a policeman could take them out through a back exit. They said that the building committee would give the money for the release. They were very shaken by father's deportation. He was their rabbi. They told me that father was actually hidden, but when he heard shots, he came down, because he wanted to be with his children. If they weren't taken to the train today, maybe it would be possible to get them out. I went to the Umschlagplatz, and I saw this huge building, four or five stories high, filled to the brim with people and around the building there was a space, a square—surrounded by a high fence, and filled with people. In the street, from Zamenhof and Niska Street, stood thousands of people—their families were inside. Everyone cried and shouted to the people standing in the windows; the people on the other side shouted something back; it was impossible to hear anything. The high-ranking policeman, who came with me, found out that they were still there. He said that we must wait till the next day. They saw that I was there, and they came to the window. My sister yelled something, all I understood was: "rescue" and my father stood there silent and just looked. Fela shouted, stretching out her little hands: "auntie, auntie—take me away from here." I sent them bread, some sugar, whatever I could. I ran home and returned running. I had to give fifty zloty to the policeman for the favor he had done for me. I yelled that for sure I would get them out and that they must stay together and keep an eye on father, and that someone has to be near the window, then choking with tears I returned to Nowolipki. In front of the gate to number 24 I saw Piniek and Abe. They had already been to number 44 to find out what had happened to us, but no one was there. By chance the head of the Jewish police lived in the building they lived in, so it wasn't rounded up at all. It was lucky for them that the boys were registered there. This head of police had a whole staff of other policemen and each one on his own was taking people out from the Umschlagplatz, for large sums of money, of course. Unless you knew someone important, you couldn't do it without money. Uncle and Aunt had to spend another night in the store, because Sarenka couldn't arrange anything in any of the workshops.

Saturday, July 25, 1942—Nowolipki 44—still no roundup. We heard that the beginning of the street would be blocked today. My "husband" came before work to pick up my photograph and wedding certificate for the issuing of a temporary document before the district rabbi would issue the permanent document for us. Sarenka and I left together with him to go to the store and bring some food to our dear ones. We reached only the corner of Karmelicka and Nowolipie. The following building numbers till the end of the street were already blocked, on both sides of the street. Our parents are there! I was holding Sarenka as strongly as I could; she wanted to free herself from me and run to our parents. "You will betray them by going there, if they didn't break down the store," I begged her. I forced Sarenka back home. "My husband" was the one with a good ID, [so he] went to observe the store from across the street. Sarenka and I had to wait. She sobbed without stopping. My eyes were red, but not even a single tear. They are waiting for me at the Umschlagplatz. I cannot move until I find out what is happening with my beloved Uncle and Aunt. Luckily, they didn't touch the store. I rushed there just to hug my beloved ones and then I ran to the Umschlagplatz. They stood at the window, pale and miserable. My brother with TB, by a miracle, is still standing. I sent a few words with the policeman, telling them that in the event of people being loaded into the cattle cars, they should stay behind. The transports with six thousand people left every day at 4 p.m. There were twice as many people at the Umschlagplatz. They posted announcements that all those who reported voluntarily, would get an additional kilo of marmalade and three kilos of bread, and they would not be separated from their family. Thousands of people besieged the Umschlagplatz, even when there was no standing room inside. They stood in the street with their families and cursed, impatient for when they would be able to get inside. They were convinced that they would be taken eastwards where they would continue living. There were some who had already heard from the deported that they had reached Brześć and found a place to live and they were welcomed by the Jewish community, etc., etc. People standing in windows yelled to their relatives standing in the streets: "Don't cry, we'll write immediately after we arrive," an old woman shouted to a boy who stood next to me and cried desperately. When he had returned home from his place of work, he found an empty apartment. He found his parents and siblings at the assembly place—"Son, don't worry, we are here together. You'll see, we'll return soon, and we'll dance at your wedding." And he smiled, but the tears were flowing down his face without stopping. This was the first time that tears came to my eyes—bloody tears.

I left my sister Fryda in the street, she could be caught at any moment since she didn't have an Ausweiss, but she cannot stay at home, and I ran to arrange the release. I went to the rabbinic association, knowing that my father was respected there. They gave me a piece of paper [addressed] to some previously rich Łódź magnates, who supposedly had influence with the German authorities. These people lived on the Aryan side and when in the ghetto, they didn't wear armbands. These were Kohn and Heller, active at the Umschlagplatz overseeing the sending to the next life of tens and hundreds of thousands of their brothers and sisters. (Later, when they wanted to leave behind more people than the authorities determined, they were executed at the same Umschlagplatz.) I approached their assistant, who promised to take care of my problem. At the same time, I went to the head of the Jewish police from Nowolipki 24, and I tried to [get him to] release them. He assured me as well, but I had to promise one of his assistants to give him a few thousand zloty to speed up the release. Simultaneously we tried to get a certificate that father was employed in the Többens shop. I returned home half dead. A policeman, who lived in my father's building, took them aside when people were taken to the train.

Sunday, July 26, 1942—Uncle and Aunt returned to sleep at Sarenka's tonight. On Sunday there isn't a blockade and people take advantage of this day to ensure that they wouldn't be deported. Everyone came out into the streets. We were up since 5 a.m. I went to the district rabbi; there was a crowd of young people getting married in a hurry. This way a man could save his girl or a relative or an acquaintance, if he wasn't in a relationship and had a job in a "shop." There were many instances now that a young man who couldn't even dream about a young woman before, because of class or economic difference between them, now he could [even get offers to] marry from ten beautiful girls. Everyone wanted to stay alive. We didn't know anything about Treblinka, this torture chamber for millions of Jews, but everyone wanted to save himself. Except for those who were lured by the bigger ration of bread and marmalade, who were dying here of hunger anyway, people fought as much as they could not to be deported. It might have been intuition.

Finally, I received the formal certificate of my "marriage"—my father's certificate was accepted without question. As a rabbi's daughter, I was released from paying for the certificate, and the price was quite high. To convince the district rabbi that I was indeed married, I wore the wedding ring of our Rachelka, which she had left with us. I visited some of my former students; one of them, a beautiful blond five-year-old boy was already gone . . . he was caught with his grandmother in the street. His father became insane to a certain degree, and he wanted to report to the assembly point himself, as he was saying, to meet his son in the east. He constantly talked about his son. The mother of this child disappeared during the fur *Aktion*;[8] she wanted to take her and her husband's furs to the Aryan side and they caught her. My pet student Fredzia hugged me and was so happy to see me. She had her Ausweiss in a little bag hanging around her neck; it stated that her father works on the Aryan side in a German firm. My sweet, beautiful girl, how did you perish? Our father (Uncle) shaved his beautiful, cultivated, nicely smelling beard, today. He left a mustache and now he looks like a muscular aristocrat. If he walked on the Aryan side, wearing his elegant dark suit and wide brim hat, no one would recognize him as a Jew. He always cared about his appearance; his shirts and neckties were always of the best kind. I can't explain why I cried when I saw him with a shaved beard. He was just as handsome, but something was taken from him, which in my mind was part of his external personality.

The shop on Nalewki 12 still didn't approve the acceptance of Uncle. Piniek and Abe want to go to the shoemaking shop at the Gęsia shop. They can get places there for five thousand zloty. I spend hours in their house just waiting for the resolution of my father's issue. The head of the police has constant meetings with the Gestapo. Quietly people say that all the policemen living in this building are Gestapo agents. I asked Piniek to take my place and make sure that my issue is taken care of, while I ran again to the Umschlagplatz, to send them some food—today there are no transports out, so there is time to get them out tomorrow. Tomorrow . . .

Monday, July 27, 1942—The sixth day of deportations. I didn't have a good Ausweiss and as I walk through the city I could be caught at any moment. My sister Fryda was already on the wagon. Only after begging for a long time with the policemen that she had left a small child at home, and she wants to take it with her—one policeman gave in and let her go. Fate was very good to me up till now. Wherever I go, a blockade was there a moment before or a moment after I passed. Kuba's father, like ours, is still without a work Ausweiss. Max, Kuba's brother, made a fake Ausweiss, identical to Kuba's, but with his photo and as of now he can walk the streets without a problem.

---

8   An *Aktion* was a German anti-Jewish operation or roundup. In the winter of 1941-1942, the Germans forcibly collected furs and other winter clothing from the Jewish population. Subsequently the *Aktionen* were mainly to roundup and deport to their deaths Jews in the Warsaw and other ghettos.

Again, I spent a few hours at the Umschlagplatz, holding on to the fence with one hand and yelling to them, as they were standing in the window of the top floor. They were so weak they could barely stand. The one in best shape is my twenty-year-old sister. I was hoarse from yelling, but I had to shout louder than hundreds of people, all yelling just like me. Someone was calling my name from a window—it was a sister of a friend of Nachman and me—Genia Sznajdler. He is somewhere near Moscow. She shouted that she and her parents had reported voluntarily, because for a few days they had had nothing to eat. "Maybe over there we'll get work, and we'll have food." Her fiancé was caught the same day and they met by chance on the Umschlagplatz.

Suddenly people started to run, and shooting could be heard. Two armed gendarmes were getting closer, and the crowd started to escape, one falling down, getting up, and running again. I was running with the crowd. To get to Niska Street, I had to go through a fence. I just couldn't; my legs felt like lead. I got closer to the mesh fence, and I was convinced that this was the last minute of my life, when suddenly the gendarmes turned back. I dragged myself home. Uncle and Aunt returned to Nalewki 12. I went to spend the night at Sarenka's, because I wanted to go to number 24 to check if there was any progress regarding father.

Tuesday, July 28, 1942—In the morning I went to Nalewki 12 to check on Uncle; someone came from number 23 with news that my father had returned. While running there I was scared to death. The streets were empty and a truck with gendarmes approached. When they saw us, they stopped and aimed their guns at us. Darkness . . . my legs refused to support me; all thoughts disappeared from my mind . . . they didn't shoot. They changed their mind and continued on their way. At number 23 I saw father, stepmother, two brothers, and sister—where are my brother-in-law and little Fela?! . . . They got out on an Ausweiss that someone gave them—it was good for a family: wife and children were included. "And you just left them there?" "Were we to stay there with them?" I ran again to the Umschlagplatz. I saw them, I sent a loaf of bread to them and a little cake for the little one via a policeman, and as I was returning, the voice of little Fela sounded in my ears: "Auntie, rescue us . . ."

Wednesday, July 29, 1942—A week has passed since this hell started. Now the Jewish policemen are not responsible for the action. Some twenty Ukrainians and Latvians get into the ghetto every morning together with one or two gendarmes and they go berserk in the ghetto, they murder, and human blood flows—Jewish policemen accompany them. Their shameful role feels bitter, but now they have no choice. They could only throw away their police hats and go together with the other deportees to the Umschlagplatz. But they are too cowardly for this or maybe they are just human. No food entered the ghetto, only on Leszno, at the gate smugglers still risked their lives—they came from the Aryan side to buy from Jews their last things; they paid pennies and sold them food at extreme prices. One kilo of butter cost as much as from three hundred up to five hundred zloty and bread cost from sixty to one hundred zloty. Who said that Jews have a monopoly of profiteering?

In my father's house they literally had nothing to put in their mouth. My brother was very ill; my stepmother looked like a corpse that moved by a miracle. Did I call her "a monster" in the past? Was she the woman, I hated a long time ago? I did a lot to help her out. I had to share with them what we still had at home. My "husband" brought the good Ausweiss for me from the shop. With this document I can walk with ease in the ghetto, but for the Ukrainians it still meant nothing. When they blocked the streets and took people, they didn't care what papers people had. When we were looking at this new document, a policeman from Mińsk Mazowiecki came in. He came by truck and wanted to take Uncle, Aunt, and me. I didn't know what to do. I wanted to be with them, but it was so difficult to leave Sarenka in this hell. My internal struggle started. I could see that Sarenka wasn't glad to see me leave. She had Kuba and she loved him very much, but if I were to leave, she would lose her last link with home. Finally, I decided to go with Uncle. Maybe he would need my care? I knew that the cousins loved him like a father, and he would lack nothing, but maybe he would feel lonely without any of his children? Yes, I wanted to go with him. Aunt packed some necessary things, and we went to the car on Kupiecka Street to find out about the journey. Kuba was to run to Nowolipki to bring some money. We reached Kupiecka Street and the truck wasn't there. A gendarme with a gun stood at the corner of Zamenhof Street. We had to hide in the gate of a building. Kuba was ahead of Sarenka and me, hidden in a different gate, and Sarenka was trying to reach him. I had to go back to Nalewki to help parents to get ready for the trip and to pack some things for me. As I was reaching the entrance gate, people running away from the roundup, burst into the courtyard. Armed gendarmes arrived at Nalewki Street in a taxi and positioned themselves on both corners of the street. They were ready for an Aktion on our block connected to Kupiecka Street. An acquaintance, a doctor, entered the courtyard and together we climbed the staircase. My Ausweiss was worth nothing at that moment. If they caught me, they would drag me to the Umschlagplatz with my good document. Someone shouted that they were coming to our build-ing. "Jump into the cellar" said the doctor—"I'll let you know when you can come out." I slid down into a dark cellar, half-filled with stuff. In the dark-ness I felt the walls and a door. I heard someone whispering. I was afraid to startle some hiding people and I returned to the opening through which I entered. I didn't know how long I stayed there, but it seemed to me that it was ages, and then I heard the voice of the doctor. I stuck my hands through the opening and the doctor helped me to climb out. I ran home quickly, and I found Sarenka there crying. Father and Mother had left in the meantime. The policeman from Mińsk Mazowiecki didn't want to wait for me. He walked our parents out, next to the gendarmes, without any problems. Fate or coinci-dence had decided for me—I was to stay with Sarenka. I moved all my things to her place, but that night neither of us slept a wink. She wept the whole time asking if we had made the right decision in sending our parents away. Kuba sat next to her and tried to calm her down and to convince her that this was the only right solution. And as for me—I couldn't even shed one tear . . . everything in me had hardened.

Friday, July 31, 1942—We received news from Mińsk. The same policeman who accompanied the parents had returned to Warsaw. He brought a short letter from Father—they had arrived without any prob-lems—"I am here like in paradise, compared to the hell I left you in. I am comforted by the fact that Ita has such a good Ausweiss (oh, yeah, so good!) and Kuba with Sarenka have a good one as well. But if you are in any danger, come here immediately. You are awaited here, and you will be welcomed." Needless to say, none of us even considered it—Kuba wouldn't leave his par-ents; Sarenka wouldn't leave Kuba; and I wouldn't leave Sarenka now that I had remained with her. If they would take us—we will all go together. Each of us always carries a tote with some medications and a syringe. I asked that she should give me, some morphine, just in case, but she refused. Sarenka wore her nursing uniform and at that time the Jewish police honored it. We agreed that if Sarenka had to be somewhere and our street wasn't safe, I would go and stay with the boys at number 24. Their place was the safest. Today I wanted to go to the tailors to pick up our winter coats. If we were to be sent away, we could use the winter coats. The policeman, who lived in the same building, notified us that today number 44 would be blockaded. He said that they would just check the work documents of the residents and anyone who was just a passerby would be able to leave. I ran to see the boys to let them know that if Sarenka was taken, I would go with her. If I didn't come during the day, they should give my last regards to my father and my best wishes to them. "Please stay with us"—asked Piniek. I didn't want to listen, and I ran to number 44. Our documents were honored—the tailor wasn't in, and I would have to go again the next day. In the meantime, we were moving some of our things and bedding from Nalewki to Sarenka's, and other things to the boys' place. In the Wrocławski apartment there was a mess everywhere. Bedding was packed into bundles; clothing, dresses, underwear were all over the room—some packed in suitcases and some in bundles. Tablecloths, curtains, bedspreads, coats, shoes, things left by Fryda and Rachelka, everything was lying on the floor, and we just walked all over it. We wouldn't be able to take it all with us if they pushed us into a train car with one hundred fifty other people. Sarenka claims that this is of no importance—if we were taken away someplace to work, we would manage. She divided the money among us. There was another blockade at my father's, but they weren't discovered in the cellar. My father is trying to get a place in a shop. Today, as I was crossing the courtyard of his building, I asked a man if he had seen my father. A complete stranger stood before me. He had cut off his beard. My sister with her husband and child and family were living in the basement of their bakery and they were just shadows of human beings. Cousin Fajgenbaum from Leszno had already been deported. In his home everyone was crying—neither Fela, nor brother, nor sister was working—it's a miracle that they are still here.

Saturday, August 1—I went to the tailor, and his sister took me to his workshop at Nowolipki 18 to return my coats. I packed them and left, but I had to go back quickly. There were lots of police in the courtyard, whistles, yelling: "out, everybody out" and shooting was heard right away. I ran up the stairs to find a place to hide. I don't want to go (to the deportation) alone, so Sarenka wouldn't know what happened to me. If I were to go, it would be only with her or to stay with her. I reached an attic but there was nowhere to hide. I noticed a gap in the wall, and I went through it, but my parcel fell. I was in a different attic. Oh, God! I lost my leather handbag with all my documents and money. This was my end. I jumped back through the same gap to look for my purse. Nothing. But this is a different attic. Again, I saw another gap and I went through it again and once more I found myself in the same attic. Had I gone mad? It seemed to me I was still in the same place. I reached a staircase and I hoped that it would lead me to a different courtyard. I heard a police whistle and the patter of boots on the stairs and later banging on the door—I ran back upstairs, reaching an attic. I didn't know what was happening to me. I squatted in the dark, in a corner, biting my finger till it bleeds and thoughts run through my head—no, no I can't go mad, I cannot lose my mind, maybe they wouldn't come in here. In my feverish search for a hiding place, I discovered a huge, iron door. I dragged it to the corner and put it down in such a way that I could lay under it. I covered my head with some garbage lying nearby. I had difficulties breathing, I was numb, my heart wanted to jump out of my chest. My mind started to go numb when I heard that someone was entering the attic. If only my heart was not beating so loudly. No, they didn't find me; no one could think that someone was hiding below the iron door. After some time, I heard voices of people asking: "who was caught, who was killed?" I understood that the blockade was over. It took me a long time to get my numb body from under the door and go downstairs. It appeared that I was on Dzielna Street and not on Nowolipki. The Aktion was in the whole complex of buildings—on one side Nowolipki, and on the other Dzielna. The attics of these buildings were connected by openings, which almost drove me to madness. These openings were prepared especially for people to flee. I entered someone's apartment to wash my face and hands, then, broken in soul and body I returned to Nowolipki 24. Now I had no documents that my "husband" works, and I was unable to survive. Piniek and Abe noticed right away that something had happened to me. I lay on the bed for a few hours without moving and without the ability to say a word. The boys brought Sarenka, but even she couldn't get anything out of me. What next? I had to find my "husband" so he could issue a new document for me. I couldn't stay at this place for long, apart from Sarenka. If they take her and I wasn't with her, how would I find her later? Sarenka tried to calm me down, saying that I needed to rest, and we'll decide tomorrow what to do. The boys' cousins welcomed me very nicely. They have a room and a kitchen, so there is room for all of us. The police in this building doesn't let unregistered people stay here, but when I asked them for help to get my father out from the Umschlagplatz they noticed that Piniek was always with me. They treated us as a couple, and they didn't make any trouble for me. But once again I was with Piniek; this was a problem. I decided to return to Sarenka the next day.

Sunday, August 2—The boys bought a place in a shoemaking workshop, for five thousand zloty. This building was supposed to be rounded-up as well, even if up until that day it hadn't happened. In the morning Sarenka brought some bread and soup for me—she didn't want me to eat there. That insulted the boys, but my wonderful Sarenka guessed again . . . She is a little under the weather. When I visited her at lunchtime, she was in bed with a high fever. Kuba stayed at home and didn't go to work in the factory. She shouldn't stay at home, because at any moment there could be a roundup and they would take her or as a sick person, they would shoot and kill her right there. People who were sick in bed were killed right there by the Ukrainians and gendarmes and other sick people at the Umschlagplatz, they give them a loaf of bread, separate them from the rest, drag them to the Jewish cemetery, and execute them right there, so the bodies fall into the ditches. Other Jews, who were at the cemetery buying food from smugglers from the Aryan side, have to bury them. So, we decided that she should go to the hospital for a few days—as for now they don't touch the hospital. We hired a rickshaw and Kuba took her to the hospital. He forbade me to come with them and Sarenka got very upset. I didn't want to upset her more and I gave in. Kuba promised to come and tell me how it all went. He didn't show up. I went to number 44 to check what was going on, and both Kuba and Sarenka were at home. "What happened? They didn't take you?" "I am returning from the Umschlagplatz," said Sarenka, "Kuba was there too." When Kuba brought her to the hospital, indeed they wouldn't admit her. Kuba left Sarenka in the rickshaw and he ran to the apartment of the head of the hospital, who knew Sarenka. When Kuba was at the corner of Leszno, they closed off the street and the Aktion started. Kuba, together with masses of others, was taken to the Umschlagplatz. When they arrived there, they checked his Ausweiss and let him go. At the same time, they took Sarenka from near the hospital and brought her to the Umschlagplatz. A moment before she was forced into a train car, she noticed a physician and a nurse carrying a wounded policeman on a stretcher. Sarenka took off her coat, threw away her bag and dressed in her nursing coat grabbed the handle of the stretcher and went with them to the ambulance. After placing the wounded man inside, she jumped into the car as well. This way she got back to the hospital. From there she went back home, where she was reunited with Kuba.

Monday, August 3—Again at number 24. Sarenka went with Kuba to his factory to spend the night there. They didn't want to let her in. The old Wrocławski couple spent all the time at the Többens shop on Niska Street. No one goes home, only for a few moments around 5 a.m., before the Aktion, to cook something warm. We packed a few warm things for the parents (Uncle and Aunt) in Mińsk,[9] but we were waiting for the possibility to send it to them. Sarenka contacted her brother-in-law, who was on the Aryan side,

---

9   These are Ita's adopted parents in Mińsk Mazowiecki.

telling him that he should sell father's fur coat and mother's fur collar and muff, as well as some jewelry, and that he should send the money to Mińsk. She gave me half of the money from the sale of a few of our things and she brought some food stocks. I quickly took it to my father. At the street where my sister lived, there were Aktionen all the time and I couldn't get to her. Our apartment in Nalewki was full of people working in a workshop located in the building. Well, they didn't work—they just sat there. But at that time, they were rounding up people working in workshops too.

Every few moments there are different rumors—that they intend to leave two hundred thousand working people, that the deportation will only last another week, that it will last two weeks, that this, that something else. One can go mad. But one rumor is true: workers from the Schultz and Többens Company, together with their wives and children, will be moved to buildings adjacent to the factories. This is true for all the other "shops." I will be separated from Sarenka . . . and I will live with this seventeen-year-old boy. The age difference and the favor he did for me—after all, he was starving with his father and sister, he could've taken a rich girl on his Ausweiss, and she would have given him thousands for it. I got chills just thinking that I would have to live with him in some tiny room and maybe even in just one bed. No, no—I cannot, I don't want to! I prefer to accept Piniek's offer, that he would claim me as his wife and register me in his Ausweiss. If we will be moved to the factory blocks, the three of us would live together. I went to my father again for a wedding certificate. Now, I already had a second "husband," and a thought bothers me, which I try to chase away.

Tuesday, August 4—In the morning, Sarenka brought soup and a big bag of rice for me. She is going with Kuba to his factory; she is scared to part with him even for a moment. Yesterday I told her about my intent to go with the boys and not with the seventeen-year-old from Nalewki. An additional argument was that Kuba's parents, the Wrocławskis, were at Többens, so we would be together. Sarenka was reluctant and even upset: "do you think that in the long run, this fictitious marriage with Piniek would work? Don't you see that this has a different meaning than with this boy? Are you so naïve that you don't understand life?" I listened in silence—I was so tired of it all, so tired. She has Kuba with her all the time, and I? With tears and a choked throat, I finally said that if this is to be my life, so at least I know how devoted Piniek is to me. I knew that she wasn't talking about her brother Nachman; not once, did she tell me that I was stuck in something that might be irrelevant. She knew about lack of feelings on my part and how much divided us in every respect. But with this boy, half-child, I had even less in common. With Piniek—his feelings for me created a bridge between us. If I had a third option, but I had to choose from these two. The next day, Sarenka obviously was sorry that she had reacted in this way. As we were saying goodbye, she hugged me, looked into my eyes, and said: "Ita, don't worry about it; whatever will happen, be strong. Our actions are not up to us; these actions are imposed on us—all we want is to save our lives. We just want to meet our father again and see our mother and to fight again about whose house they will live in when they get old. This was your dream, so you must be brave and try to survive this hurricane that is beating us down." I put my head on her shoulder and I cried quietly—she kissed me once more and left . . .

Wednesday, August 5—It's impossible to know where one is safe. Work certificates are good only for the Jewish police. For the gendarmes and especially for those twenty Ukrainians and Latvians, who get drunk before entering the ghetto—they don't care about any certificates. The Jewish police don't always honor the rights of the wives and children of the employees of the "shops." Everyone knows about it, but everyone wants to have a scrap of paper. Today I sit at home the whole day—it was impossible to go out. I don't know if Kuba or Sarenka will visit me tonight. I don't know what is happening with my father. It's been a few days since we had news from Mińsk. Policemen don't come from there anymore. Until 7 p.m. no one from number 44 came to see me. I sent Piniek to find out. He returned and said that he didn't find them at home, but that old Wrocławski said that they are busy moving the workshop. Nothing can be done. I have to wait until tomorrow.

Thursday, August 6—Today this building was rounded up too. A policeman, who has parents at our entrance, came to warn us and helped us to hide in the attic. The opening is in the ceiling at the hall; we had to bring a table, climb on it and ascend. A person who stayed downstairs moved the table, the attic hatch was closed, and a few dozen people sit or lie down under the hot roof. They took out just a few people from this building, and they didn't enter some entrances. When I came down, I was soaked, as if I took a bath. I rested a few hours and waited for the evening. I wanted to go to Sarenka. Why had none of them visited me for two days? Piniek doesn't seem enthusiastic about going with me. "I'm sure they are not there"—he says—"they might already be in the factory apartment." I didn't listen to what he was saying. "I want to drop by and if they are not at home, I'll try to visit them at the new place." Piniek went with me, strangely silent. In the hall there were lots of trunks and packages; I tripped over these at every step.

There was no one in the study. Old Wrocławski was sitting in the dining room and Kuba was standing next to the window. When he turned toward me, I thought that he had suddenly become old. Maybe it was because of his unshaven beard? "Ku!—Sarenka called him like that, and I did sometimes too—where is Sarenka? Why haven't I seen you for a few days?" "There is no Sarenka." "When will she be back? Curfew starts at 8 p.m." "There is no Sarenka." "Fine, I heard you, but where is she and when will she be back?" "There is no Sarenka!" and old Wrocławski—"don't you understand what I am telling you?" I still didn't understand, but my throat started to choke, and my eyes are wide open; my mouth opens to cry: "There is no Sarenka?!" I sat down. Someone held my head and tears fell on my head. It was Kuba holding me. He talked to me as if to a child, and he himself was devastated— there was a roundup in the complex of factory apartments. Sarenka, as the wife of an employee was not exempted from deportation. They ordered her to go down. Kuba wanted to go down with her and he was hit hard with a fist "du Schwein bleibst hier!" (Stay here you pig!) He showed his employment certificate, being sure that this will save Sarenka. If he had known that they would take her anyway, he wouldn't have shown the certificate and they would have gone together—this hurt him the most. Kuba sent his Polish friend from the factory to the Umschlagplatz, from the Aryan side, to see which train car she was in. Two others went with the train, on the outside. Their factory produced some parts for train tracks and a few laborers travelled till Biała Podlaska. They couldn't go any farther and they returned. Sarenka had two hundred zloty with her. Kuba heard that where these trains arrive, they choose strong and healthy people for a labor camp. The old, ill, and children were killed. But Sarenka is young and healthy and surely, she will be chosen for work. Maybe later it will be possible to find out where she is. His words reached me as if it was some faraway noise. My brain heard just one thing: There is no Sarenka—she left alone, I wasn't with her, Kuba wasn't with her; she was crowded among these strangers in the hermetically closed train car. Again, a cry came up in my throat; Kuba held my head strongly and put his hand on my mouth. Old Wrocławski couldn't control himself anymore—his niece, the wife of an officer and her nine-year-old son were shot and killed, and now when they took Sarenka, who was very dear to him, he broke down. Kuba, despite his absolute despair, because of his father, he tried to hold on, to support his parents. They only have him—the youngest brother Mates and their nephew and his wife were on the Aryan side. Sarenka gave me the telephone number of the brother and the address of the nephew's wife "just in case."

Kuba visited me during the day; we hugged and sat together for a long time in silence. Each knew what the other had lost . . . "If now I let them catch me, I wouldn't find her anyway. Maybe she would write or maybe she would return, and she wouldn't find me, then what? . . . I still have my parents; I must endure with them till the end." Kuba said. When I said that maybe I would like to go as well, that I don't care anymore and maybe I would be taken to the same place where she is—Kuba said: "You still have responsibilities and don't forget it. Does Sarenka's father mean nothing to you? You have to make sure that you survive; the parents might need you." "Kubusiu—can you imagine, how would I be able to stand in front of Uncle without Sarenka? It was me who was supposed to go, not her—so much more prominent, leaving behind many more broken hearts than I would. What would I bring to show my uncle?"

Saturday, August 8—The pain didn't kill me. It only wounded me, and this wound will never heal. I will find Sarenka (at the time I thought so). We all go . . . to the boys on Gęsia. They don't want to leave me there because they conduct roundups there, and I don't have . . . a wedding certificate and an Ausweiss that I am a "wife" of a shop employee—this is good for nothing . . . wives and children without exception. In this building the Aktionen are conducted only by the Jewish police. Wife . . . wink from the Gestapo not to touch this building. The "shop" was full of wives and children, laborers . . .

But they conducted an Aktion in the shop and they take out women without certificates and all the children without exception. This shop was in the basement and was spread over a few large rooms and a few smaller side rooms. The workers emptied one of these smaller rooms and in it sit the mothers with their children. Someone always stands guard at the courtyard and when the Aktion starts, all other women hide in the same room, and men, in a blink of an eye, put all the manufactured shoes in front of the door. Today I was in this room as well. It was so crowded that some people actually hang suspended in the air without touching the floor. Each mother holds her child for dear life and shivers that the child wouldn't cry out and betray us. The air is so thick that it feels like it could be held in your fist. Blood throbs in my temples and it seems to me that my skull will break in two at any moment. Finally, they remove the shoes from the door outside and I was able to get out of this over-crowded place. I declare to the boys that next time I will not, under any circumstances, go into hiding in this room. They tell me that the gendarmes took away a few dozen workers directly from the machines, and those who were hidden . . . So, what's the difference if you work or not? This day in the workshop tired me out—I will never go there again.

Sunday, August 9—Everyone must move out from the "small ghetto" (Twarda, Pańska, Krochmalna etc.) to the "large ghetto" and after two days no one would be allowed to be in the area of the "small ghetto." Everyone emerged from the basements, attics, and different hiding places. Those who were sure of their status as "safe" laborers packed all their possessions on carts and dragged them into the "large ghetto." At that moment they blocked the street from both sides and rushed this crowd, beating them with whips and shooting in the air, and sometimes shooting someone who tripped, rushing them all to the Umschlagplatz. They did the same in the "large ghetto." One side of Nowolipie Street was ordered to move out and at that moment they blocked the street and rushed everyone to the Umschlagplatz. A few buildings on Nowolipki Street were ordered to be cleared; one side of Nalewki Street was ordered out and so on. The deadly circle tightened. By that time probably a few hundred thousand ghetto residents had already been deported. Those who stayed behind don't know anything and don't understand what the future would bring. People invent different dates that the deportations will end. I went to my father's place to bring them something to eat. The boys go to the exit on Leszno Street and buy bread, butter, and potatoes from those returning from labor outside the ghetto. Butter is four hundred zloty per kilogram; bread is eighty to one hundred zloty per kilogram, and potatoes up to two hundred zloty per kilogram. They take a lot of risks buying there, but this way we and half of our building have enough food. My father and his family, by some miracle, are still there, but how they look . . . how they look! Brother lies in bed and is in terrible pain. Stepmother can barely walk and tells me crying that they should take them now, the sooner the better, because later they wouldn't be able to walk and then they would simply shoot them. (We still thought that the trains would take us to forced labor and not to death; and when it was already known about the mass murder, we still believed that it involved only the old, the sick, and the children and that the young and strong would be used for labor. They knew how to deceive hundreds of thousands of people with such satanic perfidy, so they would go without any resistance and fight.) My sister from Muranowska Street, together with her husband, child, and his whole family, went the same way as my Sarenka. Father told me that his entire family: sister, nephews with children and wives, and other cousins, had all been taken already . . . and what would happen to them, he didn't know. He didn't have the energy to hide in basements . . . I listened to all this, and my heart was like an abscess filled with pus.

Leaving the Warsaw Ghetto

Eliezer Geller [leader of the Gordonia organization and eventually one of the organizers of the Warsaw Ghetto Uprising] was a young man, but in his organization, he was appreciated for his achievements. During the whole Aktion, he tried to save his people and whoever else he could. They forged Ausweisse; they placed people where they could, and when it became clear to them what was happening to the deported people, they started to forge passes and take their people to their kibbutzim in still peaceful areas and later other people as well. Where did they get the blanks for the passes, I don't know, but they had blanks and stamps, which worked during the journey, as long as these people were not delivered directly to the Gestapo. In the beginning even there they [the Gestapo] didn't realize, but as more people with such passes were caught at the train station (Germans didn't catch anyone, because they couldn't distinguish [between Jews and Poles], but Polish railroad workers helped them and Polish police; bands of blackmailers lurked for their victims at the exits of the ghetto) only then they understood that these documents were fake. Eliezer promised us a pass for three people, but realizing that the brothers have money, he demanded that they pay for the passage of two comrades. Everything was arranged, and they just had to go once more to pick up the documents. This was a risky journey, and possibly we would be killed faster than in the ghetto, but here death is certain and there we have some chance of survival. "If you wouldn't come with us, we will not go either. In such an event you will close a rescue route not just for yourself, but you are sentencing us as well." (At that time, Eliezer already told them about Treblinka and what it meant for millions of Jews. By a sheer miracle, one of his comrades had escaped from this hell and reached Częstochowa, and Henia, his courier, repeated this [information] to her people in Warsaw. When they told this to others, no one wanted to believe it. The boys didn't tell me anything about it at that time.) "Do what you wish"—I said—"I don't care whether I stay here or I go with you. Maybe over there I can get in touch with Mińsk Mazowiecki and maybe I would even be able to reach them. But I want Kuba to come with us." We went to see Kuba. "No, I cannot leave, maybe Sarenka will write or maybe she will manage to escape and then she wouldn't find me here? My parents are at Többens, but for Sarenka I must wait; maybe I'll see her again. If you can go, you must go. Maybe later you'll reach Mińsk; maybe the parents would need you. Go and don't worry about me, maybe it will all work out." I looked at his gaunt face and I started to cry; I hugged him. "My poor Kuba!" He kissed me quickly and left: "I'll come to say goodbye." We went to Nalewki 23 to pick up the passes and to see my father. Abe went to the kibbutz, and Piniek and I went to my father. I took the rest of our food to give it to them. This touched my stepmother; they were very hungry and brother was still in pain. She took out a pair of silk stockings and wanted to give it to me. I had the impression that I had to accept her gift at this moment, so I took it, but I gave my sister some money, so she wouldn't be without any money; maybe she'll be able to buy something to eat. I told father about my leaving the ghetto. I saw tears in his eyes, and he said: "If you could take me . . . us with you . . ." His eyes shining with tears and his words stay with me forever, during the days and during the nights and till my last day, I will never be able to chase away and forget this shadow of memory. What if I was I to leave him? Despite it all, what if I was I to stay next to him? My logic tells me that nothing would have changed, that we would perish together and maybe even not. Maybe they would separate us before murdering us; that taking him with us was just impossible. He wouldn't be able to leave, if not his wife, then for sure he could not have left his three children, one of them a dying son. That if he were with us, he would cause all of us to be discovered and executed—all this is logical, but at the same time, something in my heart doesn't let me convince myself and my conscience doesn't want to stay silent. I didn't say goodbye, saying that I would return the next day to bid my final farewell.

Tuesday—The head of police Ehrlich, together with his wife and children, was executed at the Pawiak prison. May his memory live in infamy! He became inconvenient or unnecessary to those he assisted. Now he knew too much, and they were afraid that he would manage to escape, since he knew very well where all the deportees were taken—so they got rid of him. Why did he have such an easy death? He didn't shiver in fear for weeks; members of his family were not taken away from him one by one. He died before them, not going for hours toward death like hundreds of thousands of others, who later knew where they were taken . . .

In building number 24 there is confusion and excitement. The whole building will be emptied any moment now, just like all the others. The "protector" was gone, and the rest of the police were too insignificant. We were to leave today through the gate on Leszno. I burned my letters, cooking soup on this flame. I look for the last time at Nachman's letters—how beautiful is his soul and his love, in the beginning a little childish and shy and in his last letters full of awareness and manliness. I read the words of his last letter: "we settled the future plans with Mojżesz. I will go to a kibbutz for a year to gain more practice; after that I will finally go on the trip I long for, to Poland and I will take you. Together we will go to a kibbutz for another year, so you will become familiar with local conditions. Later we will decide together if we will stay longer or if we will build our life privately in the city." This letter and a few others and photographs of each of my loved ones I intended to take with me. My diary—did I really write about all these worries and grudges on the pages of my diary; could I really feel this way? It seems like an impossibility—so I burned it as well together with the letters. There were so many letters that most of them I left to the boys' cousins, for them to burn. I packed some underwear and sheets for myself and back-packs for the boys. A few changes for later and a few we wore; it wouldn't be wise to have big packs with us—it would attract attention. My heart and stomach were strangely squeezed—was it fear of the unknown? I decided not to go to my father to part from him. I felt that if I were to go, I wouldn't be able to keep my resolve to leave and I would let him convince me to stay. I needed all the fortitude for the way.

We walked to Leszno Street. This time one of the cousins walked with us. The issue with the guards was quickly arranged, we said goodbye to the cousin (Kuba couldn't come with us to the gate; we said our farewells the day before . . . it was a moment . . . there are no words . . . he gave me again his brother's phone number on the other side and we agreed that as long as it would be possible, we would keep in touch through his brother. He gave me a brown leather bag, instead of the one I lost during the Aktion on August 1. This bag is the only memento I have from Kuba.) and we passed the few meters separating the ghetto from the Polish district. A few meters separating hundreds of thousands of Jews sentenced to annihilation, from those [outside the ghetto] among which thousands, usually the most valuable people, were killed by the same hands. But among those [outside, there were] thousands of others, [who,] with blind hatred toward Jews, helped to annihilate them.

We just passed the guard booth and we turned into Żelazna Street, when a horde of teenagers surrounded us, at first not saying anything, just following us. We wanted to attract as little attention to ourselves as possible, after all our passes were fake. They were issued to Mojżesz Lewin, his wife Halina, and her brother Kleinerman. We were supposedly on our way from Krasnystaw to Częstochowa, via Warsaw. Our proof of identification was a note from the registration authority in Krasnystaw and a pass signed by *Kreishauptmann* (district commandant), all written by Eliezer Geller. This was very unfortunate, and we didn't know how to get away from the teenagers. Piniek made a mistake by giving one of them twenty zloty. This started a riot—each one of them wanted money.

And when all of them had received something, the first one starts all over again, claiming that he didn't get anything yet. One of them snatched my purse, in which I had our passes and IDs. I chased him, and breathless, I managed to get my purse back from him. Another one helped me to catch him, after I promised to pay. This horde didn't leave us all down Żelazna Street. I was so confused I didn't know which way to go to reach the railroad station. From the first moment of this event, I had to have my wits about me and for the boys. They gave up, especially Abe. At that moment some young man on a bicycle appeared; he was maybe twenty years old, and he said to us that we shouldn't let them blackmail us and that we should hire a horse-drawn carriage. I knew that taking a *droshky* was dangerous; there were many incidents that just when people were traveling by droshky, it took them to the police station. But I didn't see any other way for us. Some droshky driver, who came as if he had been called, agreed to take us to the railroad station for fifty zloty. When we were already sitting in the droshky, a few of the teenagers latched onto the cab and made a lot of noise, just so we would be noticed. The man on the bicycle tried to chase them away—he didn't want competition. Now the cyclist demanded a payment for not going to the gendarmes and telling them that we were using a droshky. Before I was able to stop him, Piniek already gave him one hundred zloty. This man started to curse us as "Jewish snouts" and he threatened us that he would beat us up for giving him only one hundred zloty. This was just about enough for me. The outcasts latching on to the droshky continued to demand money. I stopped the driver, got off the droshky and approached a Polish policeman. It was risky, but [otherwise] we wouldn't be able to reach the station. I showed the policeman our pass and explained that these people were blackmailing us, and I begged him to help us to get rid of them. I paid the driver and I decided to walk to the station and in this way get rid of the hoard of blackmailers. The policeman demanded only one hundred zloty for escorting us to the station. We couldn't be sure whether he would take us to the station or rather to the gendarmes—but having no choice we gave him the one hundred zloty and we continued. We had to get change for my five-hundred-zloty bill, because we had already spent all the one-hundred-zloty bills. Near the railroad station our policeman transferred us to another policeman—this one had to earn his one hundred zloty too. He left us at the door, and we entered the station alone. Because Abe's nose was a bit too long and additionally his hair was black, the porters recognized us right away. They have seen many like us in recent weeks. Two porters approached us and asked what direction we were travelling. When they found out that we wanted to go to Częstochowa, they advised us, while looking around, to give them money to buy tickets while we should go directly to the platform and wait there for the train. The train was leaving at 2:30 p.m. and it was only 10 a.m. We went down to the platform, and I was grateful for meeting such good people. We found a bench and sat on it and the "good people" appeared with our tickets, demanding one hundred zloty each for the favor they did. My silly faith in the goodness of people disappeared as quickly as it came. I gave them the money and asked them if now they would defend us from other blackmailers. "But of course, now just sit on the bench and wait for the train." In less than fifteen minutes we saw that a railway man was approaching us. At that time, I didn't know that it was a railway man; I thought it was someone wearing a German uniform.

In the train car, when they recognized traveling Jews, they started to talk about the Jews. About leeches, Judeo-communism, about Jews being everywhere, and other well-known Endecja slogans.[10] If anyone in the train car would say something else, it would be only to express an opinion that Jews should've been removed a long time ago, but maybe in a more "humanitarian" way. I stood in this crowded train car, and I was soaked in sweat, which permeated all the layers of my clothing up to my coat—and the poison surrounding me coming from the words uttered by the people in the train, filled my brain and my heart. Abe stood on my right and Piniek on my left. A man was standing next to Abe, dirty and disheveled, scratching himself constantly. Suddenly someone pointed at Abe and said that he could see a louse on his jacket. This is what the rest of the passengers needed to hear and there was nothing we could answer back. Who knew better than me that even during the mass deportations, when we had to hide in basements and attics, we observed the highest standards of cleanliness. Was I to tell them that we had

---

10 Endecja—the National Democratic Party was a strong movement in the 1930s, standing for Polish nationalism and also exhibiting antisemitism.

bathed yesterday and today, and we had changed all our clothes before we started this journey? Abe was telling them all this, but I just couldn't explain to them. Again, childish tears appeared in my eyes. It was clear that nothing that Abe was saying convinced the passengers. Finally, one man, sitting in the corner silently, couldn't take it anymore and he told the rest of them to behave like civilized people. Didn't they notice the man who scratched himself, the one who was standing next to the man they accused of bringing lice? I wasn't sure why, but only at this moment I started to cry.

Soon the dirty man and a few others left the train car, and there was space for us to sit. I looked out the window and I couldn't believe my eyes. Fields and forests still existed, and I really saw it. Maybe it was a dream, but two heads resting on my shoulders from both sides reminded me that it was reality. I told the boys to pretend that they were asleep so I would be the one to hand our tickets to the conductor for control. Indeed, when I handed him three tickets, he stamped them with indifference and handed them back to me. There was someone, of course, who couldn't stand this "injustice" and had to tell the conductor who we really were. A moment later the conductor returned and demanded to see the pass. I showed him my pass, he examined it and said that it looks fine, but it just couldn't be . . . I got it right away and I gave him the last fifteen zloty I had. I gave it to him with contempt, but he didn't give me back the money. His skin was too thick for that . . .

The Częstochowa Year

Finally, the journey was over. At 10 p.m. we arrived in Częstochowa. We survived the ticket control at the exit from the station. I walked first in the street asking for directions to Przemysłowa Street, that was the address of the Gordonia Kibbutz, and this was the street connecting to the Aryan side. The boys followed me, and without further problems, we arrived in the apartment filled with healthy young people, full of life. These were the members of Gordonia, Abe's comrades—more than twenty of them. On the other side of the hall there was a kibbutz of Ha'Shomer Hatzair.

They let us wash up, after we finally took off our sweaty clothes, and later we ate. They showed us where to sleep. I knew only one girl among them—it was a girl from Parczew, and I knew Henia, a courier of the kibbutz. They lived here relatively well and quietly. It was that night that I found out about Treblinka. And I knew where my beloved Sarenka was taken. I didn't yet know then about the process of murdering people in Treblinka. Later, when a few people managed to escape from there, I found out the details of the murder, the details that turned one's hair white.

So, we were in Częstochowa. It was strange in the beginning that there were no blockades, that people didn't have to hide in basements and in attics, that stores were open, that coffee shops were tempting people with their products, that there is normal traffic in the streets, elegant ladies, and well-dressed men. There were no high walls, and it didn't feel like being in a ghetto. Just the yellow signs at the entrance served as reminders that it was a ghetto, as did the armbands with the Star of David. You could see many boys and girls, who looked as if they had come from the Aryan side into the ghetto to buy something and for security had put the armbands on.

I finally agreed that a false ID paper should be made for me and with these ID papers I would go to places for a few weeks to gather news. There was tension in the air. Jews from the vicinity were being deported into the Częstochowa ghetto. More and more deportees entered the ghetto, and everyone searched for a work placement. A comrade from a kibbutz near Piotrków, Shlomo (later: Czesław Karpiński) was to arrange for my false ID. Henia (Janka) left with Dora D. (Helena Wiśniewska), but where they went was known only to the kibbutz members. Anyway, it was about trying to rescue their people. Somebody else was supposed to bring my ID from Kielce. In a few days Jews would observe the Day of Atonement. The Częstochowa Jews weren't aware that this would be a prelude to a real Day of Atonement.

Saturday, September 20, 1942—The mother of a couple of kibbutz members arrived on that day from Warsaw. She travelled back and forth with her false ID, the same that I was to receive. She looked very well, even though she was dark, just like me. Her daughter and son were both light blond and each had an upturned nose—in short: very Slavic types. It was very strange that her husband and the children's father was a very Semitic type. The mother was able to rescue him from an Aktion in the Warsaw Ghetto and she brought him to Częstochowa. Mrs. W. wanted to take her daughter with her to Warsaw, because she had arranged a position for her in a store. She was known in Warsaw as a Polish woman who had a Jewish husband and despite that they wanted to accept her daughter; after all it was "Polish blood." It was agreed that in a few days they would leave, and I would already have my new ID and I would go with them to Warsaw. I planned to go to Mińsk Mazowiecki from Warsaw; maybe I would be able to find out all the details about the Aktion that had taken place there. Maybe I would find out if Uncle and Aunt were killed right there or whether they were taken to Treblinka . . . Regarding my father and others left in Warsaw, about Kuba, I had no news. People who had just arrived from Warsaw were saying that the Aktion is still on, and that Nalewki Street is empty of people. All others were placed in buildings for laborers of the Schultz and Többens factories and they were still reducing the number of people allowed to stay there. People were still being deported, and they had made a ghetto within the ghetto, which is between Niska, Stawki, and Dzika Streets. Were the people I had left behind still there? Had they been taken to the trains? Were they killed right there? I will still not know the answer for the rest of my life. (Today I just know that they are not among the living. But how they died, I will never know.)

Sunday, September 21, 1942—My ID arrived. All that was left was to fill in the personal information. What should be my first and last name? It's very easy, but it was difficult to decide. It should fit the person on the photograph, and I don't know why I regard this photograph as average. This is the face of an average young woman with a village hairdo, a girl who walks barefoot and has never visited a city or gone to a hairstylist, cutting her own hair with scissors when it grows too long. While trying to think about a name to take, I thought of a Polish school friend, who was friendly. Her first name

was Genowefa, but instead of her last name "Ziemska" I chose Zawadzka—
let that be it. Place of birth and names of parents—the place of birth was at
that moment of no importance to me, but later it proved to have been unfortunately chosen, but I couldn't foresee that. I took a few years off, because
I looked very young on the ID photo, so I couldn't claim that I was twenty
something years old. It was incredible that I looked as if I was barely twenty
years old, so we wrote that I was born on September 8, 1922. From this
moment on I became Genowefa Zawadzka, twenty years old, born in Sieradz.
What would the future hold for this "newborn" person? As I put my new ID
in my pocket, I felt a tightness closing around my heart . . . So, it is for real, I
have to decide to take this step. I felt uncomfortable.

Sunday—today is the eve of the Day of Atonement. I ordered a travel
bag and I tried to get used to the idea that I would be leaving, and from that
moment on I would have to start playing a new role.

Monday—Yom Kippur (Day of Atonement)—Piniek went to work,
and Abe stayed with me. I made some last preparations for my journey. My
bag was packed. I didn't take a suitcase; a travel bag fits better with my shabby
coat and hat. I didn't want to look like an "intelligent" city girl—I thought that
this would be the best way. I took with me only a few changes of underwear, a
towel, washing utensils, and two extra dresses. Other clothes, my better suits,
and the rest of my things I decided to leave behind. I was aware that if during
my absence there was an Aktion, I would never see any of my things again,

German ID Card for Genowefa Zawadska in Tschenstochau, 1943. USHMM,
Acc. Number: 1998.A.0258.2 (Series 3, Box 2.7, no. 6), courtesy of Jacob Dimant.

but I couldn't take them with me, not knowing what I would face. I was jittery. I tried not to think. Piniek returned at four—there was unrest in the ghetto; something was in the air—could it be an Aktion? The streets were filled with people, gathered in small groups, and the police tried to disperse them.

Tuesday, September 22—Nobody slept that night, but we didn't exchange too many words either. All three of us sat in silence for a long time—each one of us overwhelmed by burdens. What would the next day bring? That night I burned the last letters from Nachman. For a long time, I stared into the flames, which engulfed these last pages. A few photographs of Nachman together with a few others of my beloved I left with Piniek. He promised to keep them if he would survive. He accepted it naturally. Piniek knew that apart from what Nachman was to be for me, he is and always will be the son of the man, who was for me as well, a beloved man.

At 4 a.m. we heard running and unnatural movement in the street. Our landlord went out and returned after a moment with the news that the ghetto was surrounded by the gendarmerie—so, this is it. Now it is the turn of Częstochowa's Jews. Now Piniek stopped being weak: "get dressed, we are leaving. You must get out at any price." The boys put on a few layers of underwear; we grabbed some bread and went out. It was dark outside. People walked close to the building walls and in front of some buildings there were groups of laborers ready to go to work in Raków. We walked in the same direction. The boys from Przemysłowa Street were there as well. One of them, Aron Gepner, called me and told me to stand with his group and maybe it would be possible to walk out with his labor group. But when the labor group reached the gate, a gendarme closed the gate and there was no exit. There was no way to the Stary Rynek circle either—the gendarmes were guarding this route as well. The same near First Aleja. I left the boys with the "Raków" group, and I went to Przemysłowa 2 to see what the people were doing there. A few people from there were supposed to leave the ghetto in the event of an Aktion. When I reached them, I saw them all drinking coffee and getting ready to go to work. They were convinced that working people would be allowed to go to their workplaces outside the ghetto. I returned with them, and I decided not to try to leave the ghetto again. What will be, will be. At the gate leading from Katedralna Street to First Aleja I met Abe. He caught me and dragged me back to Przemysłowa Street—"come here, you have to try here. Maybe you'll be able to jump through the fence at Piłsudski Street, or maybe this gate is not guarded yet." When we reached Przemysłowa halfway, we noticed that that a Polish policeman was at the gate. "Now!" He said, "this is your, and by the same token, our last chance. By all means you have to succeed in leaving."

I walked toward the gate like a mannequin empowered by an external will. "Halt—where are you going?" The policeman stopped me. "I want to go to the railroad station"—"And how did you get here? Are you Jewish?" "No, I'm Polish; I arrived by night train from Kraków, and I want to leave on the morning train to Warsaw. Waiting for the train I walked into town and not knowing Częstochowa, I got lost. I somehow got into the ghetto, and now the gendarmerie is here, and they won't let me out. I don't know how to explain it to them. Please, don't make it difficult for me, let me through to my train . . ." He made me beg for a long time—no and no. I appealed to his conscience, to his love of his own children, which are probably my age. On the other side a group of onlookers gathered, finally when I lost all hope of convincing him, he asked: "and what is your name?" "Genowefa Zawadzka"—I answered in such natural way, as if I'd had this name all my life. "ID papers"—"Here." I gave him my ID. He examined it illuminating it with his gas light torch, gave it back to me and said: "March, and next time don't go where you are not supposed to be." Once more, just for a second, I turned back.

Travelling in Poland

With artificial ease I purchased a train ticket and waited for the train, choosing areas where I noticed a gendarme or a Polish policeman. I believed that hiding in a corner would be more dangerous. Finally, I boarded the train, which was almost completely empty. I was the only person in the train car. On the outside I was very calm, but inside I was very excited. I sat down and I started to read a book, which I took with me especially for this reason. As I looked at the rows of letters dancing before my eyes, my thoughts were in the ghetto. The train began to move and reached the first turn—I could see a crowd of people with bundles, with children, driven by gendarmes with whips and rifle butts. I could hear a voice from the next compartment: "You see? They are driving the Jews out. Jesus, what a fate awaits them, but they deserve it." The train moved on. I listened to the clatter of the wheels, but my thoughts and the pulses in my temples were in rhythm with the clatter of the names of the boys and the names of all my beloved who were dying so tragically. "Young lady?" the conductor's voice brought me back. "So alone? It must be boring." He sat next to me and started a conversation, showing a desire to flirt. But my tired soul wanted nothing of the sort. I didn't think that I was desirable for him, but out of boredom, in an empty train, I was good enough. "When will we reach Warsaw?" I asked. "Or will I rather reach Germany?" "Oh, young lady, don't worry, if there would be a raid, I would hide you in the staff compartment." I heard voices from the next train car, and I decided to move. I saw a few village women and a young man, who looked like a workman. Instinctively I sat next to him. "May I?" I asked, "Sure, it's merrier in company. The train today is so empty. If there isn't a raid until Koluszki, they would find enough people there." That's how I met Stefan Gromuł and my acquaintance with him became so important for my future. During our conversation I found out that he worked at the ironworks in Raków. What a lucky coincidence for me. "Jews work there as well, right?" I asked quietly. (He told me earlier that he traded and exchanged goods, otherwise it was impossible to support a family. Now he was carrying tobacco and I admitted secretly that I do the same and I often travelled this route.) I told him that two men with whom I traded supposedly work in Raków, and a few days ago I came to pick up the goods and I gave them a large deposit, but when I returned to the ghetto in the evening to pick up the goods, I was told that I cannot enter, because Jews were being deported. Now I have a huge loss. But if these two men were still there, they would deliver the goods or return my money, for sure. The problem was how to find out if they were still in the ghetto. "If they work in Raków, they are still there," said Gromuł "because lots of workmen are needed there. When you come back again, come to me and I will tell you if they are still around."

The closer we were to Warsaw the more crowded it got in the train. During the two previous days there were raids on this line, but on this day, it seemed to be calm. Gromuł told me that he was actually traveling to Mińsk Mazowiecki. "Great, I am going there as well, and from there I have to go to Łuków," I said. We decided to travel together. Obviously, I looked like a good Aryan, I thought to myself. Two stops before Warsaw people somehow found out that there was a raid at the train station in Warsaw and those rounded up were sent away for forced labor in Prussia. Half the passengers jumped out, and Gromuł and I did the same.

Departure for forced labor to Germany would be the best solution and salvation for me—but I don't want it. I had some hope that the boys were still alive, and I couldn't be selfish. In addition, I was determined to find out what had happened in Mińsk. So Gromuł and I jumped out and we walked through fields until we got to the electric train going to Mińsk. Gromuł got off in Miłosna and had to walk another 8 kilometers to Zabraniec, where his parents lived. He gave me his address in Częstochowa. I told him that I cannot give him my address, because I travel so much, but that I would write to him, or I would drop by when I'll be in Częstochowa. I asked him how I could find him, and he said that I would definitely find him. For some reason he didn't tell me that he was married and had children. In Miłosna he kissed my hand goodbye (I thought to myself—if you only knew whose hand you are kissing?) and I was alone. A moment later I got off.

In Mińsk Mazowiecki I found out that from ten thousand Jews they had left only one hundred and fifty young people to clean up the ghetto, among them were some children and some "illegals," who somehow had managed to hide and after the deportation they came out of their shelters—all of them young people, at the most forty years old. They were all packed into some school building, where they stay for the night, but it was impossible for me to get in. I found out all this from a high school girl, with whom I started to talk, slowly steering the conversation in the direction of my interest. She told me that she and some of her friends tried to get into the building, because one of their teachers, who was deemed to be a Jew, was there—but they were not allowed to enter. After some time, she asked me if I maybe was Jewish? Why? I asked. "Because you show so much interest," she said. "And are you Jewish?" I asked, "Since you are so interested in your Jewish teacher." "No— she answered—but you are asking for so many details." "Some of my teachers were taken as well," I said, and I left fearing that she would bring someone official to question me. My trip to Mińsk was for nothing. My beloved Uncle, are your bones buried here or did they drag you together with Aunt, through this terrible journey to Treblinka? I have no one who can give me an answer to this question. I wasn't even allowed to ask and act openly.

I continued on to Łuków, where, as I had agreed with the boys, I would visit their friends. There had not been an Aktion there yet and the ghetto was not closed off. Piniek told me that I would be greeted with open arms and that they would help me with my onward journey. There was no space in the train going from Warsaw to Mińsk, so I traveled on the train step till Siedlce and only there was I able to find a seat inside. Finally, I arrived exhausted in Łuków. It was already 7 p.m. What was happening at this time in Częstochowa? The very moment I got off the train, a fat gendarme caught me and took me to the waiting room. Inside were only older people from the villages. I took advantage of the gendarme turning to catch additional people and I walked right out behind his back. On a side road I met a few Jewish women, who directed me to the house of the boys' friends. They were very surprised and then very happy to see me. I found out that some escapees from Mińsk were there. I went right away to meet them, and I found out that my cousin with one sister had been taken to Treblinka and the second sister, Fryda, was among the one hundred fifty people left to clean up the ghetto. One of the refugees remembered Uncle with his wife, who arrived from Warsaw to join the Miodownik siblings, but he didn't know what their fate was. Anyway, they were not among those who were left behind to clean up.

I wanted to go the next day to Parczew, and they warned me not to go by train. A good friend and a boyfriend of Tyla, the boys' sister, arranged a trip by truck, which went daily to the egg storage in Parczew. It costed just fifty zloty. After only two days, on Thursday, I went to Parczew, by truck. When I was finally in Parczew, in the ghetto—there were no wires, not even a border post. Obviously, they were confident that the Jews could not escape anyway. I looked for the boys' sisters for a long time, since people weren't eager to help me. After a while I got it and I made an armband out of a white handkerchief, and I started to ask in Yiddish. Right away Tyla, who knew me well from Warsaw, hugged me tight, crying. I met Rutka for the first time.

It was a week since I had left Częstochowa and what was known was that trains filled with Jews constantly go to Treblinka via Łuków. On Tuesday Dora D. suddenly appeared in Parczew. She came from Częstochowa. She and Henia had returned there from their trip to Kraków—Nowy Sącz, where they took care of organizational issues. I couldn't inquire too much—it was already the sixth day of the deportation Aktion in Częstochowa. They circled near the ghetto boundaries, where they met Shlomo. He left the ghetto to the Aryan side the same night I did and transformed himself into Czesław Karpiński. He certainly didn't look very Aryan, but he was light skinned and his nose wasn't too long. Czesław took them to some building, which was across the street from where the kibbutz was, and this was how they were able to communicate with some of their comrades. About one hundred people gathered there from different kibbutzim. The Aktionen were conducted differently than in Warsaw. Every day a certain street was to report at the Stary Rynek circle and after three days there was a three-day break. Since the Aktion started from the other end, Przemysłowa Street was still awaiting its turn. Raków workers didn't go to work on the first day at all, and all the others who worked outside the ghetto didn't either. She knew nothing about Piniek and Abe. She supposed that if they were at Przemysłowa Street and saw her across the street, one of them would show up. So probably they were not there. This was all she came with. She came to see her parents and to wait for news from Henia-Janka or from Czesław. We agreed that if anyone would get some news, we would immediately return to Częstochowa. Her boyfriend was at Przemysłowa Street. That night, after Dora's arrival, there was a rumor that early in the morning there would be an Aktion and that empty wagons were waiting at the train station. I sat through the night, with my bag packed, ready to get out in case the alarm was real. I decided to wait, because if it was a false alarm, I didn't want to walk to the train station in the middle of the night, not knowing the way. Rutka with her children and Tyla were hidden in a bunker prepared in the courtyard. The entrance to the bunker was through the outhouse. I sat alone in the room, and I listened to the ticking of the clock, at the same time hearing even the tiniest noise coming from outside. The alarm was false—it didn't look like they would organize an Aktion any time soon. There was an Aktion in Biała Podlaska. A young woman who managed to escape from there was saying that what happened there was the same as in Mińsk. They left only a few young men. The rest, more than twelve thousand, were driven to the marketplace—killing the old, the sick, and children on the way. At the marketplace some women with children were taken by horse-driven wagons to a small town, the name of which I have forgotten,[11] and the rest was forced to march to this town, leaving many dead on the way. Before they forced the Jews to leave on this march, they chose a group of the prettiest girls and executed them as their parents and the rest were watching. This was the Aktion in Biała Podlaska. The woman, who told us about it, knew the sister of our Mojżesz's wife, Bela. Cesia Rostowska lived with her husband, after their escape from Gdynia, in Biała Podlaska, with her uncle and family. Now she was deported, and her husband remained in Biała Podlaska (from this small town, where they were all were deported to, after a few weeks they were then taken to Treblinka).

A few days later, on Tuesday, October 5, a letter from the brothers arrived. They were working in Raków and sleeping in the Pelcery (a factory that belonged to the "Hasag" concern, the same company to which the Raków plant belonged as well. From the Pelcery to Raków, where the ironworks was located, was four to five kilometers). They go to work from there every morning, so it would be possible to see them during the march to work. The sender of the letter was someone named Zagórski, who lived at Aleja Kościuszki 23. I decided to go back the same day. Dora decided the same—she thought that

---

11 The name of the town is Międzyrzec Podlaski.

if the boys were still there working in Raków then those from Przemysłowa Street should be there as well. I wanted to make a false ID for Tyla, even though I was dubious this would work for her—she wasn't gutsy enough, if only because she was dark like a crow, even without Semitic features. In addition, the Poles, some of them, smell a Jew in everyone and they assist in hounding and denouncing them. Although Dora was not an exceptional "Aryan"—her Polish was proper, but her accent was terrible. Her pronunciation was melodic as was common in the vicinity of Lwów, but here it attracted attention. Anyway, I wanted to send false papers for Tyla. Hopefully it could be helpful to her in a dangerous situation. That evening Dora and I left— only she was again Helena Wiśniewska. Her document was a passport issued in 1939 for travel to Palestine in which she erased her old name and wrote in the new one. It was somewhat noticeable. Palestine was not mentioned, just a few southern countries, which she could visit. The crying of those who bid us goodbye didn't help to maintain our spirits. Both of us had the same thoughts—that we would never see again those we now leave behind. A difficult journey was ahead of us. There was an Aktion in Łuków, raids were everywhere and not too many young people were traveling. Every young person in the train endangered the rest of the people. In fact, the train car we entered was almost empty and only one young woman was traveling to Warsaw. It was late, after 9 p.m., and it was dark. At midnight we reached Łuków. Indeed, there was a roundup. At the last moment we backed up to an empty wagon standing on a sidetrack. Only at 1 a.m. did a railway man lead us to a train, which left at 6 a.m. for Radom. While we hid in the empty wagon, German soldiers looked in all the time, but we pretended to be fast asleep, so they left us alone. In Radom we had to change trains, but I felt relief, after the ride from Łuków to Radom with a few young railway men who wanted to flirt the whole way. (Many times, in my life—but never aloud—I lamented that nature didn't provide me with certain physical attributes—but during this journey I was sorry that my face didn't resemble the face of a monkey.)

Returning to Częstochowa

We finally reached Częstochowa after midnight and after the curfew, so we had to spend the night at the railroad station. It wasn't pleasant, not only was it difficult physically, but we had to avoid getting trapped in a roundup and caught by Gestapo agents hunting for Jews. We sat in a corner pretending to be asleep. At 5 a.m. we left the station, but where should we go? It was still dark. We decided to walk on the road leading to Raków and wait for the labor group going to the ironworks. They should be there at around 6 a.m. Dora was more familiar with this area, because for a long period she was leaving the ghetto to the Aryan side to work and during the first days of the Aktion she was in this area with Henia and Shlomo. None of the labor groups showed up till 6:30 a.m. What to do? We just couldn't walk around anymore because people started to pay attention to us. We returned to the center of town and continued to walk back and forth, thinking over what our next steps should be. It was too early to go to Gromuł. Dora had an address as well, but she couldn't go there. After 8 a.m. we suddenly met Shlomo (Czesław). He had returned the day before from Piotrków to find out who from among their people was still in town. There was an Aktion in Piotrków as well. The majority of the local intelligentsia committed suicide on hearing that the ghetto was surrounded, taking potassium cyanide together with their wives and children. Czesław hadn't found anyone here yet. Eliezer was in the kibbutz in Będzin and was to return that day. His name was now Eugeniusz Kowalski, and he was to come and take away, if possible, his people (from Gordonia) who had survived the Piotrków Aktion. Someone, who cooperates with Eugeniusz, was to smuggle all these people across the border (Będzin belonged to the Reich) and bring them to Będzin, all for a few thousand zloty per person. We still had a problem, what to do? Czesław found out that those who remained were mostly the youth taken from the building of the metal workshops and later divided into different labor brigades. Many were located permanently at their places of work. There were three thousand in the "Pelcery" factory—part of them went to work daily in Raków. Some were in the "Hagen" company (train tracks) and others with the "Luftwaffe." In the movie house "Golgotha" at Jasna Góra there were some people as well. We walked on 2nd Aleja toward Jasna Góra and suddenly we noticed a column of marching Jews, coming from the direction of the metal workshops near the ghetto. Each one of us sat on a different bench and each looked for people we knew among the Jews marching in fives. First walked the women—tall, slim, young, and mostly well-dressed. They chose the flower of the people. Later marched the men—young and well-dressed. Maybe five hundred passed and we didn't notice even one familiar face. One young man slightly lifted his hand toward his hat, not looking toward us anymore. He recognized Shlomo. We followed them to see where they were taken. We were close to Jasna Góra; we walked in the park, and they walked in the street, on the left of the convent, to the movie theater "Golgotha." They stopped on the square. Another group of the same size was already standing there. We couldn't get too close, so we stopped near the monastery looking in their direction. A strong wind mixed with rain started. They were standing and it didn't look like it would end for them soon. A few people leaving the monastery joined us and they watched the people standing in freezing rain, trying to huddle. "Mother of God, what is happening in the world" a hefty woman started to complain into my ear. I turned around and started to go down the hill. It was already 1 p.m. and we had had nothing to eat today. Czesław knew a place at a market in Zawodzie (one of the suburbs) where it was possible to buy a cheap lunch in a stall. We went there and each of us ate at a different stall, and we parted from Czesław. He returned to town, and we went to a garden in Zawodzie where Dora and a few girls from Przemysłowa Street used to work. Maybe the girls still worked there. Unfortunately, the faces we saw inside the garden were not familiar. We couldn't communicate with them, and we still knew nothing. The labor group from Raków was supposed to return only at 6 p.m., so we had some time. Where we could spend the night was a big question. Czesław rented a place to sleep from a woman on Piłsudski Street. She rented the beds to travelers. It was expensive but she didn't register anyone, and the super was paid off. Most of her customers were smugglers and peddlers. We went to look for Gromuł. I had sent him a postcard from Parczew that I would probably come to Częstochowa soon. After a lot of searching and many missteps we finally reached Dolna Street, which was somewhere between the center of town and Raków. I left Dora in the street, and I went up to apartment number 9, but it was closed. A neighbor came out and when I asked about Gromuł, she said: "You must be the one from the train, who wrote the postcard." When I confirmed that, she invited me in and sent her son to fetch Gromuł. Later, when I went downstairs with him to meet Dora, he told me that he didn't work in this factory anymore, so he had no idea which of the Jews remained in the factory, but he was sure that some were still there. "When they are on their way back from Raków, you should look, and I am sure you will find your buyers"—he said. He invited us back and his wife Marysia was very warm to us. They had a baby daughter and a three-year-old son who was with his grandparents in Zabraniec. Marysia was a very lovely thirty-year-old woman. If I would meet her in the street, I would have thought that she was Jewish. I mentioned that I have not decided yet where to spend the night and my friend here was travelling for the first time to deal in some merchandise— Marysia warmly invited us to spend the night. It was very fortunate for us, of course, but the neighbors started to come and insistently look at Dora. They didn't like her and in addition her singing . . . what could we do? It was too late. Before 6 p.m. we went out to wait for the labor group. They appeared after 7 p.m., but finally we could see them. My heart was palpitating, and I felt it in my throat. They were approaching, marching in the middle of the street, guarded by armed gendarmes. We walked slowly on the sidewalk waiting for their column to reach us. The first few ranks passed by and none of our boys were there. Apparently, someone in the back noticed us; and some movement started. I heard Piniek's voice asking to let him walk on the edge. After a while I saw both brothers.

Dora noticed just one boy from Przemysłowa Street—it was little Chaimek. I tried to comfort her saying that maybe she didn't notice them or maybe they were in a different labor group. I knew that such words were worth nothing. I wrote a few words to the boys, and we went to Aleja Kościuszki, to Zagórski, who had sent the letter to the boys' sisters. If he works with them, maybe he could take the letter to them. I told him that I come from the same town as the boys and that their sister asked me to find out how they are and to deliver a letter—naturally she would pay for this favor. Apparently, this man was the boys' foreman and he promised to deliver the letter for twenty zloty. The next day after work, he would bring the answer. At 8 p.m. we met with Czesław; we set a meeting for the next day and the two of us went back to the Gromuł family. Stefan didn't sleep at home because of a work stoppage in the factory. Marysia insisted to let us sleep in their bed and she went to sleep on a daybed. She gave us supper and was very cordial—most importantly she didn't ask many questions. It's so difficult to invent new lies all the time and to make sure that they would sound believable.

Friday, October 8—What a delight to sleep in a real bed after forty-eight hours of loitering, not sleeping, and extreme tension. The future looked dim; we didn't know what the day would bring or where we could find a safe place to stay. Marysia invited us to stay for the next night, but the way the neighbors looked at Dora was worrisome. I didn't like the residents of this building, except Marysia. I was convinced that Marysia would have helped us even if she knew who we were, apart from fear of the neighbors. We went to meet Czesław. I talked over with him the issue of the false ID for Tyla and I gave him money for it, and he promised me to arrange for it as soon as possible. He said that he would courier it to Tyla. It might be necessary to prepare such papers for many people there. I wrote a letter to Parczew, in which I described that I had seen the boys and I asked them to send me some sheets with a courier and something for the boys as well, because I thought they had nothing. I gave this letter to Czesław so the courier would take it right away. I supposed that it would be Janka, who was in Kielce at that time. We went back to the place where the girls' labor group was the day before. We walked around for a long time, but no one appeared. Finally, a cyclist came from the direction of town (Dora told me that this was the gardener) and I stupidly asked him if the girls were still working there. In response I heard: "run away as quickly as you can, as long as you are still alive!!!"

We returned to Dolna Street to wait there for the Raków group to walk by and maybe we would be able to see them. Dora was hoping to see her boyfriend, or at least someone whom she knew. But this time I didn't see the boys and even little Chaimek wasn't there. I inspected each row very carefully—they were not there. Again, I talked myself into thinking that I had just missed them. I stopped a droshky to reach the Pelcery before they would and to have another chance to check if they were in the group. Unfortunately, I gave the driver the wrong address and when I finally arrived, they were all inside. Dora was already waiting for me there and together we ran to Zagórski to ask him if he had a letter for us—"Well" he said, "those two Lewins were deported yesterday." Dora saw right away that something had happened, and I told her what I had learned. From Chaimek's letter we learned the details.

The day before, after we saw them, they entered the Pelcery factory courtyard and a truck with a few gendarmes drove in. All the people from the Raków labor group were ordered to stand in line and every other two people had to step forward. This way they chose more than one hundred people. They were ordered to take off their coats and shoes and to give away everything they had with them and then they boarded the truck. The boys were as usual next to each other, and their pair had to step forward. Chaimek was among the "chosen" as well, but he was able to sneak away and the same night he managed to run away to Raków. His foreman and other workers liked him, so they hid him. It could not last very long. If he were to be discovered, everyone would pay a heavy price. Chaimek asked us to wait for him the next day, close to the Zagórski house, and help him to escape further.

We returned to Marysia. "How did the business go?" she asked. "Not so good," I answered. "Yes, we live in difficult times" she said, "but don't worry, you will manage somehow." That night Dora and I slept very little.

Saturday, October 9—In the evening, we went to meet Czesław in a coffee house. He was to come at 7 p.m., but at 8 p.m. he wasn't there. At 9 p.m. we were supposed to meet Chaimek, but we don't know what had happened to Czesław. We walked near the train station hoping that Janka would arrive on the 8 p.m. train, Czesław had mentioned something about it the previous day. German soldiers started to pester us, seeing that we were walking back and forth. They didn't want to give up even when we walked away. Our walking in one stretch must have confused them. Finally, it was almost 9 p.m. and we went to Kościuszko Street. I was glad to see that there was a droshky station nearby; we'll take one right away. Dora had the address of the man where Eugeniusz was to arrive. This man was smuggling escapees to Będzin. In case it would be too late to go there, we secured beds for us at Piłsudski Street, where Czesław sleeps. I was there before, telling the woman who rented the beds, that while traveling by train I met Mr. Karpiński, who recommended her. Would she have three places for one night? She told me to come and that somehow it would be arranged. It was after 9 p.m. and Chaimek wasn't there. There were very few people in the street and our walking back and forth could bring attention. We entered the gate of a nearby building. We were too scared to enter Zagórski's building gate in case he would notice us. Finally, we heard steps—Chaimek appeared. He took our arms and only then I felt that he shivered, but he pretended to be carefree, and we turned toward the droshky. We arrived finally at Piłsudski Street and the woman began to spin that there was no space, and we should try to find beds with the caretaker. We went down to the basement, where the caretaker lived, but when he saw Chaimek, he didn't want to rent us any beds and nothing helped. I started to fear this man and I said: "Well, it's our money, we don't have to beg. There are plenty of other places, where we could spend the night on Piłsudski Street." We left.

For a while, we stood helpless in the gate, but we had to do something. We must find a place for Chaimek. I left them in the gate, and I tried my luck again with the same woman. I told her: "You know, it's so dirty in the basement—impossible to sleep there. I told him that we are moving to a different place, and I came back to you. Here you keep it clean, and I would gladly pay double, because I don't feel like going to the place where I usually stay." Double pay did it and finally we got two beds. I tried to talk to the woman, so she wouldn't look at Chaimek. Everything had to be done in whispers because the whole room was full of sleeping people. At night I felt that someone tried to reach under my pillow. It was the woman—she tried to find my money, I thought to myself. I asked quietly: "what happened? Is it time to get up?" "No, no, I just wanted to fluff your pillow—go back to sleep. What do you think, could it be that this Mr. Czesław is a Jew?" "Really? And why do you think that? I didn't think so when I travelled with him by train." "He talks funny, and his nose is such and he has freckles—I think he is a Jew." "Maybe" I said, "what do I care. Let him be whatever he wants; I will never see him again anyway." I couldn't sleep till dawn, scared that she would play a joke on us. But nothing happened. Obviously, she was too afraid to call the authorities. At dawn we got dressed and we went to Raków. Only now did he tell us exactly what happened with the boys. He thought that since they brought another one hundred laborers to replace the ones they took away, so maybe they had just exchanged the people in the labor brigades.

He told us what happened during the two-week long Aktion. On the day I left, they started the Aktion on the opposite side from where the kibbutz was, a few streets away. Ukrainians and gendarmes burst into Krótka Street and threw everyone out of the houses and shoved them to the train station. This was the scene I saw from the train. Later the Hauptmann [Captain] of the gendarmerie—Degenhardt—took over command of the Aktion. Until that time, he "took care" of the ghetto. Every day, he stood at the Nowy Rynek in the company of a few gendarmes and Ukrainians, holding a stick in his right hand and the people caught that day had to pass through the line of gendarmes and stand in front of him. He examined each person and if he thought that they qualified to stay, he moved the stick to the right and the person moved to the right, to the side of the living. When the stick pointed to the left—that meant Treblinka. It wasn't clear what made him decide to leave a young person or to send them to their death. The old and women with children didn't even go through the selection. They went to death without an appeal. Exceptions were the wives and children of members of the Judenrat and policemen, plus a few bakers and a few people who enjoyed "special graces." How he treated the young people depended on his mood. Sometimes he left those who had "labor cards" and other times he tore up such documents, sending them to the left and leaving people who had never worked. As a rule, he chose men and women who were tall and good-looking. The number of people who were to stay and work was decided ahead of time. Częstochowa was a factory town and almost all the factories produced for the German military. There was always a lack of people to work in these factories, so the managers of these factories, and of other places like the power plant, the Luftwaffe, the brothel, the soldiers house ("Soldatenheim"), the Hagen company, which produced train tracks, and others always asked the Gestapo or Degenhardt to leave a certain number of Jews for labor. After two weeks of the Aktion, Przemysłowa Street was sent for selection and almost all one hundred people from the kibbutz were sent to Treblinka. Chaimek escaped to Raków two days before and that's how he saved himself. Degenhardt left one man from the kibbutz as a professional (he was a locksmith) and this was Aron Gepner. Of all the girls, only one was excluded and this was due to the chairman of the Judenrat who claimed that she was his secretary—this was Regina Glanc, who was the head of the Freiheit kibbutz. The selections were still going on at the labor groups—they choose, they exchange, so no one was sure if he belonged to the living or not. We heard that the transport to Treblinka itself was horrible. They pushed unimaginable numbers of people into the train cars, taking babies out of the carriages and smashing their brains. In the wagons they spread chloride and lime and then they pushed people into such wagons and sealed them . . . I walk and listen to all this, and I look at the world around me and at the people passing by and all that is inside me is this horrendous scream: WHY??!!!

After walking for two kilometers, we reached the place where we were to bring Chaimek. Two elderly people lived there, who were the parents of the person smuggling people to Będzin. We left Chaimek there, and Dora and I returned to the "Grosz" neighborhood. I told Marysia that we met a friend, who invited us to a coffee shop and when it became late, we didn't feel like returning to "Grosz," so we spent the night with some friends. I felt quite unsafe there because of the neighbors; the Gromuł couple was very nice, and so I just pretended that everything was fine.

Monday—when we arrived in the morning at the old couple's place where we left Chaimek, we saw Eugeniusz resting in bed. Dora's happiness knew no limits. He was her leader, and he was to decide what her next move should be. I left the room. I felt completely alone; what should I do next? I wasn't a member of their organization, and I couldn't expect them to take care of me. Actually, this was the right moment to die; no one would try to convince me that I was needed by anyone or that I should live to take revenge in the future. I had so little faith that I would live until such a moment or that I have the talent to take revenge on people, who did not directly contribute to the murder of millions. I will not get the guilty ones—others will.

Should I report myself or give myself up into the hands of the executioners? I didn't have the means to commit suicide. I had no other choice but to wait passively for what the next day would bring. Let it bring what it will. Maybe they will make a small ghetto here, and then I would go in, provided that until then I do not perish on this [the "Aryan"] side. Maybe I could still accomplish something.

Portrait of Polish rescuer Stefan Gromuł holding his infant child in 1943.
USHMMPA, no. 28504, courtesy of Ita Rozencwajg Dimant.

I would not let them take me to Treblinka. For any gesture toward a gen-darme one can receive immediate death, without all of the agony from the moment of entry into the cattle car until the excruciating death in Treblinka. Dora's voice brought me back and she told me that Eugeniusz had decided to take me to Będzin and asked if I had any money for the train ticket. I told them that my decision was to stay where I was, that I still might find the boys. For the few thousand zloty that the journey would have cost me, I would be able to live here for a few months, and in addition, if I couldn't find a job in Będzin, I would be a burden to them. I didn't see any other solution, despite being desperately alone in a strange city. Dora and I went back to the Grosz neighborhood to pick up her things. Marysia was very friendly as usual, and I walked Dora back to Raków. Czesław was there as well, and he walked back with me. He told me that in a week's time a courier would go to Parczew and upon her return, she would come to see me. I knew Ewa well and there was no problem with her visiting me. Czesław left and . . . I was all alone. First, I had to find out if I could stay with Marysia for the time being. This wasn't the best place, because as Marysia in her kindness told me: "You know how people are. They insist that Miss Helenka is Jewish. But I know that you are not, so what would she do with you? I cursed them and that's it." I just couldn't look for another place; I had no idea where to turn to. I told Marysia that my friend had returned home, because it was impossible to do business here, and I wouldn't be able to travel much because of the roundups, and I really didn't want to go to Germany for forced labor. I said that if she didn't mind, I would like to stay with them for some time. Since I knew that they didn't have much, I would gladly pay rent and I could eat my meals there and pay for it as well. They would benefit from additional income and to make an extra bowl of soup when cooking for a family shouldn't make much difference to them. I even said that if there was an opportunity, we could do some business together. Marysia gladly agreed and for some time I had a safe-haven—if only the neighbors would leave me alone.

Dark Days

Days passed. I didn't do anything and I lived in mental numbness. The Gromuł family had only one room and it was always full of neighbors and their children. On the same landing were the apartments of a tailor, who was a building administrator as well, one laborer, a drunk with his wife and son, and three other families of laborers. At the entrance lived a worker from the Raków steel mill with his wife, who was the embodiment of a shrew. There was also another worker, a gambler, a drunk, a thief, and a woman expelled from Poznań—a witch—with her husband, and the owner of a shop in this building, Wizenthal. This company observed me day and night, and I had to be on my guard all the time. I had to remember each of my lies, not to say something else; I had to make sure not to show them that I know very little about the Catholic religion and its customs.

The tailor's wife, Miedziejewska, was a devout Catholic and a very nosy woman, but not as nosy and callous as the neighbor from downstairs, Kowalczykowa. This one hangs over me like a dark cloud. This woman is jealous that Marysia has such a "good tenant" as she said, and maybe if I moved into her poisonous nest (as they say—it's better to live with the devil than have him as a neighbor) maybe I would avoid everything that I had to live through because of her. In the beginning she came up all the time, smiling and observing what I was doing. The Gromuł family was very poor. He didn't work and only from time to time was he able to go to Zabraniec and sell some wool or tobacco and make a few hundred zloty. But this didn't last long. They eat dry bread and drink black coffee sweetened with saccharine for breakfast and supper and for dinner thin soup. I adjusted to this very quickly and I ate just like they did, or from time to time I bought something better for everyone. I wouldn't be able to swallow bread with butter, when Marysia ate dry bread, so I either ate dry bread or I bought butter for everyone. A week after Dora's departure, I still hadn't found out anything about the boys, even though throughout each day, I walked around the city looking for labor groups, looking for them—Stefan was getting ready to go to Zabraniec with some wool and tobacco and he wanted to bring back little Rysiek. They didn't have enough money to buy a larger amount of wool. A trip with more goods would bring more profit. I offered them a loan of a few hundred zloty, which I had for "business" and to prove that trade is my way of life I said that I could make a trip together with Stefan, to make some money. If the trip went well, we would divide up the profit. Marysia was very happy, because it would be easier to bring the child as a couple. I wanted to take advantage of the trip to prove that I was really a trader, and I couldn't wear this summer coat any longer, as it was too small and attracted attention. I would try to buy a coat in Warsaw and maybe I would recall the house on Twarda Street, where Kuba's brother was hiding. I was there once before the ghetto was sealed. I remembered that I once saw that he had a document issued in the name of

Jan Korecki, so maybe he was registered, and I could find out at the Registry office. So, one evening Stefan and I set out on our journey. I carried two kilos of tobacco leaves on my body (death penalty or Auschwitz), a bit of wool (penalized as well) at the bottom of the bag and the rest on my body, and Stefan carried the rest. At the station we had to wait till 1:30 a.m. and a few times I was very scared when I saw a gendarme or policemen entering the station, but we arrived in Warsaw and from there we continued right away. We would take care of my issues on the way back from Zabraniec. Now we had to get rid of the merchandize. We travelled by electric train to Miłosna and from there we walked seven kilometers to reach Stefan's parents. I had never imagined how peasants lived, who owned just a few acres of land. What I saw there during my three-day stay was enough to learn. It was a farm of about four and a half acres. The father works in addition as a carpenter and actually that is how he supported his family.

On Saturday morning, Stefan and I went to Warsaw. In the Registry Office—nothing. There was no Korecki and on Twarda Street I couldn't remember which building it was and I didn't remember the last name. Walking near the ghetto walls didn't bring anything either—I couldn't see anyone.

After our return to Częstochowa, I found out that during our absence "Czesław" and "Janka" had spent the night at the Gromuł place. The neighbors have new material for gossip and my stay in this household became even more difficult. But the Gromułs were not interested in the gossip—"These nosy choleras see Jews in everyone," said Marysia and as far as she was concerned, the issue was closed.

I spent whole days walking and looking for work groups, but I didn't find anyone. Marysia was happy having Rysio at home and that she had enough food to give him. He didn't leave "auntie" for a moment, because he always received something, when "auntie" returned home from the city.

It could've been a quiet life, if not for these cursed neighbors. The worst was Kowalczykowa; so tall as she was, that was how much poison was in her. The rest of them were pretty friendly, I just didn't know what they said behind my back. Three weeks had passed since I had moved in with Marysia, and that I was even registered was a great advantage. I could move around town more easily and during travel I had a permanent place of residence. In my ID card I had Włodzimierzów as my residence and an empty "moving out" form. I was always scared that they could check it in Włodzimierzów. Marysia took care of it. She went to the Registration Office and for a few zloty the clerk registered me without the "moving out" form—as if I had arrived from Włodzimierz Wołyński. We had to bribe the tailor Miedziejewski to let us use the building registration book, but it cost only twenty zloty. This registration gave me the right to have a ration card book. Only people who worked and children below age fourteen were issued ration books. The brother of Mrs. Miedziejewski offered to issue one for me illegally, because he was courting me. This didn't bother him to take fifty zloty for this favor. I preferred to pay than to owe him. I wanted to have a ration card because of Marysia, I didn't really need it, but potatoes and bread from my card were very helpful to her. She was so naïve that whatever I would tell her, it was completely reliable to her; she was telling me all her problems and she knew that she would find understanding and advice. She wasn't petty and often I had to remind her how much I owed her for dinners. "Please, stop counting how much you owe us—you are doing so much for us. Since you came our home became lighter." I know that she really meant it and she liked it that I helped with cleaning and taking care of the children. Just that the neighbors were surprised—they were not used to such tenants—if they pay, they demand. I thought about it myself—did I behave this way because I wanted her to like me? My conscience was clear—I always behaved this way.

A few days later, a new work group appeared near "Częstochowianka," some two hundred steps from Dolna Street there was a large square where trash was brought. Some Jewish boys and girls went through the garbage and helped to unload it from the trucks. Later I found out that the group belonged to the "Ravo" [Rawo] company, which took trash out as well as collecting scrap metal. Their warehouse was located closer to town, on Narutowicza Street. All the scrap and old stuff from the ghetto they bring there and Jews from this work group sort it, take feathers from old pillows and featherbeds, etc., maybe they even sorted their own things (one neighbor from Dolna Street said: these filthy Jews dirtied the whole street with the feathers. They take feathers out of good featherbeds. She said it was certain that they took the feathers out of their free will.) One day I walked with Rysio near the square, and I threw a letter to the people working there, asking them to find out if the boys from Parczew are in the ghetto. A small ghetto was established within the old ghetto and all the working groups, except the Pelcery group, were there. I noticed a commotion among those who were reading my note. I waited until they would be returning, and I walked alongside them toward the warehouse. Only one Volksdeutsche guarded them, and it was possible to talk to them. One girl said that she would take care of this and that I should come every day to find out, just now she wasn't able to tell me anything. She told me that there was a terrible chaos in the ghetto, and it was difficult to find anyone.

At the same time, I continued to follow other work groups—it became maniacal. One time I took the small daughter of a railway man to the workers canteen. She told me that Jewish workers eat there too. During the time when she took her dinner I talked to one boy, but nothing came out of it.

Sunday—On Friday, I talked to a boy from the Hagen Company as they were returning from work. When I asked him to find out about anyone from the former kibbutz on Przemysłowa Street and maybe someone who would know about two boys from Parczew—he said that he was from this kibbutz and that there are two boys from "Gordonia." This was near the factory, and I waited for them to go back to the ghetto. I walked on the sidewalk, and I tried to pass a message on for the "two." It had to be done in such a way that no one from the crowd walking next to me would notice. I managed to tell them the last name of the boys and they promised to find out and tell me the next day. But on Saturday they worked only until 1 p.m. and I didn't know it. When I arrived at 7 p.m., there was no one there. It was the same with the "Ravo" group. One of the girls was supposed to tell me something, but when I arrived at 3 p.m., no one was there. On Sunday the work groups didn't work, with some exceptions. I couldn't stay at home, and I walked out just to calm my nerves. When I reached Narutowicza Street, near the "Ravo" warehouse, I saw that some were there. From the side of the street, next to the fence, some teenagers and some adults were trying to exchange some goods or just observe. I approached and I started to look for the face of the girl I had met before. She noticed me and gave me a sign to wait. She ran into the building and a moment later she returned with Regina Glanc. "Piniek and Abe are alive and a week ago they joined the kibbutz in the ghetto. I came here today just to see you. If you like, you can enter the ghetto with us, but maybe tomorrow would be better. Go to Kordecki Street, where a few of our girls work and they will bring you a letter from the boys." We had to part ways because the teenagers were getting closer to us. The girl, who brought Regina, winked at me. "Now I have a request—my brother is staying with some people in Raków. I must write to him about an important issue and I'd like you to go and deliver this letter to him. Will you do it?" I knew it was risky for me, but after all she did a tremendous favor for me—I just couldn't refuse. I took her letter and I promised to go there the same day. She knew just the street and the name of the people, but she didn't know the house number. It would take lots of questions. Finding the boys put me in such a mood that nothing seemed difficult. I wrote a few words and very excited I returned to Grosz. But if I wanted to reach Raków before nightfall, I would have to forego Grosz.

The Brust Family

After lengthy inquiries, I finally found the Brust family's house. I asked a small girl if Mr. Brust lived there and she said, "This is my Daddy." She took me to the second courtyard leading to a one-room apartment. A cupboard separated one corner; a carbide lamp barely illuminated the room revealing a thirty-year-old woman who was kneading dough. "A Jewish woman, working at "Ravo" asked me to deliver a letter to her brother, who supposedly stays with you" I said quietly. "Here? You are mistaken, I'm sure it's someone else." I was obviously in the wrong place and in addition the woman asked me: "Are you Jewish too?" "No."

How difficult it was to utter such a denial. "Well, no one else would come" she said "but I don't care—near the steel mill lives another Brust, and beyond the factory as well. Maybe you'll find him there." I decided to leave, and I said that I wouldn't search anymore, since it was late, and I was leaving the next day. As I was leaving, a man entered. He was about forty years old, wearing work clothing. He was the husband of the woman. I told him that I was looking for this boy and I asked him if he knew where I could find him. I said that I wanted to do a favor for this Jewish woman, because she did something for me. "Yes," said Mr. Brust, "I know, give me the letter and I will deliver it to him." "Oh, but you see, I promised that I would deliver this letter myself, and in this way, I would fulfill my promise." After a moment's hesitation he said: "please wait in the hall, I'll call him from the neighbor." I left the room and when I returned a moment later, the boy I was looking for was in the room. "Maybe you want to talk—if so, go to the hall," said Mr. Brust. I gave the letter and introduced myself, but I saw that he kept a distance. After a while I said goodbye and I left taking a few words for the girl in "Ravo." Brust walked out with me, saying that he would walk me out. I told him who I was. From the first moment I had total confidence in this man. I told him in short about my experiences of the last few months. "I knew right away that you are Jewish," he said, "it's difficult to fool me, even if you don't look Jewish at all."

Henryk Brust and his wife Aniela Brust (sitting) with their daughter Ala at a
reception in their honor in the Dutch Embassy in Warsaw, 1981. USHMM,
Acc. Number: 1998.A.0258.2 (Series 3, Box 2.9, no. 74), courtesy of Jacob Dimant.

He told me that the boy was staying with him and that he was Lola's (the girl from Raków) fiancé and not a brother. He told me that the boy had lived with his parents in Raków, where they had a store. The Brust family got to know them very well after the outbreak of the war. Right at the beginning of the war, Brust and his wife were sentenced to three months in jail for crossing the border into the Reich with food. This boy gave the three Brust children food, without payment, for three months. Later this boy and his family were forced into the Częstochowa ghetto in the center of town. During the first Aktion he fled the ghetto and reached Raków, where he tried to hide in the home of a woman, who had benefitted from many favors from his family. After a few days, she said that for hiding a Jew the penalty was death and that he had to leave, so he came to Brust. "He told me that he came directly from the ghetto, and he asked me to save him until the situation had calmed down and he would be able to return to the ghetto. Fine—I said—undress and lie down in bed and rest and we'll see what to do later. I don't hold it against him that he lied to me, but if he wasn't afraid to come to me, he should know, that he could tell me the truth. Everyone tries to save himself if he can. He has lived with us for two months. If a stranger comes, he sits behind the cupboard. My wife is losing her mind, because we could pay with our own and our children's heads. But you know how it is; women have weaker nerves. I support her as much as I can, but this Lola is sending someone all the time. That's why my wife lied to you, because an hour before there was another woman from Lola, but we don't want her to know, that he is with us. My wife is scared of her own shadow." I told him that if I would have met more people like him during the last three months—I could retain some faith in humanity.

"It's true that the world is rotten and most people who live in it are bad, but there are more people who are sensitive to the fate of others like me. You have to believe it." Only after a few hours, as we walked with each other a few times, I said goodbye to Mr. Brust. When he kissed my hand goodbye it wasn't the same as Gromuł. This time I felt that he was telling me what he thought of racial and national differences. On this day not only did I find my boys, but I also discovered a human being in the wasteland.

Monday—At Kordecki Street, it was easy to communicate with the people from the work group. A civilian was guarding them, who, for the permission to trade (selling clothing and other items for food), was getting a nice reward. He didn't pay any attention to people talking. This group worked on cleaning and smoothing the gravel paths—they worked for the city administration. Near Jasna Góra they swept the park paths—it was a good place to pass by them and talk. There were many Poles around, who were exchanging goods for food, and I could pass as one of them. At Kordecki Street I met Regina. I wasn't able to go into the ghetto with the group on this day, even though they were led by a Jewish leader, who was a member of the kibbutz. Two girls had arrived that day from Warsaw, and they were to enter the ghetto. It could be that they would check IDs at the gate. Regina gave me a letter from the boys in which they instructed me where I should go. I went aside to read the letter, but beforehand I bought a loaf of bread for one of the workers, who asked me for it. I handed it to him saying that he could pay me some other time—I saw such amazement in his eyes. He was convinced that I was a Polish woman—I had to smile.

The letter from the boys was filled with joy that we had found each other. They have a lot to tell me about their experiences. I was to go to a sports field and meet a woman Cela Bylewska, who was expecting me, and she would bring me into the ghetto. I ran like crazy to the Avenue of the Blessed Virgin Mary or Third Avenue and I met Cela a short time after my arrival. She lives in the kibbutz, and she had already arranged with the leader of the group (a Jew) that I would join them. I was supposed to be there at 3 p.m. It was already 1 p.m., so I ran to Grosz to tell Marysia that I had met a friend and together we would travel to Kielce for a few days. I took my washing utensils and pajamas and I ran back. I was so impatient that I took a droshky. I waited at the sports field until 5:30 p.m. I was surrounded and questioned about what it was like living in "the other world," how it was possible to make it work and also amazement that I would enter the ghetto of my own free will. I was walking together with Cela, four in a row, toward the ghetto. If someone from Grosz would see me marching into the ghetto, it would be funny seeing their faces, but of course this would be detrimental for me. We passed the former ghetto, littered with dishes, pots and pans, smashed furniture, and broken glass. We reached the current ghetto, and my first impression was as if I had fallen from a spacious, bright space into a dungeon. I had no time to look around. I ran behind Cela, who was bringing me to the boys.

From the people I used to know at Przemysłowa Street, there were only Aron Gepner and Regina. The rest were older members of different Zionist organizations, who lived together forming a kibbutz. They live in three rooms facing the courtyard and on the other side there was a kibbutz of another Zionist organization. The whole building was taken by the two kibbutzim. The ghetto consists of the four poorest and most neglected streets: Nadrzeczna, Garncarska, Senatorska, and Kozia. The streets are surrounded

by barbed wire and guarded by Jewish and Polish police. There was a gate at
Nadrzeczna Street, guarded as well by Jewish and Polish police and two gendarmes, who go away during the day, when the Jews go out to work. When
the labor groups return to the ghetto, the gendarmes search people and con-
fiscate food, but all together it wasn't so bad. It was much worse when the
searches were conducted by the head of the ghetto, nominated by Hauptman
Degenhardt, or if Degenhardt himself was conducting the searches. There
was still chaos in the ghetto. Selections were taking place and people were
disappearing. There was a ghetto kitchen, where every worker received black
coffee before going to work. For dinner, after work, turnip soup—1 liter and
two hundred grams of black bread. From time to time there was a little marmalade, and on Sunday a little better dinner, with meat. It's clear that people
who can afford it cook their own dinner and try to eat better than two hundred grams of bread. Of course, not everyone has money and not everyone
can earn money. One can earn money by selling their possessions, if they had
any, or by stealing. On Garibaldi Street there was a warehouse with clothes,
underwear, dresses, shoes, coats, sheets, and many other things impossible to figure out. The labor group working in this warehouse had almost a
thousand men and women, cleaning out every building of the former ghetto
and bringing everything new and things in good shape to the warehouse,
and taking everything else to Ravo. They were sorting it in the warehouse.
These were the workers, who "organized" (which meant taking things which
had belonged to their brothers and sisters or were frequently even their
own) things, which they were able to bring safely into the ghetto and then
sell to those who worked in labor groups outside the ghetto. Those people
could then sell these things to Poles outside the ghetto, buying food, which
they brought into the ghetto and selling it to the people who worked at the
Garibaldi warehouse, to the policemen and the doctors (there were about
ten physicians with wives and children), to the kitchen workers, and to everyone who had a position in the ghetto. Predominantly these were people who
were very wealthy before the war and still had money. The kibbutz supports
itself in the same way; otherwise, they would all die of hunger. There were
about twenty people in the kibbutz, who worked inside the ghetto, and about
twenty who worked outside. The local authority (*gemeinde*) in the ghetto
took care of the kibbutz members issuing some food for them, but this was
never enough. A few boys and girls worked at the Garibaldi warehouse, and
they "organized"; others were going out to work taking the merchandize to
sell; the group shared the profits. Piniek worked in the technical department

inside the ghetto as an electrician and he did it very well and Abe as well. In general, both of them were very talented in handicrafts, especially Abe. They earned well and gave their share to the common cash register. One of the boys started a shoe repair workshop and made some money this way as well. From the profits they bought additional bread and butter for everybody and in the evening, they cooked a little better soup for all. A few girls don't go out to work—they stay at home, cleaning, cooking, and washing for everyone. There were just a few girls and they worked very hard.

That night, the three of us sat till the morning, recounting what each of us had gone through during the past six weeks. On the third day of the Aktion the boys had to stand for a selection. Degenhardt (captain of the *Schupo*, Paul Degenhardt) conducted it and he wasn't inclined to choose young people for deportation to death, and young men especially. He left a few women in place. Piniek and Abe were sent to a metal workshop. The next day laborers were chosen to work in "Raków," and the boys volunteered to go there. It was difficult to know which labor brigade was better. They had a few changes of underwear, shirts, pants, and shoes with them and all the cash they had left. Abe had some dollar bills sewn into the lining of his jacket. The two weeks they were at Pelcery were a nightmare—every night when they were returning from work, they were forced to run up a very narrow staircase to the hall where they slept. On the stairs stood Ukrainians who struck them with rifle butts or rubber batons. The workers were constantly searched, and their things were confiscated without any exception. They slept on the floor without any cover. Two armed Ukrainians stood in the corners and if anyone raised their head, he would get a bullet. (Heniek Brust told me the same about his time in the Łódź prison.) New tortures were invented every day, so the hours they worked at the steelworks were pure pleasure. The day they finally saw me, they had buried their money somewhere in the steel mill, because they couldn't invent any more ways to hide it during searches.

On that memorable Thursday, when we saw each other, when they went to the Pelcery factory courtyard, they were selected for deportation. They were forced to take off their jackets, but they kept their high boots. They had two layers of clothes on them. They were taken to 10 Katedralna Street, where they had to wait until enough people had been caught for the transport. They were there for three days constantly thinking how to escape. Abe cut out a passage to the adjacent room—he used a folding knife for two nights until he cut this passage—and the room had a door leading to a

courtyard next to First Avenue (1-a Aleja). People who were awaiting transport didn't believe that they would be deported, and they started to yell at
Abe that if their escape were to be discovered, the rest of them would be
killed. So, this attempt didn't work because a Polish policeman discovered
their intentions. On the third day the gendarmes forced them to go to the
train station. Abe was still frantically searching for some means of rescue and
proposed going to the toilet. If they would be noticed, they would return.
The toilets were in a small building on the side and there were a few stalls.
They reached it unnoticed, and they stood in the last, dark stall, in which
just one person could fit. But they were three. A woman was already there;
she had an arrangement that someone would come to pick her up after the
transport train had left. They stood there and listened, as all the others were
pushed onto the trains. They heard the steps of someone coming into the
building. It was a policeman checking if anyone was there—he opened their
stall door, looked in . . . and didn't see them. He didn't have a flashlight. It was
afternoon; they stood there till 9 p.m. They left and through the attic they
reached house number 12. They really didn't know what to do. They had
no other choice—they had to try to reach Raków. When they came down
to the staircase, some woman started to shout. She didn't want to hear their
appeals to stop and that she should just let them go, but she ran to the street
and called a gendarme. The boys ran back to the attic and from there to the
roof. When Piniek helped Abe to get up on the roof, the bullets were flying
around them. Somehow, they reached First Avenue and there, in some attic,
they spent the night. The next day they found a bunker with beds, bedding,
and an electric stove. Later they noticed smoke coming out of a chimney of
this building. They quietly went down and found out that there were other
people there. It was a baker with his brother and his wife and children—
they were the only people in the street still left behind. For the whole week
they fed the boys, but the boys slept in the attic of the bunker. After eight
days they took this family (the two brothers had escaped from the train to
Treblinka and returned to the ghetto). The next two weeks the boys lived
completely alone in the bunker, cooking on the electric stove from the products the baker had left them. They didn't know how this would end; their
supplies were almost gone. They started to contemplate going to Raków.
They had no idea that a new ghetto had now been formed. The labor group
from Garibaldi Street arrived to clean up and one of the girls wanted to enter
the room from which the boys reached the attic, but the door was locked.
She started to yell and one of the boys looked out and quietly asked her to

stop shouting, but she continued. They had to leave their hiding place. A Jewish policeman who was guarding the girls promised to smuggle the boys into the ghetto, but a Polish policeman had to be bribed. The last fifty dollars they had were passed on and that's how they reached the ghetto. Aron Gepner took them into the kibbutz. He took Abe, because he belonged to Gordonia and he took Piniek, because he was Abe's brother. Anyway, at that point they didn't stick to the rules. The kibbutz members supported themselves in ways that in the past were forbidden by their regulations.

Tuesday—In the morning, Piniek had to go to work in the technical department house, and I stayed with Abe and a few guys and girls. Someone came to warn us that it was dangerous to stay inside, because the gendarmes would come and check IDs. There were instances that they killed the people they found. So, we had to go out into the courtyard with everyone. Piniek arrived in a panic that there might be a selection. There was no choice. We went out to the square just outside the ghetto—Rynek Warszawski, the one where there was a gate to the ghetto and where every day at 5 a.m. the labor groups assembled. Next to the gate there was a "labor office," which had lists of all the laborers in every group. This office arranged to send the demanded number of workers to the factories and workshops. The head of this office was Kurland, a member of the Judenrat. He was very handsome, middle-aged, polite, and kind. It was he who had helped Regina Glanc, and he treated the members of the kibbutz especially well. Indeed, our group was told to stand to the side, as people employed in the ghetto, and at the first opportunity Kurland gave us a sign to go to work. At the square the German head of the ghetto, Überscherer, selected older people from the labor groups to be deported. We marched out to the warehouse to sift potatoes. After about an hour, one after another, the girls slipped out to go home and the boys stayed till lunchtime. At home the work started: I cleaned up the room in which we ate and that day we cooked (the two girls, who were supposed to come the day before, arrived only on that day. Both looked like typical Slavs. They were Regina's friends, and the rest of the group was still in Czerniaków, in Warsaw. They had avoided the big deportations of the summer of 1942, but at this point they expected that their turn was up.)

On Wednesday, I walked out with the group from the "sports field" and at the time of the arrival of a train from Kielce, I returned to Grosz (the town section). I took with me a few things for sale. The boys would try to go out with the work groups, and I would go daily to Lola to pick up letters from them. If they weren't able to go out, or if I wanted to see them, I would have to prepare a reason to go to the Jewish workplace. After a few days I told Gromuł that I had found the two Lewins and they gave me back my money. I said that at this point traveling was so difficult, I would try to trade with them together and make some money. Of course, the Gromułs would participate in the trade and would make money to support their family. They were pleased that I would help to make the local trade possible and the rest they would do alone. Marysia was very happy.

It was decided that I would not go into the ghetto to stay, that I would stay on the Aryan side, where I could be more useful, having chances that many could only dream about. The "many" imagined that being on Aryan side meant a quiet and safe life . . . I had to agree. My days were filled with constant running—to Ravo to take letters and messages from the ghetto; a second time to bring letters back, and in the evening to Brust in Raków. I had more sympathy for Heniek Brust every day. His wife Aniela kept her distance—I felt her fear that in addition to the one behind the cupboard, another forbidden person was coming to their apartment. She never said a word and was always pleasant. I never blamed her, because I understood very well that she had good reasons to be afraid, but I knew that I wasn't the reason. Even if they would discover me as a Jew in their apartment, I was registered as a Pole someplace else and my nose is adequately short, so no one could expect her to know that I was Jewish. I told Aniela this reasoning and Heniek said the same, but she couldn't overcome her fear and stay calm. I got to know and like their children and they started to like me as well. Fourteen-year-old Ala, twelve-year-old Henia and nine-year-old Szczepanek—all three are smart, even if they are just children. They are all intelligent above their age. In addition, Szczepan has beautiful black eyes and in general is very sweet. I could admire him for hours. Henia is resolute, a quite determined child. A priest expelled her from school for heretical behavior. (She asked too many questions and the priest asked one of the parents to come to school. Heniek refused to go, because he doesn't like the clergy on principle, and Aniela didn't want to go either. When the priest asked why her parents didn't come and uttered unpleasant names, which hurt Henia—she answered that her parents are not well-off like the priest, who does nothing and just gathers money. She said that her parents work hard to support their family and they don't have time for stupidities. She was expelled for this.)

Since Lola's fiancé lived in their apartment, all three children tried not to play with their friends and didn't let them come to their place. All three were brought up according to their father's beliefs; he was a real proletarian and a

former member of Polish Socialist Party. For many years he had worked in
the Raków steel mill and during the war he worked in the bakery located in
the courtyard of the building where he lived. The bakery baked bread for the
workers from the steel mill in Raków. When I wasn't in the ghetto, the Brust
household was like a magnet for me—for a few hours I could be myself over
there. I didn't have to be on guard all the time and the friendship I felt from
Heniek didn't bring up the question: if he knew who I really am, would he
still be my friend? So even though I knew Aniela's thoughts—I couldn't help
but go there.

Janka came again—this time alone. Eugeniusz is here as well. All three
of us wanted to go into the ghetto for a day. Eugeniusz had a meeting with
the Prior of the convent about placing Jewish children in the convent until
they would have a right to live again. It's doubtful that this would succeed,
but Eugeniusz is enthusiastic about this plan. There were still Jewish crafts-
men in the building on the corner of First Avenue number 14 and Wilson
Street. These were sewing, shoemaking, and carpentry workshops, working
for the Germans. The owners of these workshops with their families and their
workers were not subjected to Aktionen and they lived there quietly. One of
the entrances to the building was from Wilson Street and it belonged to the
former ghetto. The second gate is from First Avenue number 14 and from
number 12 this street belongs to the Aryan district. This way one can enter
at number 14 without anyone paying attention, since there were no guards
there. Many labor-groups returned through Wilson Street, so it was easy to
join them and enter the ghetto. On Sundays, residents of number 14 can
enter the ghetto under the guard of the Jewish police. A few of the policemen,
including the head of the Jewish police, Mr. Parasol, lived in this building.
So, if one has some pull, it's possible to enter this way as well, or if the policeman is in a good mood. I met Aron a few times in the carpenter's workshop.
I met Eugeniusz in the sewing workshop, which belonged to the Schnitzer
family. Then again "I left for Kielce for two days," and we entered the ghetto.
I left first, because I had to call to the group on Czerniaków that Eugeniusz
was coming. At Grosz, Marysia told me that Czesław was there looking for
me; he spent the night there and they all drank beer. A letter from Helena
arrived and Czesław opened it and added a few words. But what did he do?
He left the letter open, and Dora addressed her letter: "Dear Ita," and added
many Jewish names and issues, which could be only Jewish—this was underground work! But later we found out that Marysia didn't read this letter. She
behaved better than many highly educated people. This visit provoked more

gossip and the whole building started talking. I found out later that Mrs. Kowalczykowa expressed her opinion that I was Jewish, since I had so many Jewish visitors. Eugeniusz left for Warsaw. Czesław was to come, but he did not. I took Lola to Brust; she wanted to see her fiancé and both of us spent the night there. Both of us slept with Henia in the same bed; Aniela in the second bed with Ala, Szczepan, and Heniek, and I slept on the floor. I quarreled with Heniek that I should sleep on the floor and not him, since he needed to get up for work in the morning. He wouldn't let me.

He called me by my first name since I asked him to do it. He agreed on condition of reciprocity, but I somehow couldn't bring myself to call him by his first name. Later it became so natural, that it seemed strange that it used to be an issue. This sleeping on the floor while I slept in a bed was very uncomfortable for me, so finally I told Heniek that I wouldn't sleep in their place, if they wouldn't let me sleep on the floor—even if I really liked sleeping there. With Marysia and Stefan everything was going very well, except for these cursed neighbors and their constant talk about the Jews. The drunk Figzoł, the rudeness of Miedziejewski, and the arrogance of his wife, the bigot; Figzoł's wife, who has bruises all over, a gift from her husband, whom she constantly wanted to divorce; the fake pleasantries of Kowalczykowa, who digs behind my back; the idiotic courtship of Genek and the stupid comments of his sister: "Miss Genia, why don't you marry Genek; you fit so well; you are alone and he has a nice apartment—you would make such a good couple." This was my company on Dolna Street. Only Wizenthal, the shop owner, was different—he was a serious man who didn't gossip. He had a secret radio, and he is some kind of an ideologist, but I don't know what kind. But in his and his wife's way of doing business—the way they overcharged and under-weighed the merchandise. Maybe this is the basis of commerce. I obviously don't understand enough about it. A Jew is labelled a swindler, but when someone else does the same—there is no label for it. When I sat among them, and I listened to their abuse, I couldn't answer—all I could do was to clench my hands until my nails drew blood. I felt disgust with myself that I didn't tell them who I was, and I wasn't arguing with them. I knew very well that I wouldn't convince them, and the only result would be denunciation. In spite of it all, I couldn't help myself and I gave them examples of the same behavior of Poles and if this didn't teach them anything? How come they didn't show a Christian attitude. I knew that I only brought damage to myself, especially since there were enough rumors about me. I just couldn't sit there and say nothing. When I went to Brust, I could relax from it all, but even there, someone like that would come there too. Sometimes when I just couldn't take it anymore, I would go to visit one of the labor groups and I entered the ghetto. Only in the ghetto could I be myself for a day or two, just that it's exhausting to be so tense. One never knew if going to sleep at night one wouldn't wake up in a ghetto surrounded by gendarmes. Every day there were different rumors. In a persistent way a rumor circulated about the next Aktion—it was supposed to be on December 18th. So, some boys and all the girls wanted to go to Będzin.

A few days before the 18th, all those who were to go to Będzin were to leave the ghetto with different work groups, and from there I was to take them to Pucuch (a smuggler), about two or three kilometers away, at Osikowa Street. The other group of boys and girls wanted to reach the Warsaw Ghetto. Some thirty thousand were left there officially, but twice as many were unofficially in the small ghetto, created within the old ghetto. People go in and out the same way as in Częstochowa, but it is more difficult and dangerous because of blackmailers and extortionists, who stood all day long near the two gates leading out of the ghetto. One had to be ready to forfeit a few thousand zloty at the exit, if one couldn't manage to leave a labor group unnoticed.

December 16—I picked up from Lola a letter from Abe and Piniek. They begged me not to endanger myself by taking our people to Pucuch. I was uneasy that they felt this way. Despite that, I went to Kopernik Street where our girls came out and the boys were supposed to be at "Golgotha." But at Kopernik Street there was nobody. They had left without waiting for me. Now I had to go to Lola. She left the ghetto before the 18th and went to the Brusts. She will be there for a little while and then hopefully she will find courage to try to manage on her own, like me. She has excellent false papers, and she looks good, but she is not that brave, even if she is usually quite resolute. After accompanying Lola, I wanted to go to "Golgotha," but it was getting late. I decided to go to Pucuch to find out if they were all there. Aron and four other boys were there. The girls were waiting at Pucuch's partner. They were too impatient to wait for me and they went on their own, asking many people for directions, which was inadvisable. Pucuch and his wife were quite upset by their behavior, but still not too scared. The girls and three boys left the next day. Aron and one more stayed for the time being since they didn't have the whole payment and they were waiting for the sale of a few more things. I had a few things to sell, but Marysia went with them to sell some clothes at a village—it wasn't successful, because the things were too expensive.

December 18—I didn't sleep much that night. The evening before, I had returned from Brust. Heniek accompanied me. I was supposed to meet Ala near Ravo. She wanted to get news for Lola, and I wanted to get news from the boys. I went to the "garbage" with my heart in my throat. If they were not there, that would be a sign that indeed the Aktion was on. After a few moments of fear, not seeing anyone at the "garbage heap," we went up Narutowicza Street and we found them in the stockroom. Today there was no Aktion at all. Abe got out with the electricians; Piniek stayed in the ghetto.

January 10—My life can be compared to a boat without a sail, in a stormy sea. At any moment a huge wave can turn it over, but by some miracle the boat is still floating, avoiding the dangerous wave at the last moment. How does it happen? I don't know. For many months death has been circling over my head, but always at the last moment, some chance lets me escape death, while I do not participate in it, and I do not direct it. I always assure Marysia that I definitely do not feel any fear, but I know that the moment the police would come to pick me up, I would be lost. My identification papers have no meaning, but the fact that I do not have a baptismal certificate is really bad. I tried to find out how to get one, but to find a "macher" is very difficult. I cannot "organize" just any birth certificate and a *Kennkarte* (ID card). To prove that I am not a Jew, I must have an ID, and a residence registration from the same locality with a date of birth. Otherwise, I cannot reside in Częstochowa at all, in case someone from 9 Dolna Street might meet me anywhere and would recognize me. I see how this issue bothers Marysia and how she tries to be so much nicer to me. This naïve woman is so certain that I am not Jewish, that she would vouch for it with her life and Stefan feels the same way. At one time Marysia said to me: "Miss Genia, don't say anything good about the Jews in front of these people; they are ready to take it as a proof, these deplorable creatures. Do you think that they wouldn't start to curse the Jews, as they like to do, even if none of the Jews did anything bad to them? Just the opposite, this woman worked for a Jewish family for many years and told us that she had a good life. Would she do anything today to help any of her previous employers? Before they made a ghetto, during the first two years of the war, a Jewish tailor used to come to Mudrzejewski and worked for him fourteen hours a day and maybe more. Would they give him a safe place, even for one hour, if he would avoid death by this? Let them think what they want. I have to tell them what I think."

January 12—Marysia and Stefan travelled into the country at dawn to sell some clothes and to buy food. I stayed with the children. I took advantage of the time when Alusia went to sleep, and I ran to Ravo to see Lola. She gave me a letter. It's quiet in the ghetto. So why do I sit here and worry so much? Rumors wind me up and I go down to Kowalczykowa: "please tell me why you spread gossip about me; you see that in these dangerous times you expose me to harm. Did I do something bad to you? I am not afraid of the gossip, and I am not afraid to die as you perhaps imagine, but you will bear the responsibility for spreading rumors." "Me? I never say anything. Everyone else gossips, that you entertain Jews and that you are a Jew yourself. For hiding a Jew, the penalty is death and the whole building will pay the price for you." "If the Gromuls want to keep you, let them do it, but I will go to the police (Polish police) and I will report them and you." Well, she told me very clearly. My decision to go to her was the right one. Otherwise, I would've found out about her deed directly from the gendarmerie. But I cannot leave the building today; I am alone with the children, and I have to wait for Marysia and Stefan to return. I am waiting for a gendarme to appear at the door any moment. I am so upset, and it takes all the strength of my will not to show how distraught I am.

Mr. Figzol came by and said that I shouldn't take to heart "old women's talk," and he assured me of his friendship (a few times I had lent him money for vodka). I tried to think quickly: If I have to run, and I won't be able to return to this place—I would have to go back permanently to the ghetto, which will be liquidated any moment.

When Marysia and Stefan returned, I told them about my conversation with Kowalczykowa and I told them that I had decided to travel to the Lublin area, because my birth certificate is there in my friends' house. I explained that it would be difficult to get a copy, or it would take a long time, and I want to show them all that they are gossiping for no reason. I explained that I would leave in a few days, because I didn't want them to think that I am afraid of them. "If the gendarmerie comes for me during this time—there is nothing I can do about it, but you would be in the clear and I guarantee that nothing will happen to you—I did tell Mrs. Kowalczyk that she wants to betray you and to make orphans out of your two children—but in reality, you have nothing to worry about. I have identification papers and I am registered; and even if I were Jewish, it is not your fault that I lied to you." "But I am not afraid"—said Marysia. "But what if these horrible people really report you and they (the police) would shoot and kill you right away, without asking any questions?" "What could I do? Nothing would happen; one can die only once," I answered boldly. I talked about it with Wizenthal as well. He knew that I was afraid of the gendarmerie for a different reason. Since I met Heniek, I brought to Dolna Street every edition of "*Gwardia Ludowa*" (a Communist publication) and "WRW" (an underground publication of the Sikorski Army). This is the reason that Wizenthal and Gromuła, as well as Genek, "know" that my frequent travels are for the underground and not commercial, and that I have good reasons to be afraid of the Gestapo. I found out that Wizenthal is a nationalist or "Endek" whatever,[12] but at this point in time he is an enemy of the Germans. He told me that I am doing the right thing by going away for the time being, so it didn't matter if I would bring the birth certificate, but the gossip would disappear when its object would disappear. And anyway, he will shut the mouths of the worst gossipers. At night, every noise kept me awake and jumping out of bed at every real or imaginary movement I heard, and during the day—every step on the stairs made my heart stop with the absolute certainty that they are coming for me—somehow, I managed to withstand it for six days: from Saturday until Thursday. During these few days at the Brust family I didn't sleep, not even through one night. I told Heniek about the situation, but I asked him not to say a word to his wife. She shivered each time I appeared, but I wouldn't have been able to relax if I had been in their place anyway. On Thursday I packed my things; luckily Mudrzejewski had just finished my coat. He totally botched it. Marysia's parting words to me were: "Please return to us quickly and write to us"—I left for the "Lublin area" or actually I entered the Częstochowa ghetto, after taking my things to the Brust home.

Again, life outside the ghetto seems to exist in a fog. I wrote a letter to Marysia, and I asked Regina, who travelled to Warsaw, to send it from there. I wrote Marysia that I had given the letter to an acquaintance, who was going to Warsaw, so it would reach her quicker. I gave her the address of Halina Wiśniewska in Parczew; after all I had to give some address for her to write back. Later I will tell her that the letter was probably lost. I wrote to the Brusts as well. Heniek sent me some encouraging words. I sent a few letters to Marysia via Ala; I wrote that I had already obtained my birth certificate, but that I am still busy there. Abe recognized his own jacket, worn by a guy

---

12 *Endecja*—the National Democratic Party.

from "Hasag Pelcery" and he managed to reclaim it. In return he gave him a coat, which he had "organized" before. It still had dollars inside . . .

Wyga and Tadek had just arrived from Warsaw, and they arrange these issues. One Sunday in the middle of February, I left with the "Fourteen" together with Wyga.[13] We were supposed to meet at Mr. and Mrs. Szuyer. I promised them that I would bring Wyga to them, because they want to talk to him as well. That night I will spend at their place and take the first train to Warsaw, where Wyga was to arrange a birth certificate for me. He left at night and left a phone number for me. No address and no last names—these are not to be mentioned. In the morning it was impossible to go through the gate; a gendarme was on guard and checked everyone's papers. Tension spread quickly. Some said that the Aktion was in this building and others said that it was in another building; that the Hauptmann with the gendarmerie was to come and check if only the people on the list were in the building. Well, I arrived at the best possible moment . . . I tried to keep calm and to plan, but I concluded that nothing can be done. In addition, the Szuyers might have big problems. Everybody was so upset that going back to deliberations was out of the question. The younger of their two daughters, who was dressed in a long skirt and an adult blouse, to look older and able to work, started to cry inconsolably. At 11 a.m. a Jewish policeman came from the ghetto and told us that after the first few work groups (*placowki*) marched out, suddenly the gendarmes arrived and ordered all the work groups to come out to the main square and all those who were hiding in the ghetto; and they chose some three hundred people to send to Skarżysko-Kamienna, a penal camp, worse than hell. One of the boys from this group took out a revolver and fired a shot toward a gendarme, but the gun was rusted and jammed. The boy dropped the gun and attacked the gendarme with his bare hands, but all he accomplished was breaking his finger. A few gendarmes dragged him away and the man who was attacked ran to the phone and a moment later a few cars with gendarmes arrived. They executed twenty-nine men and the attacking boy. Later I found out that ten girls from the kibbutz were taken as well and from them only two went to the camp. A few escaped on the way to the train; two jumped from the train near Koluszki—one with a broken arm and the second one limping, but they somehow reached Częstochowa. The Ghetto was calmer again; no one was standing at the gate so I ran quickly to Ravo to tell

---

13 The "Fourteen" is a reference to a labor detachment from the ghetto.

Lola what happened, so she shouldn't return to the ghetto. Lola told me that Abe left the ghetto with the work group and Piniek stayed in the ghetto. So long as I have not found out what happened to them, I cannot go anywhere. I take a droshky, so I wouldn't meet anyone. I arrived at Ravo, where I stayed for a few days, and after finding out that the boys stayed and that it seems that it will be calm for the time being, I left for Warsaw. I have a recommendation letter from Marysia to Uncle Stefan on Furmańska Street, in which she wrote that I am her cousin. She asked that they should let me stay with them for a few days until I had taken care of a few things in Warsaw. I was supposed to go to Marysia's dear friend, who recently married a policeman. At Furmańska Street I found only Uncle Stefan; his wife was travelling. After lunch I met Zyga in a coffee shop and after a few hours, when we met again, he handed me a birth certificate. It has a stamp of a diocese in Wilno (Vilnius) and an identical signature of a priest (many birth certificates—blank, stamped, and signed were stolen). Nothing could be done about it, I was born in Sieradz and baptized in Wilno, since he wasn't able to obtain a blank form of a baptism from Sieradz. I spent that night at Marysia's best friend, who was very nice to me. Her husband guards the ghetto and of course he got rich doing that. And I thought to myself: "if you only knew who your guest is now." The next day I obtained a certified copy of my birth certificate, because when my personal information was written in, there were stains, and it was clear that things were changed. Any Christian could risk having such a birth certificate, but I couldn't. I walked back and forth near the gate of the ghetto, on Żelazna Street. I was watching to see if it was possible to go in. It was impossible. I went to the main train station. I wanted to go to Łuków and from there to Parczew, to find out what is happening with the boys' sisters. Since the letter received via Janka, there had been no news, not even a word from them. The boys had wanted for a long time for me to go to check on what was happening there, but something always interfered. It was difficult to decide to go on such a journey.

Forged Baptismal Certificate for Genowefa Zawadska, born in Sieradz, 1922.
USHMM, Acc. Number: 1998.A.0258.2 (Series 3, Box 2.7, no. 1), courtesy of
Jacob Dimant.

My throat hurts and I have a fever; it would be best to go to Częstochowa
and go to bed. But I will not come back after travelling halfway. The train will
arrive only tomorrow; it's impossible to stay the whole night at the train station; there is even no place to sit. I went to Furmańska, and I asked to spend
the night. I was let in, but begrudgingly (he was afraid that gossip would
reach his wife that a young woman slept there, when his wife was away), but
I just couldn't go to look for a place to spend a night someplace else. I spent
the whole night lying on the edge of the bed, fully dressed. I suppose that this
old man, with a seriously damaged liver, didn't have to worry about the gossip
of his neighbors. The next day the Terespol train, which was supposed to
leave in the morning, was moved to the evening. I waited at the train station,
trembling from frost. I had a high fever. I left the train station and at Nowy
Świat Street I went into a movie house. I had two hours to get warm and to
doze off in the dark. Finally, the overcrowded train took me to Łuków arriving at 3 a.m. It was impossible to stay at the station through the night because
of roundups, so I went with other passengers to a hostel nearby, where I sat
till the morning. I had no idea where the ghetto was located and if any of the
people I knew were still around, but I heard conversations of other people
about trading with Jews through the wire fence. I surmised that it was possible to approach the ghetto. After a short walk I found the fence and soon after

I was behind it. The family I knew was intact except for the father, who was killed. There was no need to go to Parczew; only some twenty Jews are left there, and the rest were killed. Rutka with her husband and children and with Tyla went to some peasant not far from town. He was to hide them for a huge amount of money. At night he attacked them, robbed them of all they had (as far as I know they had about two hundred thousand zloty and jewelry) and in the morning he went to the gendarmerie to report that Jews came to him. All were executed . . . I left the ghetto in the afternoon; I was sick and devastated. The train to Warsaw was only the next morning. It was my fifth day of travel and [I had slept] only one night, which I spent dressed. Fever was burning me up, and I couldn't swallow. I spent another night in a hostel, on a mattress on the floor. I was coughing so badly that the landlady brought me hot milk. The next day there is a notice that the train will leave not in the morning but at 7 p.m., but all the people were standing on the platform, in a biting cold, for many hours, since it was unknown when exactly the train would arrive from Terespol. By pure miracle I got into the train car, pushed by the crowd. I spent the whole night suspended in the air, supported by the arm of some gentleman, who had a fur collar. It served as the only protection from the frosty wind blowing from a window without any glass. I spent the next day in Warsaw and at night went back to Częstochowa. We arrived at 6 a.m. in Częstochowa; for me it was too early, because none of the work groups had marched out yet and I needed to find out what was going on in the ghetto, and if I could enter the ghetto and finally go to bed. I decided not to wait at the train station, but I entered a pastry shop nearby to have something hot to drink. A moment later the gendarmerie surrounded the train station and took away all arriving passengers and those in the waiting hall. Among those taken away was "Motek," a boy who was in charge of the ghetto underground. He was able to escape, and he returned to the ghetto. At 8 a.m. I went to 54th Avenue. I found out that the ghetto was calm. Mr. Szuyer, seeing my condition, asked a policeman to take me with him. In a few minutes I was already at 70 Nadrzeczna Street, in the kibbutz, where two happily surprised boys welcomed me. But I was thinking only about how to tell them the tragic news, which I brought? I wasn't strong enough to console them or to participate in their despair. I just wanted to lie in bed and not to think . . . not to think!

I have to decide to get out and go to Dolna Street—I have to convince them. On Sunday I leave again with the "Fourteen" and I reached Dolna Street at the time the train from Warsaw usually gets in. When I entered the apartment, I was greeted with: "Holy Spirit, praise the Lord"—you are finally here! Pleasant, smiling faces; what caused this change? A little later Marysia enters, and she was genuinely happy to see me: "there was no need to be away so long for a birth certificate. The gossip had subsided; now everyone is behind Miss Genia and Mrs. Kowalczyk is scared that after your return, you will file a complaint against her for libel. Now you will stay with us. You know, I saw these Lewins often. They gave me clothes to sell, without asking for money and I brought them food. I made some money for myself. They often asked after you, when would you be back . . ." There was a change at the Brust home as well; their attitude toward me was much warmer and very sincere.

One day, unexpectedly, Helena came to Dolna Street to see me. She had arrived from Będzin with Aron, and she wanted to enter the ghetto. I told her about the issue of the "kike" and that this place is unsafe. The next day, I escorted them to Ravo, and they entered the ghetto. I wouldn't like to meet Piniek anymore. At a certain moment he has seen me with Eugeniusz and heard that he calls me by my first name. At one time Eugeniusz was so careless, that he sent Piniek to fetch me at Dolna. Now, when I see him sometimes in the street, I imagine that he would send a gendarme for me. I spent two more days in the ghetto; the underground group gets bigger all the time. There were some guns already. In addition, they had accumulated sulfuric acid and most importantly there was contact with the Aryan underground. It was published in "WRN" (Wolność, Równość, Niepodległość—a publication of the Socialist underground organization—GL) that General Sikorski had testified in the British Parliament that about one million Jewish Polish citizens had been murdered. About a million! Almost two million had perished . . . A member of the Polish government in exile, a Jew, committed suicide after getting the news about the events in Warsaw. Sealed cattle train cars travel through Częstochowa, packed with Jews taking them to Treblinka. Among others, the Białystok [ghetto] was sent away too. Were Fryda and Chaim taken in these trains, or did they die before? In the Warsaw Ghetto there is a new Aktion again. But this time it looks different. When the gendarmerie entered the ghetto, a rain of grenades and bullets welcomed them. No one obeyed orders to come down from the buildings. A group the gendarmes succeeded in pushing to the Umschlagplatz managed to escape and return to the ghetto with guns in their hands. When gendarmes entered apartments, their guns were taken away and they were thrown out of the windows onto the sidewalks, to die there. Street battles are continuing. Buildings were blown up [by Germans]. Eugeniusz was one of the leaders, himself fighting like a lion. We get the news from boys and girls who were on the Aryan side in Warsaw. There was contact with the ghetto; half the ghetto was burning. Germans entered the ghetto in tanks and bomb from air, blowing things up building by building. Only individual Jews survived out of sixty thousand. Those people escaped through underground canals. After the Germans razed the ghetto to the ground, they cut off the exits through the canals, but a few managed to escape anyway. Eugeniusz most probably fell in action; otherwise, he would have come to Częstochowa or to Będzin. In the "WRN" publication, the article about the battles in the ghetto ended with: "we salute the heroes of the ghetto!" They will be a part of the history of battles of Polish citizens against the barbaric invaders from West. (Or something of this sort.) The appeal by Sikorski to the Polish nation: that they should stop blackmailing and oppressing the hiding Jews, as news reached him—they should reach out and help those in despair. The blackmailers and others should know that punishment would also reach them. This appeal came too late. It should've come a year earlier, but I have a feeling that even the government in exile, deep down is happy that the "Jewish question" in Poland was so radically solved. Now they would just shed a tear for show. The "Jewish question" was solved in all of Europe. Cattle trains from half of Europe, packed with Jews, travelled continuously to Treblinka and later to Bełżec. In gas chambers millions of Jews were murdered. Just a few gendarmes, and a gang of Latvians and Ukrainians managed this mass murder.

A certain lawyer came to us, whom we met while arranging registration in the Częstochowa Jewish community before the Aktion. He lived with a friend, an engineer, who had escaped from Treblinka. This young man had white hair and wasn't completely sane. What he told us was supported by others who by some miracle had managed to escape. This engineer was deported together with his wife and child; when they arrived in the overcrowded train car, in which many died on the way, the cars were opened, and a gang of rabid Latvians and Ukrainians started to push them out with whips. The weak were killed right away. Men were separated from the women and children. All were ordered to undress, and to put clothes on one pile and shoes on another. Money and gold had to be deposited in special boxes. A few young and healthy-looking men were chosen to sort the clothing. (From every transport a group was chosen, which was later destroyed, and another group was chosen from another transport—they were all killed so there wouldn't be even one witness to the bestiality, but the world will find out anyway . . .). Women and children were driven right away to a barrack; after a moment, a terrible, inhuman scream was heard and after a few minutes there was a deathly silence. The men were forced to run till they couldn't breathe and at that point they were pushed into a different barrack, from which this terrible scream was heard and then the same deathly silence . . . The engineer managed to escape during this run and joined the group selected for labor. He was selected to drag corpses. Using hooks, they had to drag corpses, which were melted into each other and were unrecognizable. He did recognize the corpse of his wife and the body of his child, as if it was part of her body. How did they burry tens of thousands of corpses—I don't know. Some said that corpses were burned, and some said that they were buried with the help of a tractor, but how it was done in reality, I don't know. The engineer managed to move to a labor group and later he hid in a train car filled with clothes taken from the victims and after two weeks he arrived in Częstochowa. All this was done in the heart of Europe, among people pretending to be civilized and cultured. It wasn't done in any other country, only in Poland (Gen. Sikorski wrote that it was done to blame the Polish nation). But they knew very well that in any other country there is no such antisemitism; that Jews from other countries seeing where they were taken (all those condemned—from France, Belgium, Holland, Romania, Bulgaria, and other countries occupied by the Germans) didn't believe it when they were told that they were going to their deaths. They believed these treacherous creatures that they are just being resettled to Jewish colonies, especially created for them. If the people among whom they lived had known, where and why they were taken, they would have given them refuge and shelter. Even in Germany not many people knew where the German Jews were taken. After all they could take twenty-five kilograms of luggage, even furs, even musical instruments. Talking to many Germans, trying to find out what their feelings were, I didn't feel the resentment and the venom of antisemitism. One German woman told me that she worked for a Jewish family before 1933 and "for sure I would not have had it so good in any Christian family, for sure." Of course, the youth brought up under Hitler and people who were members of the Nazi party have this venom in them. The older generation doesn't have it. But while living among the Poles, it is rare not to hear some insulting invective toward the Jews, even if their mentality, level of knowledge and the way they live their own lives could certainly be improved. A couple of cousins I met here—wife of an officer and a painter, so people rather cultured and intelligent, people participating in the uprising against the Germans and deported by them here; turned into slaves, they expressed their opinion in the following way: "Hitler did one thing right, he removed the Jewish nation from the body of Europe." "Maybe it could've been done more humanely" (just like the humane slaughter of cattle, according to Mrs. Prystorowa, a member of Polish Parliament). At the same time these two people treat me with respect; the man kisses my hand for welcome and for farewell—I have some value, but the moment that they find out who gave birth to me, all my personal worth would be lost. Heniek Brust is a much more valuable human being, who knows how to appreciate other human beings regardless of where and to whom he was born. In addition, he has a heart. His sister, Henryka hid a young Jewish woman in her own apartment, for many months, risking her own life, not taking a penny for it. His brother helped Jews who were imprisoned for forced labor at the Raków ironworks, as much as he could and in any way he could; one friend sent letters to me here . . . we owe him our gratitude and we feel great respect for him and his brother. Our letters were sent through him (he worked at the ironworks) and Heniek's letters to me, and back. Heniek's brother was killed by a guard; he didn't allow the guard to search him, because he was carrying something for the Jewish forced laborers.

Early March 1943

I couldn't recover after my last trip to Łuków. I had a urinary tract infection again. I went for a few days into the ghetto to get better there. Dr. Lipinski, an old doctor, visited and kept me company. Later on, I was uneasy to ask him to take care of me, but I liked talking with him. In addition to the urinary infection, I got some woman's ailment. I was constantly in pain, and I had high fever, but despite that I left the ghetto one evening and I went to Dolna Street. On the way I went to Wizenthal's shop to buy something for the children. Genek was in the shop and seeing me he grabbed my hand and said: "Miss Genia, the Gestapo is looking for you; you cannot go up." He went out to see if anyone was waiting in the street; I left the store and I started to ask questions about what happened. Apparently just half an hour earlier two Gestapo men in uniform and one agent not in uniform came by to search for Jan Zawadzki and Helena Wiśniewska. In my false papers, the name of my father was Jan. They looked for Zawadzki at the Gromuls and for Wiśniewska they looked at some neighbors. Marysia understood that they were looking for me, but she told them that there was no Helena Wiśniewska in this building. They asked if she rented a room to anyone, but she said "no."

She forgot that they could check in the registration book, but luckily Mrs. Miedziejewska and her husband were away, so they couldn't check it. So, they didn't find Helena Wiśniewska, and they left, asking how to get to Osikowa Street. The whole thing was very strange, but they were obviously looking for me. In my opinion it was due to Mrs. Kowalczyk, but the rest of them thought that it had to do with my "underground activity," since Genek asked if I had illegal newspapers with me. As far as Marysia was concerned, she knew that it was all about me, because at the time when I was in the ghetto, she sent a letter to me addressed to Helena Wiśniewska in Parczew. The letter was returned with the annotation that I had moved and there was no forwarding address. Anyway, I wasn't able to spend the night at Marysia's place, since they could return. We all decided that I should sleep in the Miedziejewski apartment, since they would not look there. I undressed only partially, and I couldn't fall asleep—I just listened for every noise. Marysia came a few times; Genek was still at her place. I was feeling really sick. I blamed Piniek for it all; why would he want me to die right here? Why didn't I stay in the ghetto, then I would have spent the last few days of my life in peace? At 10 p.m., the Miedziejewskis unexpectedly returned home. They weren't surprised to see me in their apartment, because before their departure they had asked me to sleep in their place during their absence. Unfortunately, Genek told them about the Gestapo, and I could see that Mr. Miedziejewski got very scared. He told me that it was a bad idea for me to sleep in their place and if they would return and ask him about me and find me in his apartment—that would not be good. But where could I go at ten at night? I decided to go to Raków, even though after the curfew it was very dangerous. Finally, someone said that it would be best if I would spend the night at Genek's. At that point I didn't care anymore, but I felt uneasy to spend the night in my buddy's place. But he behaved honorably. I didn't sleep at all that night. Marysia came in the morning and said that no one had come during the night. I left for Raków. I explained to Marysia that I would come in a day or two to the carpentry workshop where Stefan worked, to find out if they had returned.

After a few days I returned to the ghetto, but I was very sick. Every other day I received a shot, which caused my temperature to go up to thirty-nine degrees and an inability to move. Again, I spent a whole week in bed . . . A roundup occurred in the ghetto . . . if it was the Jewish police doing the roundup, they did not enter our building. If it was supposed to be a more serious matter—the gendarmerie or the *Hauptmann*—they let us know to hide. So, for the most part I spent quiet time in bed. This tranquility was interrupted one day when the entire "Fourteen" labor group was brought back to the ghetto; they were driven back without any warning—some three hundred people—and brought back to the ghetto, where they were searched. A few people were arrested and taken to jail. Two men, who were very ill, were taken to the hospital. The next day the Hauptmann ordered their execution at the Warszawski market. Nurses brought them out, supporting them under both arms. They begged the doctor to give them poison, but he didn't give it to them. The Polish police were not guarding the ghetto anymore; Ukrainians, who were brought to town just to fulfill this task, were guarding. A week before Easter, I left again for a few days. I had to buy some more injections and I had to show up at Dolna Street. Marysia insisted that I shouldn't "travel" during Easter. I told her that I would try to come, but I had to travel. Our Passover started a few days earlier, so I hoped to fulfill her wish.

Passover—we prepared a traditional meal together with three others from our building—two brothers and the wife of one of them. The married couple slept on the "married" side of our home; brother Zyzek (Zyskind) Szmulewicz slept for a long time on our side of the kibbutz and later on "bachelors" street—with friends. (He and a few others have some kind of secret job—I suspect that they make grenades—Zyzek was a mechanic, and in addition they prepared an underground tunnel leading to the Aryan side.) I like this quiet and good-natured boy very much and I have the impression that he feels the same way about me. At the meal we had traditional wine and everything else, even a piece of Matzo. We didn't want the depression to get to us, but we had to remember our dearest and beloved, who had tragically passed away. Just a year ago each one of us sat around the table with them, celebrating this traditional meal. The boys, Abe and Piniek, were together with us in Warsaw, but they knew that they had a home and family. So, after a short while, each one in a different corner, sobbed desperately. I drank too much; the fourth cup we drank to live long enough to get retribution, which would at least in some tiny way pay them back. But those who died could not be brought back, not even by the bloodiest of revenge. My crying became the weeping of a drunk. Out of the six people who participated in the Seder, four were dead for a long time. Was Zyzek still alive? I didn't know.

On the second day of Passover, I had an attack of appendicitis. I had to be operated on right away. On Thursday, April 22, I was in a hospital for the second time and on Saturday I was on the operating table for the second time. It was a miracle in the practice of Dr. Sz.; the cut was closed with just two clasps. Apparently, the doctor was so delighted with the procedure, that he carried me upstairs by himself and put me in bed. The first two days were horrible. I felt I was losing my mind; I couldn't withstand the pain—the other patients and nurses felt I was a very good patient.

Suddenly there was a restless atmosphere in the ghetto. No one knows anything for sure, but the air was poisoned. On Thursday, on the sixth day after the surgery, only four women remained. People feared coming into the hospital, because if something would start, being in hospital was the worst. I tried to get out of bed and on my wobbly legs and with clenched teeth, I walked along the wall; most important was to start.

On Saturday, none of the work brigades was allowed out of the ghetto; not even Pelcery—this most important work group had to stay in. No one knew what this means. A day passed and there was no Aktion. Some people said that it was because of May 1; others said that negotiations were going on in Radom about the fate of the ghetto, because the factories demanded workers. But nothing was certain. If an order to liquidate the ghetto would come, no demands from the managers of the factories would help. Maybe these were our last days or even last hours. But I am inside and because of that I don't have a chance to rescue the boys. The boys said that this time they would join the fight; it is unclear if they would be able to reach the fighting group; there were very few weapons.

Saturday evening, on the eighth day, I returned from the hospital. On Sunday morning it was calm. I reached the fence on wobbly legs just to see if I could escape this way, but I couldn't even walk, so how would I run? They told me to leave. I said: "leave me alone, I will stay with you. Whatever happens to the others, the same will happen to me; I have no strength to go on." Somehow, I felt indifferent about death. It's not so easy to get used to the idea that this is it . . . right now—and then return to life and again build up an indifference to death. It's as if a convicted man is brought to the gallows and at the last moment he is pardoned, but after a few days he is brought back to the same place and then pardoned again and after a few days . . . don't make my acceptance of reality any more difficult than it already is."

"No, you cannot be here! Ituś, snap out of it, collect yourself! You can still save yourself. What was all this effort for, if now you are to perish here with us? You will not be helpful to us, just the opposite. It will be easier for us to die knowing that someone will remain, someone who will remember us. Maybe, one day, you'll be able to tell our sister in Mexico how her family ceased to exist. You are the only one, who has the chance to do it in the future. You must leave!" And so on, and so on . . . But I couldn't; it was out of the question. On Sunday night many people crossed over, but many were caught. Blackmailers arrived even here. Everyone demands that I should leave, but I firmly refuse. I knew best that I wouldn't be able to get far enough. What was I to do? Should I voluntarily go to die on the other side? On Monday— no change. The work groups did not go out, but there was no Aktion. There is a better chance for getting out. Garbage from the ghetto was taken out in handcarts to an empty square, near the Warszawski Market. There was a possibility to leave the ghetto with the garbage cart and to escape from the square. Lots of juveniles stood at the square selling bread and other food staples and they pay attention to any escapees. If I were fully recovered, I would try anyway, but in my state at that time, I just couldn't, and all Piniek's appeals were lost on me. We spent Monday night sleepless. Apparently, the gendarmes are walking around the ghetto, and they are observing our building as well.

On Tuesday, till the afternoon, the situation was unchanged. Again, appeals for me to leave. I became so upset with it that I started to get dressed to leave, but at the same time a trumpet sounded, calling "Hasag" to work. (Every morning at 5 a.m. and in the evening at 9 p.m. a special bugler announced the start and end of the workday.) The ghetto exhaled. Again, a little more time to exist was gained. I went to bed with a feeling of relief that I didn't have to go anywhere. After eight days of resting in bed I finally started to feel stronger, and finally I could walk. The next few weeks I left the ghetto for a day or two, I returned for a day, and left again etc. etc. It was permitted to go close to the barbed-wire fence. When I stopped at Warszawska Street, near the marketplace, I could see the window of our apartment, to see if someone I knew was standing close to the fence.

Many of the work groups were incorporated into the Pelcery, but there were enough groups, which I could join. It was more difficult to leave, since the leader of the group had to agree, as the guards check the list of workers in the group. Sometimes I would go to the labor office to see the man who had replaced Kurland (Kurland himself and three others were hiding on the Aryan side, somewhere) and I told him that I wanted to leave. He knew me, where I was from and that I wasn't living permanently in the ghetto. So, he would give an order to the leader of the work group to integrate me into the group. But there was a better opportunity. There was a bathhouse on Garibaldi Street and to reach it, they had to walk through Warszawska Street. A group was formed every day, which went to the bathhouse, around 4 p.m. and it was led by a Jewish policeman. So, I could walk with the group up to Warszawska Street and there I would walk away. One day I was walking with Ala on Warszawska Street when a boy I knew from Garibaldi asked: "Do you want to go in?" I gave Ala my purse, I took off my coat and a moment later I was in the "kibbutz." (For some time, none of the boys went out to work. I spent the days sitting in the attic or I would work taking garbage out from the ghetto and at Warszawska Street I bought food, or I would bring food for them together with Ala or whatever Aniela was able to buy, or Stefan would come.) I remembered that I was to do something for Marysia, when a group was walking to the bathhouse. I joined the group and Piniek too. On Warszawska Street I stepped on the sidewalk and again I was Genia. I went to Grosz, I took what I was supposed to buy, and I returned in the evening with some other work group into the ghetto. Of course, it was risky, especially since the Polish police together with the Ukrainians were guarding the entrance. One of them could recognize me and in addition quite often I carry "Gwardia Ludowa" and "WBN" underground publications. When in the ghetto, I usually sat with half of the residents of our building in the attic, until the work group returned and at that time I would get down and cook dinner. I did not wash the dishes. The boys usually did this. Sometimes, when I cannot come, Abe is doing it. My time outside the ghetto is divided between Grosz and Raków, and when the boys were in a work group—I went to see them. One day Piniek said to Marysia, when she told him: "This Genia is a good girl," he answered: "You know, I like this Miss Genia. If I'll survive this war and if she'll want me, I'll marry her. So, make sure that no one should take her away." "Oh, no—said Marysia—she is not so easy—she would make a good wife for you . . ."

One day we were all sitting in the attic, when suddenly a squad of the Polish police and a few German gendarmes appeared out of the blue. They went to search the building of the workshops. Again—we could not understand what this meant. Abe was at Ravo and a moment later the "underground" people came by. "Be ready to fight"—there were just a few handguns and the rest had to pick up whatever they can: hatchets, knives, and the girls picked up vitriol. One explosive charge for breaching fortifications was taken into the street and, when needed, it would explode. We moved from our attic to another attic on our side, where we were able to stay lying down only. It would be easier to shoot from there and to pour vitriol on their heads—they would have to climb up to reach us.

Piniek stood on guard and refused to come up to the attic. He said that he wanted to be the first. We, up there, lay down and waited. But minutes

passed and hours passed and nothing... They didn't come. We were psychologically and physically exhausted, just by waiting for a few hours. As if it was
the hardest physical effort. The police took almost all the people from the
workshops and went to three other work groups. They selected some people
from there and sent them to some camp similar to Skarżysko or maybe even
worse. (Some time ago, five men from our building were taken there. After a
few weeks they organized an escape, but only one of them returned here. The
others were shot and killed in the vicinity of the camp. The one who returned
went with many others into the forest to join a partisan unit.) Again, there
was a period of calm. Pentecost was approaching and this time I promised
Marysia that I would spend the holiday with her. Stefan's mother was supposed to come, and I would help her to prepare for the holiday. "I prepared
so much for Easter, and you didn't come—she said—this time I will not let
you stay away." She didn't know that I ate her cakes in the ghetto. She had
brought the cake and some wine to the boys in Ravo, and they brought it to
me in the hospital.

Pentecost—our Shavuot—I spent in the ghetto, and two days before
the Christian holiday I left. The first day of the holiday I spent with Marysia.
Her mother-in law and her niece came to visit, and I took advantage of there
being no place for me to sleep and I went to Heniek and his family. No one
would have to sleep on the floor because there was a folding bed. I usually
slept with Henia, who always fought with Ala about this privilege, and she
usually won. On the second day of the holiday, we went with Aniela and
Szczepanek to see an exhibition of paintings from Gdańsk, which was at 1st
Avenue and on the same occasion we went to visit Marysia.

We reached the ghetto from the Stary Rynek (Old Marketplace) side
and we saw Piniek standing at the fence. He was very upset, because I hadn't
come two days in a row, and he was convinced that something had happened
to me. We talked for a few minutes, from a distance. Szczepanek took two
letters through the fence from Piniek, for someone, and we left. We looked
back a few times and we saw how he stood there not moving, just looking at
us. "What a horrible world and how this barbed-wire fence, and these people
walking behind it, make a terrible impression"—sighed Aniela. I said nothing.

It was the middle of June, and I entered the ghetto again. In the ghetto
there was a strange restlessness. It was dangerous to stay in our building. They know that the center of the underground was there. There were
rumors about the liquidation of the ghetto very soon and placing the workers
in "Hasag." Some said that that they preferred death to moving into such a

camp and others try very hard to get into "Hasag," so in the event of the liquidation of the ghetto, they would stay alive for the time being. The elderly and the children knew well that there was no salvation for them. Every child who still has some brains, talks about death and even if they do not understand it completely, they know that it would be something horrific. Many of them have seen a lot and gone through a lot . . .

Friday, June 18—In the morning, I left with the work group of Mrs. Mosiewicz, who used to be a patron of the "Fourteen"—now the former residents of 14th Avenue go to her to work in the workshops, which she built. The leader of the workshops is the old Valkod, who is called "grandpa" by the workers. When we reached Wolności Avenue, I escaped. Abe left from Ravo, not at the same time as I did, and I catch up with him at Narutowicza Street. I walked on the sidewalk, next to them and I accompanied them to the storehouse. They had stopped working at the garbage place. After they entered the courtyard, I managed to talk a little with Abe. He asks for food, which I was to bring over. I went to Grosz. Stefan bought some food in a village, and they waited for me, to give it to me. I told him that I had just arrived from the Kielce area and as I was passing by Ravo, I noticed one of the Lewin brothers. Stefan went with me to talk to them. "Hello Miss Genia!"—said Abe. Stefan and Abe talked and agreed that since the guards take away all the food at the entrance to the ghetto, Stefan would come in the evening, and he would throw the food through the barbed-wire fence. We said good-bye and we left. I still had to go to the registration office about my Kennkarte—it was supposed to be ready that day. They told me to come the next day. I had nothing special to do, so I started to fix my summer dress; all the dresses, which the boys had purchased for me together with Zyzek, were too expensive for me. At 4 p.m. Stefan came and said: "Miss Genia, something happened at Ravo." There was a search, and they found an illegal newspaper. I stifled a cry. The only person who had an illegal newspaper was Abe. A few days before I had brought it into the ghetto and Abe was the last one to read it. I heard Stefan saying: "It was one of the Lewins, for sure, because they said that he had black hair; wasn't it you who gave it to them?" I answered "yes, I gave it to him." Stefan and I went to Ravo to check exactly what had happened there, but it was empty. We just found out that the gendarmes took this boy to some unknown place, and the work group returned to the ghetto.

I must reach him today. Stefan and I returned to Grosz; he wants to take a bike and go to the ghetto to find out what was going on. I would walk and we decided to meet at the Warszawski marketplace. Marysia was sincerely worried. "Maybe it wasn't him," she said, but I knew that it was him. I met Stefan at Warszawska. He said: "I cannot find anyone; apparently all the work groups have already entered." I just knew that I had to get inside the ghetto, but first I had to lose Stefan. After all, I cannot enter when he is around. "Let's go to the Old Market, you will stand guard near the fence and maybe I would see someone, and I would ask to call the older Lewin. If indeed it was his brother, I will go to Raków to sleep. I wouldn't be able to sleep at home. I was sure that Lewin would not give me up, but you never know. They might look for me. You don't need to worry. You are not responsible for me."

After a few minutes of waiting, a Pelcery group shows up, but I couldn't enter with them, because armed Ukrainians guarded them. But I didn't care; it was the last work group returning to the ghetto. When the first five women and a few leaders showed up, I just joined the group, not even worrying if someone noticed. I said to the leader: "kibbutz."

After a moment I was with Piniek. He was so frazzled, that he wasn't even surprised where I had come from. I was as devastated as he was, and there was nothing I could say to console him. But he had to go to the barbed-wire fence, to Stefan, to tell him that he has seen me and that I went to sleep at Raków. He returned after a few minutes and told me that a gendarme caught Stefan and confiscated his bicycle. At least he was safe and managed to get out. The two of us stayed helpless. We already knew that Abe was at the Polish police station on Piłsudski Street. Our previous neighbor from Senatorska Street talked to him there—she works there as a cleaning woman. She was there when Abe was brought in. She said that he was calm. The whole evening long I tried to find ways to get him out of there. No one is ready to try to do it, all because of the illegal newspaper. If he was caught exchanging goods, maybe something could be done. I understood that all the efforts were for nothing, but I couldn't just sit and doing nothing. There was no place to sleep. That night I spent with a girl, whom I had befriended in the hospital, at Kawalerska Street.

Saturday—I crossed to the Aryan side. I had to take a few thousand zloty from Heniek; I had to see Stefan—I wanted to get the handgun we had talked about before. I needed to take care of this and, if possible, to get some more guns for the fighting group, but now I just want to purchase the gun and try to deliver it to Abe. This is the least I could do for him. In Raków, they see right away that something has happened; they sent for Heniek from the bakery. I told them what happened.

Aniela accompanied me and waited for me when I was arranging matters with Stefan. He was to take the gun hidden in a loaf of bread, to the ghetto fence and give it to Lewin. In return Stefan was to receive three thousand zloty from Lewin. I couldn't tell Stefan that I already had the money. Aniela and I went to pick up my Kennkarte. It was ready. I saw that Aniela became calmer after seeing the document; maybe now she won't be afraid that I spend so much time in their apartment. We passed the police station a few times. Nothing. I said goodbye to Aniela, and she cried parting from me. I went to Wolności Avenue to join one of work groups. In the evening the handgun got safely into our hands, but I still didn't have an opportunity to send it on. People who were at the police station and belonged to the work group were unsuitable. Someone would have to join them and go in, but as of this moment, there is no suitable person to do it. May he stay a few more days at Piłsudski Street . . .

Sunday—Abe sent a few words; he is very calm, and he knows that this is the end. If possible, he asked to send him a screwdriver and a drill. He thought that it would be possible to get out of his cell through the ceiling to the roof. In the next cell was a group from Garibaldi, caught trading things and he was afraid that he would be taken with them. "Ituś, don't despair, maybe at least you will live to see the day of revenge for us." I was to write back, but what should I write? How would I be able to tell him what I feel, not being able to do anything for him? Zyzek was with us the whole time; he didn't say much, but his presence helped. I cannot recall if during these days I ate anything at all; I still had no place to sleep. During the day we sat in a cellar; a flap leading to the cellar was covered by some piece of furniture. Someone from the people working in the ghetto dragged the furniture on top of the flap. At night we were in the attic of Hone Manowicz. He used to be placed in Pelcery. The atmosphere in the ghetto was getting very tense. It's been four days since Abe was locked up on Piłsudski. When we finally sent him the tools, it was too late. He was already transferred to a common jail cell. Whatever we bought for him, it was impossible to deliver to him. No one from outside the work group could get even close; besides, the women had already been sent to "Hasag." The only thing we could send him, apart from food, was cyanide. He asked for it. He didn't want to give the satisfaction to the hangmen, to perish at their hands. He wanted to die on his own terms. I received the cyanide from Majtek, the leader of the underground fighting group. Apparently, someone had already delivered one pill of cyanide to Abe, so I kept this one for myself. I am convinced that I will use it one day.

Thursday—It's difficult to get out of the ghetto with a work group. All were searched. Only one was ready to march out. I approached the leader and asked him to take me with the group; he answered that he would try. One of the Sznycer daughters was sick, so maybe it would work out. I stood at the exit, and I waited hidden in a gate. When the group leader called me to join the group; I didn't even have time to say goodbye to anyone (Piniek). At the marketplace I looked back, and I saw how he looked at me and took his hat off. At the corner of Warszawska, the group stopped. "The Grandpa" who led the group forgot something and he went back. I couldn't leave at that point, because we were visible from the ghetto gate, full of police and gendarmerie. I stood there talking softly with Cesia Berkowska from the kibbutz, who once escaped from the train to Skarżysko. When "Grandpa" returned, I saw that he noticed me. I whispered to Cesia: "call the group leader, he noticed me, and I have to arrange it with him." Before she was able to call him, the group leader approached: "Well, and what do you want here? You are not Jewish. Get out of here immediately and if not, I will take you back to the ghetto. Goodbye to you." Cesia said loudly: "Goodbye" and I went a few steps back and I left. At the corner I looked back, and I saw people laughing and Cesia waving to me. I walked through Zawodzie to Raków, in order to avoid Grosz. I look for a long time into the barred windows of the prison—Abe, my dear boy, maybe he is standing at one of the windows and will see me for the last time. And maybe he wasn't there anymore . . .

At Okrzyja, I saw Szczepanek in bed with a wounded leg. He was supposed to go to his First Communion that day and this was the reason for my leaving the ghetto. I had promised a long time ago that I would spend this day with them. Now the communion was delayed until July 15th. I stopped at Grosz. Stefan told me that he has one "piece." "If you could just bring it to the fence"—I told him—"I'm supposed to meet Lewin, so you'll be able to talk it over with him." We left, and when we reached a cross street with Warszawska Street, we went to Kozia Street, from which the ghetto was visible. A strange feeling of death emanated from there. With my heart in my mouth, I ran to the next cross-street, and I saw a gendarme wearing a helmet with a gun in his hands chasing someone close to the fence. Stefan and I ran to see from the Old Market side. He begged for me not to despair, that I should remember our purpose, because I was the only person, who could help those inside . . . (Ha! Ha! I was still needed by someone.) Along the fence gendarmes and Ukrainians stood guard. At that moment I knew—this was the end.

Raków . . . when Anula and Heniek came home around 9 p.m., they found me stiff in bed. They had already heard about what was happening in the ghetto. I heard what they were saying to me; I felt Aniela's tears on my cheeks, and I felt that Heniek took my hands in his and kissed my forehead—he talked to me as if I were a child. My teeth were clenched, and I couldn't utter even one word. I heard that Raków did not return to the ghetto that day and that a few hundred additional people were brought from the ghetto to the ironworks and that they were all supposed to stay there permanently. I heard that there was shooting today in the ghetto—"calm down, dear—tomorrow we'll find out." Oh, God, these two people next to me—they touched some chord in me, which I was sure was broken into pieces. Only thanks to them I was able to cry. "Cry, cry Genia, maybe this will bring you relief," said Heniek. He sat with me long into the night, until I asked him to go to sleep. He had to go to work the next day. Aniela came down a few times during the night. Heniusia hugged me, sat next to me, and cried: "our poor Genia." Alusia stroked my face and asked me not to be sad, saying that the next day it will turn out that there is hope. The next day Heniek and Ala went downtown to find out what had happened in the ghetto. I couldn't get up. When they returned, I heard about trucks filled with women and children, taking them to the cemetery. They had to undress there and were executed into the pre-dug trenches. I heard about trucks filled with the corpses of people shot and killed in the ghetto—so there was a battle. Later an ironworks worker brought a few words from Zyzek. Piniek was dead! He was shot and killed. Zyzek reached Raków; his brother was taken a day earlier, and no one knew what happened to him. His sister-in-law was taken to Pelcery. His friend Jacek and one other were together with Zyzek. I wrote to him, through Heniek's brother, asking him to write to me the details of what happened. On Friday most work groups were integrated into Hasag, but many still marched out. The whole day was very tense; policemen with families were sent to Skarżysko, with some exceptions. Before 5 p.m., Zyzek and Piniek came to the ghetto gate to find out what had happened to Zyzek's brother. Suddenly, at great speed, a truck arrived with gendarmerie and before they had time to hide, gendarmes chased them, shooting non-stop. The boys ran in the direction of the building at Garncarska Street, where there was a place prepared for such an event like this. Zyzek wasn't able to reach this building and ran into another one, where he hid in some dark corner. A moment later he saw through a crack in the shutter, a group of gendarmes leading Piniek and four others from the underground. A girl from the kibbutz recognized their bodies later. Majtale was killed right there during the shootout—he was very ill. A few escaped with the crowd and just these five were taken and later executed. Zyzek and others were forced into the square, from which they were all taken to Raków.

July 14, 1943—Tomorrow is the First Communion for Szczepanek. I don't have a fever anymore, but I still wear a scarf around my neck. My bed still stands behind the cupboard, but I started to walk a few days ago. Aniela and Heniek slept after a long trip; they walked for miles to purchase some food. I haven't been at Grosz since June 25th. I have no idea what is happening there. Marysia didn't know Heniek's address. In the past I told her that it would be better if she wouldn't know this address, just in case something happened to me, and she might be interrogated about me. She connected it to seeing illegal pamphlets in my possession and she felt that this was the reason for me not wanting to involve her. This morning we talked with Aniela about going to visit the Gromuls. I felt a strange reluctance, I just didn't want to pretend to be carefree. Hidden Jews are denounced and discovered all the time. People who gave them safe haven, now they just tell them to leave. It happens all the time. Those who hid Jews, for huge amounts of money, like the sister of Lola's fiancé with her small child, who was told yesterday to leave. She was discovered in Rakowo; she just stood with her small daughter in a public lavatory. Maybe she was waiting for someone. They took her to Zawodzie. I said: "You know, my dear ones, actually it's my turn now. Why should I be an exception?" A few hours later Marysia walked in—"After all, I found out where you are hiding from me." I had a very strong feeling that something had happened and when I was accompanying her back, I found out that my instinct was right. "They all went crazy in our building and everywhere, about the Jews. They hunt; they sniff and check every face. One man took a passerby in the street to the police station, claiming that this man was a Jew. The identification papers of this man were not enough for him. He had to prove it in a different way. [*Pulling his pants down*]. Some woman was standing near Wizenthal's store, and she was accused of the same and with great difficulty she was able to get out of this predicament. And now they dragged out the old story about you. Miedziejewski got angry and he and Stefan decided to bring a foreman from the police station, so he would close this issue once and for all and close the mouths of these hags. So now, you must come and show this foreman your IDs." I answered that I didn't intend to do it, because even this would not shut them up. In addition, I wasn't healthy. I asked her to say that I was sick. But I knew that I was trapped. If I wanted to go and live someplace else, I had to have the registration from Dolna Street or some other documents. So, I could not remain in Częstochowa anymore. I was telling all this to Heniek when Stefan showed up. He didn't know that Marysia was already here. Stefan found the address only knowing that Heniek worked in a bakery and the names of the children. Now I had to go with him to show my IDs, otherwise neither he nor I would have a moment's peace. It was just a formality; the foreman had already visited the building, he asked questions and yelled at Kowalczykowa that she should pay attention to her pots and pans and that people were crazy. He would just look at my Kennkarte pro forma and in this way, he would shut the mouths of all these witches. I made up my mind; what will be, will be. Maybe it will work out and then I would be able to live in peace or I would be lost. But I knew one thing—I would not drag anyone else with me. I threw away the unfinished cigarette and I put the cyanide pill in my shoe. I took my coat and my purse (huge mistake), and we were on our way. I didn't say goodbye to anyone, because of Stefan, even though I thought that I might never see any of them again. We almost ran because Stefan wanted to meet the foreman before noon.

In Police and Gestapo Custody

A thought passed my mind that I shouldn't have taken my purse. Once more I looked at what's inside. My photograph with Nachman was hidden under the lining. I moved it into my pocket. When we got to the police station, the foreman was already gone. They told us to wait because he might return. After three hours he still wasn't there. Marysia came by; she was worried. The police chief entered, and we didn't want to take care of this with him. All my papers: Kennkarte and birth certificate were already with the secretary. The chief called me; he didn't ask me about any details—it was all in the documents. He asked me to recite the Lord's Prayer and the Hail Mary—I did; then he asked about the seven sacraments—I kept mum. "I forgot," I said. He continued with some more questions and then led me and Stefan to the second floor where two civilians were seated. "Where had I come from, what was I doing, and how did I meet Stefan and when?" (Stefan told me before that he had answered this question two weeks earlier "Because there was an Aktion then, so they could've got stuck on this"—said Stefan.) "Why was something rubbed out and corrected in the birth certificate?" "I wanted to be younger, so I wouldn't be taken for labor to Germany, but I didn't do it well, so I put the same date again," I answered. "But I made a copy, and you can check it with the notary," I added. "And why were you so afraid of going to Germany? Thousands are going there, and all are doing well." He tried to catch me in a mistake, but I didn't move a muscle in my face: "I don't understand." Stefan was told to bring his labor card from Raków, and it showed that he had left his job on his own. The chief and the civilian wink to each other and say in German: "these birds should've been caught a long time ago and sent off." They took us downstairs and ordered us to take everything out of our pockets. They took my purse and at that moment I remembered that I had a photograph of father (uncle) as well as a section of the WBN bulletin hidden under the lining of the purse. I would be a goner if they would find it. I asked if I could take a handkerchief out of the purse. They allowed me this courtesy. I managed to take out, together with the handkerchief, all that was hidden under the lining. They put me in a cell, in the basement, and there I swallowed all of that. Stefan was kept in the next cell. Will they really send us off to Germany? If so, Stefan was caught because of me, I felt very sorry, but there was nothing I could do. They called me to come up and do some cleaning—I was to wash and wax the floors in three rooms. A young civilian was watching me; I asked him for a pencil to write a note to my landlady and maybe he could give it to her. He agreed without any problems. I wrote to Marysia that she should ask the foreman for help to release Stefan. After finishing the work, I was returned to the cell. The night ahead of me . . . Marysia brought soup and bread, but I couldn't eat. A policeman brought me a blanket; obviously he was convinced that I was not Jewish, because on the same occasion he tried to kiss me. A pig. I put him in his place—sleep didn't come. What will happen the next day? I knocked on the wall for Stefan and he came to the cell-door, and we started a conversation from across the corridor. I asked him to remind me of the seven sacraments and a few other things. The night didn't want to end. Finally, dawn arrived. It was freezing. At 8 a.m., Miedziejewski came to the window and told me that when the chief arrives, they will let us go. Marysia brought us soup and bread again. I heard her voice and the voice of the children coming from upstairs. When the policeman brought food, I gave it all back, except for a slice of bread, just in case. That was the day that Szczepanek was going to Holy Communion, and this was to be our holiday . . . Stefan went upstairs, and I waited for them to call me as well, but they brought Stefan back into his cell. What does it mean? I feel that something bad is coming. They called me. They started the questioning again from the beginning; the interrogation included many questions, to which it was difficult to have ready answers and I had to think quickly on my feet, so one answer would not contradict the previous one. The police chief took me to a different room, where he showed me my photograph with Nachman and the letter I wrote the previous day to Marysia. The guy who guarded me was a spy and a photograph must've fallen out of the coat, or he searched it when I cleaned the floors. For some reason, he took this photograph to be a proof that I was Jewish. Nachman looked Jewish in the photograph. The interrogation started again. I felt that all was lost. But some basic instinct didn't let me admit that I was Jewish. I knew that when the last sign of hope would disappear, I would throw in their faces all I was thinking about them, but I wasn't sure if this was the end. First of all, I asked to separate Stefan from my case. First of all, I wasn't Jewish and even if I was it wasn't Stefan's responsibility to know, because I showed him my documents. They took me downstairs again. I was so glad that I took the cyanide with me. I will not let you kill me, you hangmen. I made a small ball out of bread, and I poured the powder inside. It will be easier to swallow. Again, I heard the door opening and I put the ball in my shoe. And who was in the door—the previous head of the ghetto together with the chief of police and one policeman. "Jude?" asked the gendarme. "I don't understand." "Are you a Jew?" "No"; "Ja, ja, du Jude." The chief said to the policeman in German: "take her out and shoot her." "Yes, sir," answered the policeman. I kept my mouth shut, still pretending that I don't understand. But apparently, I paled, because the police chief claimed that I revealed myself that I knew German.

He had said it with this purpose in mind. They took me back to the prison cell. Stefan was taken upstairs, but this time he didn't return to his cell. Probably he was released. After a moment they took me back to the police chief. There were questions about what I had been doing each year since I had graduated from school. When did I go to communion; what does one say going to confession and during communion? My "biography" was typed up in German, but I didn't have answers to the questions asked at the end. I wasn't prepared for this. "A Jew!" said the male police typist. Again, he took me back to the prison cell, brutally pushing me: "You just wait, I'll hit you in the noodle," he yelled pushing me into the cell. I decided not to swallow my bread ball. Why? I have no idea. A policeman led me to the German gendarmerie. On the way I frantically tried to think of a way out. But it was impossible. He walked behind me with a gun. My lips were parched, and my tongue was like a piece of wood. I haven't eaten at all since the day before and I just had some water. At the German police station, I saw gendarmes, whose faces I knew from the ghetto. They looked at a photograph, which was supposed to be the proof. One of them said that he was sick and tired of people constantly being brought in, accused that they were Jews. "Let her go," but someone said that the decision has to be made by a higher-ranking officer. I didn't have a chance with him. I knew this from many similar cases. They ordered me to sit on the bench and wait. Suddenly two men in tattered clothes ran in. One of them, rubbing his hands and with a sucking up smile; he reported that he works at the cemetery and that he had found a Jew in hiding. They left one worker to guard him and these two hurried up to report about the Jew. "And . . . when will I get the two hundred zloty, promised for each reported Jew?" One man at the German police station knew Polish, so the two could make themselves clear. A few men left to "take care" of this Jew. My heart was on fire, and I felt that my skull was about to explode—I sat alone; there was just one man sitting at the table, writing. I got up and I reached the door; he didn't notice me. The courtyard, maybe fifty steps long, was empty. Not think- ing and completely instinctively (it was absolute nonsense to escape, without any documents, impossible to hide, even impossible to reach any place, with- out a pass) I walked toward the gate and only at that point I started to run in the direction of Jasna Góra. But one gendarme was chasing me. I continued run- ning; surprised that I didn't hear shooting and that I didn't feel a bullet hitting me. I was very close to the park when people there created a barrier, by holding hands and catching me. Then they take me back, holding me by the hair on my head; later a rubber baton split my head. I flew into darkness, and only the pain caused by being hit in the face brought me back. It didn't want to end . . . noise in my ears, blood running from my nose, and I fell onto a bench. The sight of blood calmed the torturer. He sat across from me like a furious animal. When I finally came to, I felt like a washed-up rug, but the thoughts were spin- ning in my head. They returned from the cemetery; they threw onto the table the money they had taken away from the Jew they had killed. They looked at his ID and threw it in the garbage bin. It was the pharmacist Paszkiew. Later two gendarmes on bicycles with a dog taller than my knees escorted me to the Gestapo. There were a few women in the cell, all shivering from fear at what the interrogations would bring. Apparently, they torture people. Suddenly I was engulfed by peace. Walking there I parted from trees in the Avenue, from the sky, and the sun. I didn't think about people. I thought about all those who had died. They all stand in front of me, lining up. I am coming to you, my beloved. The thought of death doesn't bother me in the least. If I had been able to reach this state two weeks ago, I could've avoided the last two days. Maybe this was my fate to have to mourn my beloved and those dearest to me, one by one, and

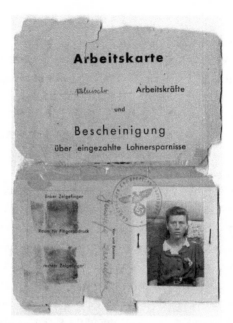

German Work Card for Genowefa Zawadska, 1943-1944 (front). USHMM,
Acc. Number: 1998.A.0258.2 (Series 3, Box 2.7, no. 3), courtesy of Jacob Dimant.

German Work Card for Genowefa Sawadska, 1943-1944 (back). USHMM,
Acc. Number: 1998.A.0258.2 (Series 3, Box 2.7, no. 4), courtesy of Jacob Dimant.

at the end to go through the very same thing that they did, and to end this ago-nizing life. When these women will be taken for interrogation, and they were supposed to go soon, I will swallow my bread. I am amused by the thought of the reaction of those who will come to fetch me for interrogation, when they will see that their victim has escaped them. I sent my thoughts to Heniek and his family—I wasn't able to thank you for your heart. What remained of me in your place does not constitute thanks. I dreamt about having influence on the future of your children and you; I hoped to help you in your daily strug-gle. I heard steps; I heard a key turning: "Zawadzka Genowefa!"—So, it's me now? Already? Apparently, I have to go through this interrogation. I followed the man, without my coat. We entered a bright, large room. Two young men were in the room—one in uniform and the other, even younger, in civilian clothes. I asked for water, and he gave it to me. I was asked the same questions as before at the police station but asked politely. "If I'll admit it, they wouldn't do anything to me. I would go to Pelcery, where Jews work"; "you can take me there." Going upstairs I decided to take off this mask. I will not die pretending to be somebody else! But at the last moment my survival instinct didn't let me utter these few words of truth. The second, younger, Gestapo-man entered the room to hear my answers. Again, they ask about prayers—I recited. The Seven Sacraments? Now I knew them well. They both looked at each other; next question: where did I live previously; answer: near Lublin; is there anyone who knows you? Yes, my relative, Bara … These two looked at each other: "why do they bother us; this is not a Jewish woman." After ten minutes I am handed an appointment at the Arbeitsamt (Labor Office). Some boy agreed for twenty zloty, to go to Marysia and deliver a note. I wrote that they would be able to come and see me the next day and I would explain it all.

Despite it all, danger came close, but this time it was Heniek who res-cued me at the last moment. He didn't tell me about it, as he could've done. In the Arbeitsamt a blackmailer threatened me that he would take me to the Gestapo. This time, if I would reach the Gestapo, I would not get out alive. When I told Heniek that someone started to blackmail me, he asked me to show him this man. When he saw him, Heniek told me: "don't worry, I'll try to arrange it. Don't panic Genia, and don't show that you are afraid." Heniek returned after a few hours and said that all is good and that this guy would not bother me anymore; the next day I was to leave.

Leaving for Germany

On hard planks, among the shrieking and noise of hundreds of people, full of little children crawling around. Heniek and Anula with one of their children stood waiting next to the fence for hours. Marysia only came that day. On the second day, Stefan and Wizenthal were arrested along with others; it was a political case, and Marysia was in total despair. Alusia with Heniek brought me all kinds of things to eat on the way. I packed it as well as some of my own things. Szczepanek came as well: "I want to see our Genia too." Halinka asked, "Please push two fingers through the hole in the fence, so I can kiss." And we kissed one another, putting our lips on the hole in the fence, on both sides. I was so touched by their dedication. I was torn away from the arms of death once more, and once more I would have to fight to remain calm all over again.

One day before my departure, Monday, July 19th, I was together with everyone, at the farewell Mass. This time I couldn't avoid it.

Tuesday, July 20—I went with the whole group of about one hundred other Polish men and women to the train. Heniek, Anula, and Alusia accompanied me the whole way to the train. Anula was very upset, because there were roundups in town. She was the first to say goodbye to me, together with Ala. Heniek takes me all the way to the station and we say goodbye through a small fence. I made him promise that when an opportunity will present itself, he would send the letter I had left addressed to Dora in Brazil. I didn't have the exact address of Nachman and his brother; I would locate them quickly . . .

I was on the train for an additional five days; the train stopped twice for the night. We slept in special barracks. We had an additional disinfecting bath—men were assisting us—and our things were disinfected too (my bread with cyanide I hid in my hair). On Saturday, July 24th, I finally arrived at my destination, Kerstlingerode bei Göttingen. But if I had hoped that I would be able to rest, and to get rid of the fever, before starting to work—I was very mistaken. On Monday they drove me to work.

Kerstlingerode bei Göttingen

On July 24, we arrived in the city of Göttingen, at a place where Germans, mostly women, were waiting to take the workers they needed to factories or farms. I was chosen to go to a thirty-acre farm in a small village named Kerstlingerode. The owner was a woman whose husband was in the army, and she had only one young, mean-looking, man to help out. He caused me a lot of trouble. As sick and tired as I was, I could rest for only one day. The next day at 5 a.m., a bell over my bed woke me up to start working. Over the next twenty months and twenty-one days, until the US Army liberated me, I worked very hard for my bloody enemies. For nine months of the year, I worked sixteen hours a day; in the three winter months I worked twelve hours a day. I milked the cows three times a day, feeding them and two oxen, pigs, and chickens, and cleaning up after them. I went with a wagon drawn by the oxen into the fields and worked all day ploughing, fertilizing, planting, and, according to the season of the year, doing all the work which usually only men used to do. In addition to the work in the fields, gardens, and inventory chores, I had to clean the house and help with whatever else was needed. In the winter months I mostly chopped firewood all day. I slept in a very small room under the roof of the house; my bed was made of a wooden frame with a sack of straw. A very narrow window was covered all winter with snow or ice, which made the room very cold.

I had to wear a "P" [Polish] patch on my right breast and eat at a separate table, as did all the Polish workers. Later on, when sometimes I heard the chatting German women praising my work, I had to fight back an enormous impulse to reveal who was beneath the letter "P." I dreamt of living up to the moment when I would be able to tell them. In the meantime, I felt terribly lonely. I was friendly with the other Polish women, but I had to keep my distance because they still expressed themselves in hateful terms about the Jews.

At that time, I started to write my diary during sleepless nights in my room to ease the loneliness. It was impossible to get any paper and so I washed the margarine wrapping paper and used it to write on. It was a real miracle that I managed to do it for so many months without being discovered. It could have been the end of my life, but luckily nobody looked inside the straw sack that I slept on . . .

And at night I have nightmares, and they all come to me one after another and they look at me and accuse me because it is only I from among all of them, who is still alive. Every few nights I live through my own death, in different forms—from a bullet, on an electric chair, by poison, by hanging. I feel it so clearly, that I wake up drowning in my sweat. For a few moments I am unable to realize that I am alive and that I exist. I suffered from terrible loneliness—the only person I met here who was a valuable human being, was a twenty-year-old girl. The best relief from this gloomy existence came from the letters sent by Heniek, Anulka, and Marysia. For some time, I received letters from Zyzek. Later Adam found me, and he is here till today. When Stefan was in prison, he found out that Abe had poisoned himself. The correspondence with Zyzek stopped because Heniek's brother got killed, when he was carrying something for Jews in the ironworks and he refused to let them search him and started to flee.

Then, one day, I received a letter from an unknown man with regards from Aron Gepner. He had left the Częstochowa ghetto sometime before the liquidation and went to Będzin, and I did not know what happened to him. In the letter, I found out that he is in a camp for foreign citizens as a Uruguayan citizen. This was a happy moment for me, and after that we exchanged letters until the end of the war. His girlfriend, Dora-Helena, was caught on one of her journeys and taken to Treblinka. She jumped from the cattle train, trying to escape, and was shot by a German guard. (Today Aron lives with his wife and children in Israel.)

Freedom

On April 11, 1945, in the afternoon, after a night of hearing guns shooting, US Army troops marched into Kerstlingerode village, and I was liberated. It is very hard to describe those moments after a sleepless night, full of exciting expectations, standing in the streets to welcome the liberators. The frightened Germans closed their doors, and only we, the slaves whom they brought from all the occupied countries to work for them, stood along the streets shouting, clapping, and crying with joy. The next day I could finally accomplish my dream of telling the owner of the farm who I really was and that from then on, she herself would have to do all the work and that I hoped her nation would pay for all the terrible crimes to so many nations, and especially to us, the Jewish people. I think she had the shock of her life when she realized that she had kept, for almost two years, a Jew in her house. On the same day, I, with two other girls, Baska and Eva—who had arrived several months earlier to work on a neighboring farm—left the village and walked all the way to the city of Göttingen. We found a city with empty streets and closed doors. Not a single place to buy some food, not a place to go into. After a few hours of walking, we found a US army unit, the 555 company, and they took us to work in the officers' luncheonette as waitresses. They gave us a room in an empty house and food. I immediately started to search for Jewish soldiers and found quite a few, and they sent a message from me to my relatives in Palestine and Brazil. They took me to the Buchenwald concentration camp to see if maybe some of my relatives had survived there, but the only person I found there was my friend Zyskind Szmulewicz (Zyzek). He, with three other men from the camp, came later to work in the garage of the 555 company. After the dramatic and exciting announcement of the blond Baska—who came with me from the village—that she was Jewish, we were six Jews working for the 555 company of the US army. (The amazing thing was that all that time before the liberation, I thought that the black-haired Eva was Jewish and tried to take special care of her, but she turned out to be a "pure" Polish girl . . .)

On one of the Saturdays, the six of us went to the Sabbath sermon for Jewish soldiers and we met Rabbi Marcus. Soon after that he started to convince me to leave the company, because—as he said—I did not belong in such a place. Rabbi Marcus told me that after the liberation of the Buchenwald camp, a Rabbi Shechter took sixteen Jewish men and settled them on a farm, where later more and more survivors from other camps joined them and it became a kibbutz. They called it Kibbutz Buchenwald because of the sixteen men from this camp that had started it. Rabbi Marcus was taking care of the needs of that kibbutz and insisted that I join them: "Where you belong," he said. To convince me further, he told me he was going to Paris to the British embassy to get certificates for the members of the kibbutz to go to Palestine and he wanted me to go with them. It was only about four months after the war, and this kind of event sounded unrealistic at that time, but it was the dream of my life to go to Palestine, so I left the 555 Company and my friends there and joined the kibbutz. A few weeks after I had joined them, the unbelievable event came true, and we were on our way over to Palestine. We were eighty young men and women, and in France twenty other survivors joined us. Rabbi Marcus came with us, because as he said, "he wanted to have the privilege of bringing the first survivor group to Palestine."

We arrived in Haifa on September 8th, 1945, the day of Rosh Hashana. And again, it is hard to describe all the feelings of that day in which a new chapter of my life began . . . The only relatives I had then in Palestine were my beloved uncle's two sons, who welcomed me very warmly and became my closest family. A few months after I arrived in Palestine, I married a Buchenwald camp survivor from our kibbutz, Symcha Dimant, and gave birth to my two sons Jacob and Menachem. I had the privilege of celebrating the new-born state of Israel in 1948. I also lived again through the experience of fear from new enemies, who desired to destroy the state together with all of us. But all these years in Israel through the five wars I experienced, worrying first about my husband and later for my sons involved in those wars, I felt the pride of being a free citizen in my own country, whose people, like every human being in the world, have the right to live and defend their freedom.

During all the years since I left the Brust family, I corresponded with them, sent them whatever support I could, despite the post-war financial tough times, and I still keep in contact with their children. In 1980, together with Zyskind (Zyzek) Szmulewicz, we planted a tree in the Alley of the Righteous Among the Nations in Jerusalem in honor of Henryk Brust and his wife Aniela, his brother Marian, whom the Nazis killed for helping Jews, and their sister Henryka who saved the life of a young Jewish woman hiding in her apartment for two years. We also sent, via a representative of Yad Vashem, a gold medal with their names on it. In 1984, I went to Poland to meet the Brust family and to go to the death camps. It was a very emotional meeting and a heartbreaking experience in the camps. A year after my visit, Henryk Brust died, and two years later his wife died. I have remained in frequent contact with all their children and grandchildren. I found Abe and Piniek's sister in Israel and we are still in a close relationship. The Kibbutz Buchenwald members, with the beginning of a new life in Israel, chose a new name—Netzer. (Netzer means a shoot or a sprout growing out of a stump of a tree that projects out of the ground after most of the trunk has been cut down.) In 1948 they settled on a large farm between Tel Aviv and Jerusalem. Because of health and personal reasons, I left the kibbutz and lived in Holon, a town near Tel Aviv. My two sons grew up there and became medical doctors. They came each at a different time to New York to accomplish their Internships and Fellowships. They got married and have children and are now American Citizens. My husband died in 1983 and since then I live partly in New York, near my children and grandchildren, and partly in Israel.

Ita and Symcha Dymant in Israel with their two sons Jacob (right) and Menachem (center), circa 1957. Photo courtesy of Jacob Dimant.

Epilogue

Jacob Dimant

At Kibbutz Buchenwald, Rabbi Marcus offered to arrange for Ita's emigration to the United States, but she chose to join the group of survivors who went with Rabbi Marcus to Palestine, hoping to reconnect with Nachman. Upon arriving in Palestine, she reconnected with Moshe (Mojżesz) and his wife Bella, and with Nachman, who had married Esther Elkind. But her love of Nachman never abated. She started to correspond with Malka in Sao Paulo, Brazil, and Rachelka in Poland. Rachelka lost her husband and child to illness early in the war and managed to escape to the Soviet Union, where in 1944 she was mobilized as a nurse into the Soviet army. She returned to Warsaw in 1945, where she met her husband Szymek. They remained in Poland. Other then Rachelka, only a few of Ita's cousins survived the Holocaust from Ita's entire Rozencwajg and Miodownik families. In Palestine (later Israel), Ita was able to find comfort in her close relationship with Moshe, Nachman and their families, and her few cousins who were living in Israel. She was also close with Zyskind (Zyzek) Szmulewicz and Aron Gepner, who survived, came to Israel, and built new families. She kept a close relationship with many members of Kibbutz Buchenwald (renamed Kibbutz Netzer Sireni). She became the magnet for the family and amazingly remained in close touch with the group of survivors, her family close and far in Israel, Poland, and Brazil, and the younger generation of her family.

Many Holocaust survivors were able to leave their past behind and restart their lives. Unfortunately, Ita never left the Holocaust, and the Holocaust never left her. She kept reliving the events of past years. As my brother and I were growing up, the events of the Holocaust were always in the background. Ita wrote and gave testimony to Yad Vashem, the Israel memorial for the Holocaust, and made sure that the memory of every person in her family who perished was preserved. Yet, given the existential threat to the young state of Israel, she never felt completely safe, particularly when we, her children, were young. There was always a fear of recurrence. She was always ready to run away, and made sure that myself and my brother attained independence at a very young age and always had good shoes at the ready, just in case . . .

While raising her family, Ita also developed a career as a merchant running a retail optical store and additional business for many years in the center of Tel Aviv. After Symcha's death in 1983, Ita moved to Brooklyn, New York, to be close to myself, my brother, and our children and families. At age sixty-five, she started a new chapter in her life. She found many new friends and a few relatives, who, unbeknown to her, had survived the Holocaust and moved to the US. She developed a new career working in a nursing home with a mission to improve the quality of life of the patients at that home and was particularly dedicated to assisting Holocaust survivors.

After coming to the US, Ita spent much time working with Barbara Engelking, an academic from the University of Warsaw and a researcher of the Holocaust, writing a book (in Polish) about her life and her experience during the Holocaust, which became a best-seller in Poland. She provided much testimony to the United States Holocaust Memorial Museum, Steven Spielberg's USC Shoah Foundation, and the Kean University Holocaust Center in New Jersey. Unfortunately, but not surprisingly, the events of September 11, 2001, caused her to have a severe emotional reaction. She had felt that she and her family were finally safe in the United States and immediately realized that the events were an act of war, again coming too close for comfort.

Ita's courage never abated, and she never gave up. Toward the end of her life, she successfully fought disease, remaining active and in touch which her family despite increasing disability. Even from her nursing home bed, she continued to communicate with family and friends, many of whom made the trip to visit her. She passed away in peace in 2010 at the age of ninety-two. Her original diary, documents, and photographs were donated to the United States Holocaust Memorial Museum and remain in their permanent collection.

Courage and Survival— Symcha Dymant[1]

Jacob Dimant

My great-great-grandfather Chaim Rozrozowski, born circa 1810–1815, lived in Radomsko (in Congress Poland, then part of the Russian Empire). As a young man, he worked as a mail carrier, driving a horse and carriage between the towns of Radomsko and Piotrków. Getting mail was so rare at that time that lore has it that when he delivered mail, he was often invited to celebrate with a meal at the receiving family. Around 1845, when the Warsaw-Vienna railroad (then the second railroad in the Russian Empire) started to be built, workers were sought to lay the tracks. The Jewish people in Radomsko did not volunteer, and Chaim was the only Jewish person to take the job, losing a finger in a work-related accident. He eventually rose to become the railroad's local Station Master, and thereafter started a sheet metal business needed for the rail cars, a business that made him a wealthy man. Chaim had a long life and died at the age of 104. It was thought that any child blessed by him was destined to live a long life. Family members brought their children to be blessed. His grandchildren who survived the Holocaust all lived to their late nineties. Some of his descendants who survived the Holocaust believed that their sister, Sara Wislicka Lenchner, left for Israel and was spared the Holocaust because he blessed her when she was a baby.

Chaim had four daughters and a son. His daughter Pessah (also Pesla) was born in 1865. She married Jozef Symcha Wislicki (born 1867 in Zdunska Vola to a family of Dutch origin), and they eventually moved to Sosnowiec. Jozef was also a tinsmith, who worked in the sheet metal business. They had several children. One of their daughters was Kajla, born in 1889.

Chaim's daughter Breindl (Brajdel), Pessah's sister (1861–1933), married Josef (Josk) Dymant in Radomsko. Their son Aaron (born 1884)

---

married his first cousin Kajla in 1909. They had three children: Ziskind (Fischl), Symcho (born February 18, 1913 in Warsaw), and Alexander, the youngest. Aaron became a watchmaker and was offered a job in Warsaw, where the family moved shortly before Symcho was born. When Symcho was seven years old, his father Aaron died while travelling to a new job offered to him in Switzerland, and the family moved back to Kajla's mother's home in Sosnowiec. Kajla married again and had a daughter named Henia (Hindy) with her second husband. Symcho grew up at his grandmother's home in Sosnowiec. As a young man he worked in Oświęcim (later the site of the Auschwitz concentration camp) and subsequently became a master carpenter and settled in Częstochowa, where he had a bicycle repair business. On August 23, 1936, he married Tonia Wargon. They had a son, Aaron, born in September 1936. They lived in Stary Rynek, a square near the Jewish quarter, which later became part of the ghetto (and eventually an assembly place from which Jews, including Tonia, Aaron, and Henia, were marched to the nearby train station on their way to their deaths in the Treblinka death camp).

On September 1, 1939, Germany invaded Poland. The German army occupied Częstochowa on September 3, 1939. Symcho and his family were forcibly moved into the ghetto after it was established on April 9, 1941. Symcho was involved in the underground resistance in the ghetto. On Yom Kippur, September 21, 1942, the Germans started the liquidation of the Częstochowa ghetto. This took the underground resistance by surprise, as, knowing what was coming, they were preparing for armed resistance, but were not yet ready. The first Aktion took place on September 22, 1942. The Jews were forced to gather in front of the Metallurgia factory, where a "selection" took place. About seven thousand Jews were marched to the railway ramp, where they were pushed into railway cattle wagons. The death train consisted of sixty cattle wagons, each occupied by around one hundred thirty people. The train made its way to Treblinka upon some of the rails that Chaim Rozrozowski had laid almost one hundred years earlier. All were murdered upon arrival at Treblinka. Among the deportees were Tonia and Aaron, who was to turn six later that month. Many of Tonia's and Symcho's family members, including his mother Kajla and his sister Henia, were all deported to Treblinka, but it is not clear if it was on the same day or in one of the subsequent transports to Treblinka, the last of which was on October 4, 1942. Almost no Jews remained in Częstochowa, except a few young people who were left for slave labor, mostly in the nearby ammunition factory. These events are mentioned in my mother's diary.

Symcha Dymant with his first wife, Tonia Wargon, who was murdered in Treblinka with their child. This photo is dated November 17, 1936, shortly after their child, Aaron, was born. USHMM, Acc. Number: 1993.34.13, courtesy of Jacob Dimant.

On the same day, September 22, 1942, some three hundred other Jews were shot dead in the streets of Częstochowa and buried in a mass grave in an empty lot on Kawia Street. Among them was Tonia's mother. The site is now a small garden with a small gravestone memorializing the event. I went to say Kaddish on that mass grave in 2010. On September 22, 1942, Symcho escaped the ghetto. Because he spoke German without an accent, he was able to get work in a German military installation near the town, run by the German army. Seeing the extent of the atrocities around him, he did not believe that any Jew, himself included, would survive to tell the story of these atrocities. In May 1943, a sympathetic German officer helped Symcho evade censorship and send his sister-in-law, Hela Wargon, and her husband Karl, in Bronx, New York, a letter telling them the fate of the family. That officer was later executed, having been suspected of espionage. The letter is stamped "geprüft 9" (examined 9) probably indicating that the letter made it past the censor. The original letter is now part of the permanent collection of the United States Holocaust Memorial Museum. The letter (written in German) includes the following paragraphs:

> "Wonderfully good people are giving me the extraordinary opportunity to send you a letter and I hope that it will reach you . . . And if this letter should reach you, then you should think of this good person.
>
> The letter is from your brother-in-law Symcho, who, together with Kerner, is the only one left of this whole family. I prefer not to give you the details of this brutal tragedy now, but the most important events were as follows:
>
> Your mother was shot by sadistic cannibals on September 22, 1942. Your sister Tonia, my dear wife, with whom I was so happy and of whom I was so proud, was deported with our child, who was about to turn six years old this month, to Treblinka, and we all know what was done there. My mother, your brother Morie, the dear fourteen-year-old Hela, and the whole family, except Kerner, were deported to the same place.

Prisoner Card from Buchenwald for Symcho Dymant no. 15349, issued on December 24, 1944. The card notes in red ink that this Jewish prisoner was registered by a Hollerith Machine, which was a primitive computer made for Nazi Germany by IBM. The Nazis used it to keep track of the prisoners in concentration camps. USHMMPA, no. 95314, courtesy of Jacob Dimant.

My dear Hela, I am writing you this letter for two nights now, but I have to end. I can't write any more. The horrors are so overwhelming that no one could describe them (especially not I). Only two thousand out of thirty-five to forty thousand people are left, and even these people don't have any more hope."

It appears that in the next paragraph Symcho is asking his sister-in-law to visit the mass graves . . . "and once you are there, think of revenge, but only against those that are guilty."[2] Hela, Symcho's sister-in-law, never made it back to Poland, but in 2010 I went to Treblinka to visit the mass graves and

---

2   The original letter is in the permanent collection of the United States Holocaust Memorial Museum.

say Kaddish. The best revenge is the multiple descendants of Symcha and Ita. The extermination plan failed.

Symcho remained in the German military installation near Częstochowa working as a mechanic. In 1944, the SS discovered that Symcho was Jewish and demanded his arrest. The camp commander refused to release him, and it took an order from Berlin to do so. He was charged with political crimes, as well as being a "Pole" and a "Jew," and was deported to Buchenwald concentration camp in Germany. He arrived there on December 24, 1944. He was assigned prisoner number 15349. His identification card at Buchenwald was registered by a Hollerith machine (an early computer made by IBM, used by Nazi Germany in concentration camps to keep track of the prisoners).

While in Buchenwald, Symcho was sent for slave labor in a nearby military factory in Weimar, where airplanes or parts for airplanes were produced, so his mechanical ability was useful to the German war effort, and he was spared. As a political prisoner (and possibly due to his work at a military factory), he was assigned to the German prisoners' barrack, which protected him somewhat from the atrocities happening at the camp. Buchenwald had an active communist underground resistance as many of the German political prisoners were members of the Communist Party. Symcho was active in the German underground resistance at the camp. Among other deeds, this group was able to hide and save some eight hundred children who arrived in Buchenwald shortly before the liberation, having been on some of the last transports of Jews from Hungary to Auschwitz and other camps in 1944. Among them was Elie Wiesel. The youngest child on that transport, Rabbi Yisrael Meir Lau, who eventually became chief rabbi of Tel Aviv and later of the State of Israel, performed the ceremony at my first wedding in 1967. In 1978, talking to a patient at Maimonides Medical Center in Brooklyn, NY, I discovered that my patient was one of those eight hundred children.

On April 11, 1945, Buchenwald concentration camp was liberated by American troops. On April 13, Rabbi Herschel Schacter, a Chaplain in the US Army, celebrated a belated Passover Seder at Buchenwald for the Jewish survivors. Rabbi Schacter later organized a group of sixteen camp survivors to settle on a farm near the US Army camp at Fulda, Germany, which later became known as Kibbutz Buchenwald.

Symcho was able to obtain and save various documents from Buchenwald, including the above-mentioned identification card, all of which are in the permanent collection of the United States Holocaust Memorial Museum.

Symcho's brother Ziskind (Fischl) with his family and twin children also perished in the Holocaust. Symcho's younger brother, Alexander, with whom he was close, made it to the Soviet Union, and after the war was spotted there by his cousins Cesia and Issak Wislicki, but on the same day he was arrested by the Soviet police and was never heard from again.

Immediately after the war, because Symcho spoke many languages, he worked for the Allied Expeditionary Force, traveling through Germany gathering information on refugees from concentration camps. He had moved to Fulda displaced persons camp by the summer. Then he joined Kibbutz Buchenwald, where he met Ita. Rabbi Schacter and Rabbi Marcus, the US Army Chaplains, were associated with the group. Rabbi Schacter went to the British Embassy in Paris and was able to get certificates for emigration to Palestine. After a long train ride that took them through France and a harrowing journey by ship, on September 8, 1945, one hundred young survivors, men and women from the Kibbutz, including Symcho and Ita, arrived in Haifa, one of the first large groups of survivors to reach Palestine. Symcho changed his name to Symcha. In 1946, Symcha and Ita married and had two sons. They lived in Holon, a town south of Tel Aviv. Symcha, age seventy, died in 1983. He was finally at peace.

Although my father talked a bit about events at the Buchenwald concentration camp and the events following the liberation, he never talked about what happened in Częstochowa. The mental scars of his Holocaust experiences were visible for the rest of his life. When I moved to the United States in 1972, he handed me the jacket he wore at Buchenwald and an envelope with documents. Some years later, Hela Wargon called me and asked to see me. I did not know who she was. She gave me the original letter she had received in 1943, an invitation to my father's wedding with her sister Tonia Wargon, and a photograph of my father with Tonia. I first looked at the various documents when I learned about plans to create the United States Holocaust Memorial Museum. They needed restoration, and I donated them to the permanent collection of the museum in 1993 and additional documents in 2014. A list of some of these photographs, artifacts, and documents in the museum's collections is appended (see appendix 3).

APPENDIX 1:

The Brust Notebook Diary

Preface

This notebook was written by Ita Dimant in Częstochowa sometime between September 1942 and July 1943. It appears to be a letter to Mania (Malka, sometimes Dora), a daughter of Menachem-Mendel Miodownik, who left for Sao Paulo, Brazil before the war. She had hidden it at the home of the Henryk Brust family, and it was left there when she was deported to Germany for slave labor. According to Mr. Brust's daughter Ala, he found the original, which was in bad shape, and he re-wrote it in a notebook. Ala gave me that notebook in 2010 when I visited her. I do not know why Henryk Brust did not give it to my mother when she visited him, but perhaps he found it afterwards. The notebook is now at the United States Holocaust Memorial Museum. The following translation was made by Teresa Pollin and edited by Martin Dean.

Jacob Dimant

The Notebook Diary

I have been thinking for a long time about leaving if just a memento of our and our parents' last days; to disappear without leaving even a sign that we were here, alive, and living, just does not make sense. When I think about those who are alive, I think about you, Mania, as well as Mojżesz and Nachman. You, Mania, are in some way closer to me because I know where you are; I know your address. All I know about them is that they are in Palestine, but I am not sure where. I am sure you know where they are, and if you will ever receive these pages, make sure that they should get them as well.

Maybe Rachela or Fryda are still alive somewhere, even if it is hard to believe, but maybe when the war will be over, one of them will be alive; I am sure they would be in touch with you. So, this is for them as well.

How to start? How to describe this inhumane tragedy of the whole nation? Even if a hundred of the best writers tried to describe it, they wouldn't be able to explain everything that happened during this war, what we went through since the mass murder of millions of Jews took place. I am unable to describe it all. I will try, in the hope that it will be easier to die knowing that you will be aware of how our parents, and we, perished.

In July 1942, the destruction reached Warsaw, we, in the Warsaw Ghetto, didn't understand that this is our final destruction, our death. Lublin was already without Jews, even though my sister Henia together with her child was deported together with tens of thousands of others to an unknown destination. Even at that point I did not realize the truth. There were all kind of rumors and differing accounts, but no one could envision or believe something so brutal and cruel.

I don't know how long it was before this disastrous July that you, Mania, received any news from us. Since the US joined the war and the contact between us was severed, we were completely cut off from you and the boys. We knew nothing about Rachela; we corresponded with Fryda till the last moment, until the outbreak of the German-Soviet war. Is she alive? Difficult to believe, but maybe.

We received a package from Fryda; it arrived in the first days of the murderous Aktion in Warsaw. She lived together with Chaim in the Bielsko ghetto. In every letter, she begged us to sell all her things, just not to be hungry. If we should survive, we would have new things. Sara (Sarenka) and I had just one goal—to protect our father and mother, not to let them starve, and how to hide them. We guarded them like a relic for us all. I didn't think about myself at all. All my thoughts were concentrated only on how to work for our parents. I regarded our father as a reflection of my own identity. I was happy to undertake any job, any effort for him. I know that you all loved him beyond words, but I loved him with every fiber of my heart and my pride. Even you all couldn't love him like that. Please forgive me, I understand, you were his children. I became his child because of his enormous heart and my unlimited love for him. Even my feelings for Nachman were rooted in my love for Father. Now I can admit it. I saw in him, most of all, a son of a man

I cherished and only later I fell in love with him. The thought that I will be one with him and I will go through life with him filled me with happiness, because I knew that it would be a double happiness. I would have Nachman, and he would be the father in a double way. It was not to be, I was robbed of it. How much this man was a father, only I knew. How many tears did he shed when he mentioned separately each child? Cruel fate took away each of his children, and each time a piece of his heart was gone. He was a great man and always said: "Follow your happiness, my child." He had so much love for his children, so much understanding. He was young in his soul and had so much life in him. During the last years, his attitude toward me changed, and he started to treat me like an adult. This made me very happy. I was childishly angry when he treated me as a child; I would give so much to be able to return to those times, but they are gone.

Who didn't love him? Every new spouse of a child became his child, and each loved him. Chaim and Kuba [Fryda and Sarenka's husbands] were dedicated and loving till the last moment. Even Leon [Leon Zuk, Rachelka's first husband], who was far from sentimental, loved him. Everything was good in this last year before the war. Sara married Kuba, and they lived in their own, nice room. They worked and supported themselves. Fryda and Chaim were supposed to move to a different apartment; their relationship improved; they both worked. Rachela and Leon managed well, and I was the only one at home. Fryda and Chaim lived at home too, as long as they were looking for a new place. We returned from vacations, sun-tanned, rested; we were getting good news from Mania with wonderful photos of her children. Bela and Mojżesz had a few problems with his job, but their little daughter gave them so much joy. Nachman graduated from school, he didn't know what to do and decided to go to a kibbutz for a year and after a year he was to come for me. This is what he wrote in his last but one letter. I received his last letter at the post office during the general mobilization. He wrote that he had heard bad news, and who knows what will happen. Well, all was finished on the day the war broke out on September 1, 1939. Actually, each one of us received our death sentence on that day, but to implement so many death sentences, it takes time. So, some of us are still alive. It is a question of days or weeks.

Rachela and Leon left on the seventh day of the war. They went east. We lived through a horrible month of bombing. All of Sara's possessions were burned, but it wasn't important, we were all alive. Three months later Fryda and Chaim left us; they went to Chaim's parents. The Soviets were there, and they were happy there. We were left, just the two of us: Sara and I. Sara lived with Kuba's parents, and I lived alone with our parents at home. Sara was able to earn a bit; I did nothing; mother was in bed with a broken leg for three months. I took care of her, and I took care of the household. The repressions against the Jews had started already. Jewish men were taken for forced labor, to labor camps. Jews were deported from some localities, but all in all, the first year in Warsaw wasn't bad. We had letters from Rachela and Fryda; from Mania and from the boys we received regards. I got no news from Nachman anymore.

After the first year we started to feel hardship. Sara didn't have a constant income. We worried, because we had decided not to leave our parents and to make sure that they would be taken care of. It took a lot of effort to convince our father that he should come to terms with the fact that he would not be able work, that it was our turn to support the family. He knew how to work honestly, so it was good for nothing in wartime.

A year after the start of the war, I finally started to work. I opened a pre-school. This was not enough to support us all. It was altogether impossible that one person could support four, maybe with the black market, but none of us knew how to go about it. I was able to make enough for about half, so together with Sara we managed to support the family. There was no hunger. We felt bad that we were unable to give father, who suffered a chronic cough and weakness, all he had before the war. Mother lost a lot of weight and definitely needed better nutrition. I was in very good shape, on the other hand, despite working hard. I worked from early morning till late at night and quite often I didn't sleep for a few nights in a row, because I was busy doing laundry or cleaning up. I wanted to do everything and not to leave anything for mother to do. There was a lot of work, because when you work with children everything must be absolutely clean. Despite all the hard work I was gaining weight and I felt very well. How strange with this bad nutrition and often I went hungry, but I never told anyone. The thought that I am helping my parents, that I can be useful to my mother and give back for all I got from them—all this gave me so much joy, that I didn't feel hunger. I told myself that I do not exist now, that my heart has no rights; my longings were buried deep down. All I wanted was to be a machine, working with one goal only—to help our parents. I wasn't looking for social or cultural life. I have a home and Sara, and this was my world. You all know who Sara was for me; all of you who will be reading these pages realize how important she was for me and there is nothing more to add to it.

Two more years of the war passed, this horrible war, which took place not on the military front but in every inch of land occupied by the enemy. The war was not declared against us Jews; we were cruelly, slowly murdered. The treacherous means of murder, never heard of in the history of the world, were so enormous and so precisely thought through, that no resistance, no protest could arise.

At first, they transferred Jews from the small towns and villages to larger cities. People were forced to leave all they owned, all they were able to amass throughout their lifetime and go to an unknown city, where there was no place for them. Most people weren't able to support their families; those that were wealthy and were able to bring money and gold, they could live. But what was the fate of the paupers, who barely made a living in their hometown? What was he to do in a city where he knew nobody; he had no money and no job? These poor people were forced into barracks; into frightful living conditions where many died every day and the ill and the crippled were murdered right there before the transfer. At least they didn't have to suffer, even though it happened that the sick were transferred, and only after suffering all the horrible conditions, they died. Men aged sixteen to sixty had to go to forced labor. The Germans created labor camps where the only goal was to make sure that the prisoners die, because the conditions were such that no one could survive there longer than a few weeks. If one managed to escape, the Germans killed ten others, for the one who fled. They organized roundups in the streets and took people to these camps. Many times, I felt happy that Nachman is not here, and he doesn't know this hell. We worried about Kuba, but he managed somehow. Life continued despite it all. People, who were not touched personally by these horrors, were so busy with their own issues, news, sadness, or brief joys. In some places the Jews were in more or less closed ghettos. In 1941 our ghetto in Warsaw was surrounded by a two-meter-high wall, hermetically sealing it. At the same time my father and his family were deported from Lublin to Warsaw. The first four weeks they lived with us; later he somehow managed. After all he was still a rabbi, and he was respected. Little Fela, Chaja's daughter, stayed with us. Chaja and her husband went to her in-laws. Life again went its own way; people died; some were born. Our Rachela had a son and my sister Henia, who was married in Lublin, had a son. In June 1941, the war between Russia [the Soviet Union] and Germany started, and it was a long time before we heard from Fryda. We were depressed, but we tried not to give up and to keep parents' spirits up. Finally, we received some news from Fryda, but we didn't hear a thing from Rachela, unfortunately. As if she had disappeared. So many tears were shed while we were reminiscing. Jewish tears are not tears, anymore, these are droplets of blood—but so what? A second year of the war passed; two years of tears; two years of Jewish corpses. This was just the beginning. There were more and more hungry people in the ghetto; at the same time those who made money from this tragedy, danced on the corpses of their sisters and brothers. There were theaters, dancing clubs, elegant ladies in the streets and on the sidewalks—paupers and small children begging. Inside—hunger and destitution. It didn't matter; all of them went to their deaths. At night— roundups for forced labor camps; during the day—roundups of men for labor in Warsaw. It was like living on a volcano. The whole summer I took the children to the small garden—a few trees, a little grass, and some benches. Things were going well. There were a few such small "parks," and the Jewish people showed their strength and will to live. I am not making things up, far from it. My (biological) father was not doing so well; they were slowly starv- ing, and I couldn't help. My attitude and feelings toward my father changed and his whole household changed completely during these miserable times. My home was someplace else and even though I did whatever I could, yet there was so little I could do. I had Fela to take care of, who became part of our household.

1941 ended, and at that time we were displaced from our apartment. We had to move from this street because they changed the borders of the ghetto. After long searches we were able to rent a room with a kitchen in someone's apartment and at the same time troubles started to mount from all sides.

My (biological) father contracted typhus, and I had to take care of him, but at the same time I had to continue my work with the children during the day. Sometimes I spent five nights in a row taking care of my father— never undressing, never sleeping. Sara was on call, and she couldn't help me. I worked so hard, and I was telling myself that I helped him to overcome the illness. Two weeks later my sister Chaja was laid up with typhus. I took care of her as much as I could. She died in my arms. We were not very close, but her death shook me up. Now I know how lucky she was, she died a natural death, when she was unconscious, and she had her dear ones nearby. So much luck- ier than I am—I am at the endpoint of my life for eight months already and I have no one; I'll die alone and like a bedbug, helpless, and without any pos- sibility of revenge.

Soon after that time there was the deportation Aktion or rather murder action against the Jews in Lublin. No one knew where they were taken, but there were rumors of dozens of sealed train cars, which went in an unknown direction. Some talked of the gassing of these people in the train cars; others said that they were deported somewhere—no matter what, they disappeared like a stone in water.

My sister Henia was among them. Her husband later described how it all happened. One day all Jews, who were not employed by or working for the Germans, had to report to a certain square or near the synagogue. It was done by residence or by age—I don't know exactly, but at this place Germans selected young and strong men and took them to the concentration camp at Lipowa Street and the rest were herded into the wagons and taken away the same day. When Henia with her one-year-old baby and her husband were supposed to report, it was rumored that this was the last day of the Aktion, and all the Jews left behind will remain. Henia's in-laws stayed behind, so her husband gave them the baby. Henia cried that she wanted to be with the baby, but her husband explained that it would be better for the baby. The very next day his parents were taken, and they gave the baby to some friends— they wanted to make sure that someone from the Eiger family should survive. Well, this family together with two thousand other Lublin Jews were taken to Majdanek and from there they were taken out together with the baby. [1] So, from a few tens of thousands of Jews in Lublin, only about two thousand were left as of now. Many thousands were shot and killed right there and then; many were taken to *Toten-Lager* (death camps) near Majdanek as well as to Majdanek. It was even worse there. Only a few were able to escape this hell and fall into the next hell. We were so naïve at the time that we didn't under-stand that the same end was prepared for us.

I was, of course, dejected on hearing about these tragedies, but our daily life was so stressful and exacting that I had no time to think about anything. Work at home and work with my parents took their toll and furthermore in our house there were two additional people—two brothers from Parczew. They had to flee from their hometown; their father was arrested, and they managed to escape. They are mother's distant relatives. Now we have more responsibilities, but this had little meaning. All-important issues were left to be taken care of "after the war." We were so sure that we would survive this war and the only important thing was to be healthy and have enough money for food. Jobs and other issues were immaterial. Maybe not for all,

1   On Majdanek in this context, see note 5 on p. 42.

because people loved, got married, had children, argued, cheated each other, planned for after the war, dreamt. A small group of people like me couldn't do it all; I really wanted to survive this war and to look forward to all of us being together again, but I had very little hope that I would live that long. I felt that for me all is lost. Is it possible that Nachman would wait for me all these years? His bond to me was not very strong. I realized that all I dreamt about was lost forever.

So many issues were coming up, unrelated to my outlook on the future, which I had to take care of. I couldn't solve any of these issues, but life took care of them. Again, there was spring all around us and again I started to take the children to the so-called park. If I had a free moment I would go to Sara or for a walk with the boys from Parczew. I never had a free moment. There were always a few hours more I could use, but I didn't complain. I had lots of difficulties at work, but it gave me so much pleasure. The children loved me, and I liked them so much. Money was always a problem, but Sara and I managed somehow. If necessary, we would sell some of the things left by Rachela and Fryda, and Sara was selling her own things and we used the money for what we needed. More or less, everything was fine. Mother felt well, grandmother died, our beloved father didn't feel too good. Sara and I suffered greatly because we couldn't feed him properly and we couldn't give him enough good air to breathe. If we only knew what was awaiting us, we could've eaten like kings, but we thought that we would have to survive like that for a long time and we stuck to the budget. Fryda's packages were of great help to us. In every one of her letters, it was clear that if she only could, she would've sent us her soul. I understood her feelings completely. A short time before the start of the deportation Aktion the atmosphere changed, and it became unsettled. Many Jews were taken from their homes at night and shot in the ruins; many were taken to the Pawiak prison and killed there, but it all started on Tuesday, on July 21 or 22, 1942. On that day the children didn't arrive at my daycare, the whole city was anxious, but no one knew what was going on. We heard something about deportations, but we didn't know who they would deport. Anyway— mothers wouldn't let their children out and all the people ran around, from place to place, very upset. The food prices jumped up. During midday I noticed that the Jewish police were taking away the child beggars and other beggars; they took them to the police. I could see big children crying and explaining that they are not beggars only that day they didn't dress well. But nothing helped. In the evening they issued the announcement that as of today all Jews who are not working will be deported to the East. People who work for the Germans or in German companies would not be deported, nor would their wives and children up to the age of 16. Youths able to work will be placed in special buildings within the ghetto and they will be put to work.

The first thought that occurred to us was to assure father and mother that they will be safe because Kuba worked in a factory, which produced for the Germans. Anyway, Sara as a nurse belonged to the medical staff, which was excluded from deportations. I thought that in the worst-case scenario I would be forced to move into these special buildings for workers in German workshops. At the same time, I frantically looked for a different solution so I wouldn't be separated from our father. Sara had a problem with her father-in-law—the only way not to be deported was to be employed by some workshop working for the German Army. It wasn't so easy to get a placement there; one had to pay a lot of money or to have a sewing machine.

On Tuesday evening, the chairman of the Jewish Community, Czerniaków, committed suicide. On Wednesday the Jewish police blocked some house units and took people out. As of now they take just the poorer ones, but those who had work certificates, they left in peace. Of course, the people, who were able to bribe the policemen, were left alone as well. All the people taken from the buildings were forcibly put on horse-drawn wagons and taken to the so-called Umschlagplatz. It was a huge square, with a school building on one side and it was from there that the people were loaded onto the freight-train wagons, hermetically sealed; two hundred people in each; the daily quota has to be six thousand people.

Sara and I did all we could to find a sewing machine for father, so he would be accepted to the sewing "shop." We didn't have enough money to purchase a "workplace" for him in a workshop. We decided to stay all together in Sara's apartment, just in case. The boys were hurt by our separation from them in difficult times. They were on the verge of deciding to escape from Warsaw, but somehow it was not easy to make such a decision. They stayed and moved to their cousins' place. They kept a grudge against us, especially the older one, who from the moment of his arrival in Warsaw had feelings for me. He was despondent that in such a tragic and decisive moment, we wanted to be just with our own family.

It's just that I cared only about guarding father and to be together with him and with Sara. It was impossible to take these two boys to Sara because she lived with her in-laws and her father-in-law opposed bringing additional people. Sara sent a telegram to Fryda in Mińsk Mazowiecki to take the parents and me to her. At that time, we didn't understand that no matter where we are, the same fate awaits all the Jews. Death was the only outcome for Jews, no matter where they were. I couldn't believe that Fryda in Mińsk Mazowiecki would be able to do anything, but Sara was sure that all that would be possible would be done. All throughout the war they showed incredible interest, sent packages whenever they possibly could and kept regular letter correspondence with us, at least twice a week.

On that same day we had a brilliant idea for protecting me from deportation. The son of our landlord had a job in one of the most important of the workshops. My father issued a "Ktubah" (marriage certificate) for this boy and me, and the boy got a certificate from his workshop officially protecting me.

We were able to get a sewing machine for father and we placed it in a workshop just opened in our building. The list of newly accepted workmen was not yet certified, so parents were still in danger of deportation. Sara was preoccupied with protecting her father-in law—this was difficult too.

In the meantime, they started to block entire streets and one had to turn away, escape, and hide. I don't trust my Ausweiss (ID card); if they'll catch me, they'll take me away. It's just that this piece of paper gives me courage to walk the streets of the ghetto. Every day I walk around the whole ghetto— I visit my father, where Josef is in bed half-dead with tuberculosis; Chaja's husband with little Fela the same. Fela is scared to be in her place; his parents were already deported. Then I go to Fryda's in-laws (the second daughter of my father in Mińsk Mazowiecki)—they are thirteen people and not one of them has the protection of employment in a workshop.

The sleeping conditions in Sara's place are not conducive for that many people living there, and I feel that father is uncomfortable. Mother goes to sleep with the Kadenczyk family, and this is dangerous; after all we moved here to be all together.

Friday
Aktion in my (biological) father's building; everyone was taken out. I have seen police and the wagon at the entrance from far away, but I was not allowed to come through. I left crying, but I still had a shadow of hope that maybe other residents wouldn't let them take him. After all he was very respected in the building. After a few hours I entered the courtyard; all the windows were boarded; silence; emptiness. My brother-in-law and Fela were

gone too. Father could've saved himself, but he volunteered to go, according to the residents left behind. The chairman of the house committee called me over and told me to start efforts to release father and his family from the Umschlagplatz; he told me that he would help with money. What to do? I ran to some "macher" (trickster) and he promised to see what he could do. Any moment they could be taken to the wagons. I ran to the Umschlagplatz; Fryda was already there. We search the faces in the windows in case maybe we'll see father's face or any of the children. The huge school building is filled to the brim; the whole square is filled with people; Jewish police are surrounding the whole area. May each one of them burn in hell for joining the police. One policeman agreed to go and search for father. Finally, he appeared in the window. I really wasn't so attached to him, but when I saw him, I felt that my heart broke and I burst into tears. There was no time—I had to run away because they started shooting. I only had time to yell that they should stay together and that I am doing everything to get them out. I had to yell at the top of my lungs for them to hear, because everyone, from both sides was screaming and shouting. I started to run around, here and there, wherever anyone was willing to tell me that something can be done. I searched for people with influence, and I tried to bribe. It seemed to me that I succeeded in saving them—and then nothing. It was already 10 at night and I had to go home, and I had to drop into Sara's place to see what's going on there. When I reached home there was not a soul in the street. A few steps away from the gate to our building I saw a group of gendarmes, maybe ten of them, shooting. I sneaked from gate to gate, finally reaching our building. Our father exhaled, he worried about me. His situation was still not clear; the list of workmen still wasn't approved. I went to sleep, tormented by what tomorrow would bring?

Saturday
I got up at dawn and ran to the Umschlagplatz. A crowd was already there—everyone had someone inside: parents, a brother, sister, children; everyone was crying. I was able to send them some biscuits and sugar. It's impossible to buy bread at all. We still have some cereal and flour at home, which we kept for a rainy day. I am so busy trying to rescue my father and his family that I can't even think of food. It seems that I have to be in several places at the same time and sometimes I have to hide when they are having the roundups. Many people try to release father, most of all the rabbinate, but I have to make sure that they do what they promise.

The Judenrat put out announcements that it is true that the Germans deport Jews to the East, but the rumors that people are deported to their death are not true, so people should stop panicking. The notices called for unemployed people to report to the Umschlagplatz together with their families and they were promised three kilograms of bread and one kilogram of jam for each person. These announcements caused crowds to migrate toward the Umschlagplatz; people carrying bundles; clutching babies in arms and holding children by the hand—all walk toward the square and say: here we will die of starvation and over there we'll get bread and a job. Oh, the horror, the square is overflowing to such an extent that the police won't let anyone else in. People complained that they have to wait. Then I felt sorry for them but today I envy them. They had no idea that death awaits them and when it came, it was sudden. Those still remaining alive today have been dying day in and day out for a whole year. In addition, they are keenly aware of the fact.

There are these two creatures, Kohn and Heller, who take people out of the Umschlagplatz. I am trying to get to them.

The boys from Parczew, Piniek and Abe, live in a building in which the head of the Jewish police lives, who works for the Gestapo. Half of the building's residents are just like him. In this building, there are no roundups. They are safe.

This mafia takes money for taking people out of the Umschlagplatz. I managed to get to them, and they promised me (everywhere they promise) and in the meantime Saturday passed and father is still there, at the Umschlagplatz. What is miraculous is that father and his family were not forced into the wagons yet. I sent them food and notes asking them to avoid going to the trains. My feet are swollen from walking throughout the day, and I lost my voice from yelling and shouting, so they could hear me. My Sarenka runs around as well and tries to get a place in a workshop for her father-in-law and his niece, who lives with them.

Our father and mother again sleep at home. Father has a temporary certificate that he works in the Többens workshop. Kuba goes to work every day. I go to the families of the children who attended my preschool to get the money they owed me, but in general I come back empty-handed. News of the tragedy had already reached most houses and I couldn't talk about silly sums of money. I visited the sweet Fredzia, the sweetest of all the children from my preschool. She hugged me so long . . . Her father went to work in a camp outside the ghetto and this protects the rest of the family.

I am concerned about my sister Fryda. She and her husband do not work, and I am afraid that they could be deported any day. Troubled and tired in the evening I went to sleep at Sara's; I am scared to go home so late.

Sunday

Pause in the deportations, apparently it is not allowed to work during holy Sunday. Sara and I pack some basic clothes and food into bundles, in case we might be caught, so we would have something for the journey. My father is still being held. Some buildings were ordered that all residents should report to the Umschlagplatz. Some obey and some move to a different place, where such an order had not been given. Between the roundups the streets fill with crowds of people carrying sewing machines. This is the way they figured they would be saved from deportation. They don't know that this journey is one way—to death. The price of bread goes up and up and it's almost impossible to buy it. I had to take waffles from Fedziunia's mother to send to my father—how can it feed seven people? Josef with TB—Oh God! Oh God!

Monday

Up until now the Aktion was conducted by the Jewish police and about twenty Latvians, Tartars, hard like a stone. Now there are more and more of them and more and more victims during the deportations. When they surround a house and order everyone out—they warn that those hiding, when found, would be killed right away. My (biological) father is still there; mud in the square reaches people's ankles. There is no food and no water. My father already received a certificate that he is employed in the Többens workshop. Maybe he will be released. The secretary from Kohn and Heller went to take them out, but no news in the meantime. The one thing that was done is that when they take people to the train, they leave him and his family in the building. Again—I go home tired and resigned.

Tuesday

In the morning, I sat at the table with our father and the order came for our building to report. Our father has the certificate, which is not worth much, because there are swindlers in the workshop, who sell workplaces, so we worry. I have just a temporary ID card. My new husband is still supposed to bring me the real ID. Suddenly someone called me and told me that my father had returned. What? Where? I ran like crazy and in the street a German police car stopped abruptly. There are just the two of us and no one else. The shotgun is directed at me. I stood still. They passed.

I entered my father's apartment; he left my brother-in-law and Fela behind. The certificate was issued in his name and covered his wife and children. How horrible. I can't calm down. How could he do it? There was no other way—he said. He will try to get them out. I know that it's too late; I can see their faces, my brother-in-law and little Fela stand in a window at sundown, I could hardly see them. I sent them some bread hoping that they all were still there. My brother-in-law yelled that my father and his family came down and little Fela shouted: "Auntie, save us, get us out of here." I was sure they will all get out together and I shouted back that they shouldn't worry, that they would get out. Tears choked me: they stayed and who knows what would happen to them. I heard that they kill all the children. At that time, we thought that only children . . .

Wednesday

The streets near our houses were all closed. In the morning, I went to my father, and I brought them some food. Josef feels very sick. They don't have their own apartment. The Kibbutz of the Shomer took their place and now they must stay with strangers. I argued with the boys from the kibbutz, so they would leave the apartment of my father, that they are healthy, and my brother is so ill, he has a fever of forty degrees Centigrade and has no place to lay down.

My worries are not over, after all, my father doesn't work anywhere, and they can be taken in the next roundup. From there I ran to Sara to see what is going on there. Was everything quiet there? Was everyone at home? Kuba didn't go to work today; Sara and Kuba came to us; our father is in the workshop, trying to get accepted for work. We called to him to come home. I couldn't get used to how our father's face looked—it's been a few days since he shaved off his beard. Each time I looked at him, tears came to my eyes. He looked so handsome with the beard, not that now he looks bad, it's just that he looks different. We all sat around the table to discuss what to do with my father. I finally got my permanent ID, and our father was happy that I was protected. The boys—Piniek and Abe don't have jobs yet, but they are arranging a place in the shoemaking workshop, for money, of course. Suddenly someone knocked on the door—it was a policeman (Jewish) from Mińsk Mazowiecki. Fryda and Mojżesz sent for our parents and in their note, they ask that I should come as well. We started to confer frantically—what should we decide—yes or no? The policeman says that in Mińsk Mazowiecki all is quiet, no one knows about the situation in Warsaw, and that Fryda and Mojżesz are doing very well, and they will be able to support our parents and me. I feel tortured—should I go with my parents? I would like to be with them, but I cannot decide to part from Sara. God, what should I do? We decided that our parents should go, there is nothing to gain by staying here and maybe over there they can be saved. And what about me? Finally, I decided to go as well. During the whole time of the war all I did was for my parents, and I will continue being with them. I will not be apart from my beloved father. The automobile was parked on Kupiecka Street. We told mother to pack the essential things and Sara, Kuba, and I ran to the car to arrange things with the driver, because Kuba has to return home to bring money. The very moment we arrived at Kupiecka Street we noticed a taxicab with a machine gun standing at the corner. The street was empty. The car was there, but no one was there. Kuba decided that I should return home to help with packing and they will find the driver. I returned through a gate at Nalewki and at the corner is another taxicab with a gendarme holding a shotgun. I was trapped. When the gendarmes participate in an Aktion, an ID is of no help. I stood in an entryway and waited. I expected that this is my end, and I would never see them again. The building belonging to the entrance I was standing in is rounded up. At the last moment I climbed through a small window into a cellar. I sat there for a long time; it seemed like an eternity. Finally, I heard people moving in the courtyard and someone calling me to get out. It was a doctor who stood next to me before and at that time they didn't take medical personnel. This whole Aktion lasted about two hours. I ran home like crazy; too late. Our father and mother had left already, and the car couldn't wait, so I didn't even say good-bye. I didn't cry. I couldn't. I had Sara. I moved the same evening to be with her. We packed everything into bundles, and we were to move it all in the evening. Suddenly Sara started to bawl her eyes out and I couldn't calm her down. She worried that maybe this was a mistake to let our parents go. I couldn't show her my own despair and together with Kuba we reassured her. I swore that now that I have only her—whatever would happen to her—would happen to me. If we were to be deported, then we would be deported together.

All we wanted was to get a letter from our father to know that they had arrived; how are they? We spent days walking around asking different people if they received a message from Mińsk. Every day I went to see my father; our cousins Fajgenbaum and Piniek and Abe (by chance their last name was

6

Fajgenbaum too) and then I returned to Sara. The days were terrible, with frayed nerves.

For hours one had to hide while trying to go from one place to another. Sometimes going from one street to another the journey lasted five or six hours. The list of people we knew who were deported became longer and longer. Chaim Shloyme was deported, and the children wandered in desperation. People looked like shadows. People spent whole days in cellars, in attics; at night no one slept quietly, and no one knew what the next day would bring? When would all this end? People invented new dates to reassure themselves. Only the Jewish police partied, convinced that nothing would happen to them. How they dragged the people who resisted; how exacting they were in fulfilling the orders. Oy Jews, Jews!

One day, after our parents left; our building was surrounded, and we all had to come down to present our IDs. All of us had good documents, but no one could be really sure. Kuba's cousin hid under the sofa. She became hysterical and the rest of us almost went crazy. I ran to the boys to tell them that there is a possibility that we will be taken and, in any event, if Sara will be taken, I will go too. I just wanted them to know what could happen to us. Piniek ran after me and begged me to stay with them: "please stay" and I said: "no, goodbye forever." But they didn't take us together; I wish they would take us together. This was a few days after our parents' departure; we received a letter that they were well and life is like in paradise, just that leaving us behind, in hell, makes them miserable. They asked if we would like to join them and if yes, they would do everything in their power to make it possible. Kuba didn't want to go; he didn't want to leave his parents so we decided that we would stay as well. We wanted to send some clothes to them, because our parents left without anything, but we just couldn't. The situation got worse and worse every day. When people parted, even just for a few hours, one wasn't sure if you would ever meet again. When I was still trying to release my father from the Umschlagplatz, a young man stood next to me, yelling to his whole family. He left for work outside the ghetto in the morning and when he returned, they were all gone—parents, sisters, brothers—at a stroke. They shouted to him from the window: don't worry, don't cry—we are all together; we are not worried and when we arrive, we'll write you a letter; we will dance at your wedding; eat drink, do not worry. The boy cried like a child, and I cried with him. They lied to us, they made idiots out of us; they spread rumors that letters had arrived from Brest-Litovsk from those "resettled" from Warsaw; that they are alive, and they are working.

Later people started to whisper that children and the elderly are killed, but the healthy and young go to work.

Desperation grew in the ghetto; people sold everything for pennies. My father still didn't have his own place to live. All of them starved—when I just think about it, I am unable to swallow a bite. I had my meals with Sara; we cooked twice a day and after all I just couldn't bring food for five starving people. I tried as much I could, but all for nothing. One day, I entered the courtyard and asked if anyone had seen my father and this man answered: he is standing next to you. I looked and I couldn't believe it. This is my father? I was speechless; if I would meet him in the street, I would just pass him by and not recognize him. He had shaved and it changed him completely. People did everything to avoid deportation. My father shaved his beard and put a regular hat on his head and wore just a regular jacket and he worked in a workshop— may I not live to see such a transformation.

I was always radical and opposed to everything he represented—but this was just horrible.

I started to visit the boys (Piniek and Abe) more often; I felt more secure there. I didn't have to hide during the roundup. Sara went often to Kuba in his workshop, and I was with the boys at that time. In early July we gave our winter coats to a tailor for repair. Now Sara reminded me every day to get it back, so if we were sent away, we would have our winter coats. That's how we thought at the time. About a week after our parents' departure and about two weeks after the deportation Aktion started, I went to get our coats. This part of the ghetto was quiet, especially at this hour. I left the boys' apartment telling them that I was going to visit my father. I was very depressed, because there were rumors that every workshop would put their workers in special workshop dorms and the wives will live there as well. That meant that I would have to live in the dorm of the Schultz workshop with my husband! Brrrrr!! This is an 18-year-old boy. He is a good boy, but to live with him in one room, and with just one bed. Oh my God, what will happen? In addition, I knew no one in this workshop. I would prefer to live with Piniek and Abe in the Többens dorm, even though I argued so many times with Piniek already and so many times I told him that I am unable to accept his feelings, but if the worst comes to the worst, I would rather be with them. I realized that such a shared accommodation had to end with what from the first moment of the meeting I dreamt about; but the fear of living with this complete stranger, makes me prefer to live with them.

I felt that Sara held a grudge, and it made me feel even worse. They were strangers to me too, especially Piniek with his bourgeois views and his small-town behavior. On the other hand, his burning feeling for me, his turning into ashes at my feet from the very first moment after their arrival, despite knowing that there is someone else in my life—diminished my dislike toward him. I never knew how to resist people who had feelings toward me. I talked about it with Sara this morning and she told me to do what I want, but in her opinion, I should make it official. In Sara's opinion such a man would treat a wife differently from a girlfriend and she wouldn't want that he would say something to me, which I would not be able to take. How wrong you were about him, my dearest Sara. Filled with these thoughts I reached the tailor, I put the coats in a bundle, and I look at the tailor and I see that he didn't look like a human being. During the day, when he was working in the workshop, they took his mother and four-year-old son and deported them to Treblinka. He said that his baby was thrown into the fire and his wife was in prison since they had confiscated furs from the Jews. He heard that all Jews from the prison were already deported. I left him with my bundles, in addition I had some sheets which I took from home and a dress in which I had all the documents and some money. Suddenly I heard the police whistle, and the building was surrounded. I heard yelling: all come down! I hear the guns rattle. What should I do? Should I come out? No! These are gendarmes and they just take people away. I ran upstairs; maybe there is an attic? When I reached the last floor, I noticed that I had lost my pouch. Oh my God! My ID, my certificate, and money. I am lost and I ran back to look for it. I didn't remember where the bundle fell apart and I tried to reconstruct it, but it's not going well. I hear shrieks from downstairs, it's the end. No one would know what happened to me; I let go of the bundle and run into the attic. Where should I hide? There is only a space to hide in a hole in the wall. Behind the wall there is another attic—am I mad? Whichever staircase I approached I hear the same whistle and the same yelling: "all down," and the same gunshots. My heart beats like a hammer and my eyes are protruding. I jumped from one attic to another until I saw an iron shod door on the floor. I lay down under the door; it pushed me down and I could hardly breathe. I saw some hay, which I put on my head and other garbage too. I lay there knowing full well that if they discovered me, they would kill me. Please, may it not hurt when they are killing me. Maybe they will not discover me? Who would look for a human being under such a heavy door? My whole body was numb; it was so stuffy that I couldn't breathe and my heart beats in my throat. Someone passed through the attic, and I think it was a Jewish policeman and I was sure he would hear my heart-beat, but he left. I was completely numb; I didn't know how long I was there. Was it a century or just a few minutes? Finally, I heard movements in the courtyard; people were calling to each other. I got out with difficulty, and I walked down. I saw that I am on a different street. Probably the attics of the buildings were connected in a whole block. Maybe during the roundups for forced labor, someone made this escape route. I thought that I am going in circles and that I am going mad. I was all dirty. I entered someone's apartment and asked the people to let me have a wash. When I got out into the street— as if nothing ever happened. I could hardly walk; this experience shook me up. I thought it was the end of the world.

I walked along Nowolipie Street. I wanted to go to Sara, who lived at number 44, but I just couldn't muster the strength and I went to the boys at number 24. I barely made it to the fourth floor, and I just fell on the daybed. I looked so bad that I frightened everyone. After a few hours Sara came by; she was worried what had happened to me; she wanted to take me home, but I just wasn't strong enough to get up. I had no documents of any kind; not any document which could protect me from deportation. My only protection was that the building in which the boys lived was never rounded up. I stayed there. There were three girls and two boys, so it wasn't too crowded. In the morning Sara brought me some soup and some provisions for cooking. She was on her way to the workshop with Kuba. The boys didn't want to accept the food from her, but both Sara and I didn't want to accept food from them. I would eat with them if they would work like everyone, but they just had a lot of money. At that time, they still had this cult of money and believed in money and for me it was repulsive. Actually, I didn't see anything too expensive there.

For a few days, I just couldn't move, and then Piniek arranged for an ID (Ausweiss) for me, in his last name. They were in Warsaw under a false name because they were afraid that the Gestapo from Parczew would search for them. My father wrote another Ktubah for Piniek and me and this way I already had a second husband. It didn't matter much because they stopped leaving the families of the employed and deported them like all the others. Only the employed were protected. Kuba was told that he would have to move to his workshop's dorm and Sara was with him all the time.

For the first two days after this incident, I didn't leave the apartment. Sara would come early in the morning before going to the workshop with Kuba. On the third day Sara didn't come. I asked Piniek why Sara didn't come. He answered that she probably wasn't let out. In the evening, I sent Piniek to check up on Sara; after he returned, he told me that she is busy moving into the dorm. I decided to sneak out and to see her myself. It was just a few houses away. Oh God! Sara was sick; she had a high fever. In the present conditions that shouldn't surprise anyone. She cannot stay at home, because there wasn't any hiding place and Kuba is supposed to move to the workshop housing. She wouldn't be able to rest there. And anyway, she is no longer protected by her husband's workplace. Sara must go to the hospital; I prepared everything, and we started to set off. Sara and Kuba took a rickshaw, but they didn't allow me to go with them. I went back home, but after a few hours again I sneaked into their place to find out about Sara's condition. I found both of them at home. They were both taken to the Umschlagplatz, but separately and somehow both got out. The hospital didn't want to admit Sara; they told her to go to a hospital for infectious diseases. Kuba went to a friend, a doctor, to arrange that Sara should be admitted, but in the meantime . . .

Number 1

After a few days, they were taken out, and my brother-in-law and little Fela left. Many influential institutions took care of my father. In the first days it was possible to take people out (naïvely), only so they would suffer a little longer.

My older brother had TB for a few months, and father recovered from typhus. After he shaved off his beard and when he started to wear a regular hat it was difficult to recognize him. Their bodies looked like skeletons and they had absolutely nothing to eat.

Number 2

The starvation was so terrible that when they posted announcements that people who report to the transport point will receive three kilograms of bread and one kilogram of jam, hundreds of families with bundles on their backs walked there of their own free will. Oh horror! To be so naïve. I wasn't able to take to heart every detail of their criminal perfidy. I wasn't even able to cry when someone from my family was missing. After losing Sara I became numb; I hurt when I looked at my father and his family. They could've been taken any moment. After Sara was taken, I wanted to report myself, but the boys guarded me. Piniek didn't leave me for a moment, and I just couldn't get rid of him. Abe, the younger one, showed me a lot of compassion. Both of them tried very hard to bring me back to life.

Number 3

I was numb; nothing mattered to me. Piniek fought from the very first day after their arrival to make me his wife. I wouldn't let him even think about it. The fact that it actually happened did not take me out of my stony numbness. He fought for me so hard, that even though he got what he wanted, he could not enjoy it. He cried and he threatened, and nothing helped.

In the middle of August, Piniek came home and said that he had purchased three passes to Częstochowa for a few thousand zloty and that we were going. The Gordonia movement issued these passes. The heart of the Gordonia movement was a young man, Eliezer Geller. They forged employment certificates for workshops; they were able to get blanks of different documents and forged passes. They rescued people from a burning hell to places where it was not burning yet. Abe was a member of Gordonia and that's how this contact was made. All this happened on the day when the Gestapo shot and killed the head of the Jewish Police, Erlich, and our building stopped being protected from deportations.

Number 4

There was no place to hide. Since nothing made any difference, I agreed to go. I believed that we would be caught on the way and that we would be killed. I told my father that I will most probably leave, but I didn't go to say goodbye. I just couldn't. I tried to talk Kuba into coming with us, but he wanted to stay in case Sara would write of her possible return. When I think about it, all I want to do is howl like a dog. Maybe she'll write, maybe she'll come back—now I know that she was not alive then.

We left, I think, on August 20th. I don't know when my father and his family perished and when Kuba died. God, it's a fact that they perished. We left, but I still had our beloved parents, my beloved Father. This thought gave me some energy when we were leaving the Warsaw Ghetto. Maybe I'll be able to go to see them. I will be able to write to them. We passed the guard booth pretty easily; it cost nine hundred zloty taken from us by a Jewish policeman and here, on the other side.

Number 5

. . . a new hell started. We left the hell of the Warsaw Ghetto at eight in the morning, but we left for Częstochowa at ten at night. It is impossible to describe the nightmare of this day. First of all, tens of street urchins yelling: "Jude! Jude!" They chased us like mad dogs. Some wonderful people rescued us from these locusts for one hundred zloty. Jews were not allowed to travel in a droshky, but we had no choice and we jumped into one. A few street urchins again caught the droshky and yelled for us to give them money, and if not, they would call a gendarme. The boys got confused, but I didn't give in, and I called a Polish policeman, who politely took us to the train station, for a few hundred zloty. This was just the beginning. We sat for six hours on the platform; different individuals constantly blackmailed us. They knew very well that if they denounced us that would be the end of us. And we knew it too.

Number 6

In the end, I couldn't stand it anymore and I started to shout that they should just take us. I couldn't take it anymore. Abe behaved like a child and cried. I had enough pride not to shed even one tear. I was sitting and watched the clock. Every fifteen minutes another one came and threatened that he will go to denounce us. It was all about money. In this way they took from us one thousand five hundred zloty, our watches, and a gold wedding ring, which I had from our Rachela and was wearing. I just cannot understand how we arrived in Częstochowa alive. I described it for you in such detail because we were not the only people who experienced these tortures. All Jews who escaped the Warsaw Ghetto or some other hell, were exposed to such tortures. Not one perished on the way. Of course, one should not judge the whole nation according to some individuals. To encounter persecution from people from whom one is looking for deliverance—it was awful. We arrived in Częstochowa half dead, not looking like human beings.

Number 7

We arrived at Kibbutz Gordonia. They greeted us warmly. We had a feeling that we had emerged from darkness into a different world. Here there was a ghetto as well, but there was no wall or barbed wire around it. At the boundaries of the ghetto yellow boards were posted with signs that from this point on it was a Jewish district. Poles could enter, which almost never happened in Warsaw. The stores were open, pastry shops, coffee shops were open. Just like in Warsaw before the Aktion. Immediately I wrote to our father in Mińsk. The boys had their whole family in Parczew. We moved in with some people and we all lived in one room. After two days in the kibbutz, we found out about Treblinka and what it really means. And only at this moment did I realize that Sara is dead. I wasn't the only one who lost my dear ones. New people, who had lost many or all of their family, arrived in the kibbutz. There were girls and boys that didn't have anyone.

Number 8

At that time, I thought that we had only lost Sara, but a week after our arrival in Częstochowa we received news from Parczew that there had been an Aktion there. The boys lost their mother, sister, brother-in-law, and two nieces. They were all hidden in the ice room but the woman, who was fictitiously registered as the owner of the factory, thanked them in such a way for becoming rich off their backs. The mother was shot three times in the head and lived for two more weeks. Their sister died immediately and her husband with a child and another girl of their sister from Lublin went on a transport to Treblinka. Only two sisters remained: Tyla and Rutka with their children. I had to forget about myself and take care of their immense pain. They worshiped their mother and now their spirits were broken. I started to worry that there was no news from Mińsk and ultimately everything ended in Mińsk as well—there was an Aktion. Everything collapsed into rubble; the goal of my life from the moment of the outbreak of the war was, together with Sara, to save our father and mother; that they should survive this devilish war and that they would be able to be with all their children.

Number 9

Oh God! All my personal dreams, wishes, sacrifices—all these I locked up just to fulfill the needs of our father. I worked beyond my abilities, and I was happy that I could earn enough to buy them a piece of bread; that I could repay him for his enormous heart and all the love he showed me. I dreamt of that wherever fate would take me, and even though my desire to be reunited with Nachman was not fulfilled, because he couldn't wait for me for so many years; but father, I would not give anyone for you; he would always be with me, and I would be his footstool, and he would be for me a holy relic. Fate is brutal. I don't even know when he perished; were they killed right there or were they deported to Treblinka. Oh, no! Just not Treblinka, no, no, no! It's a hundred times better to be killed right there. From hundreds of thousands there were a few who managed to escape from this massacre. They told us what was happening there.

Number 10

When the train arrives, bringing a transport of Jews, they open the wagons and twenty Ukrainians with whips start to make the Jews jump out. Then one gendarme who is in charge selects a few men for labor. Women and children stand separate from the men. They kill the sick right away. They order everyone to undress so they are naked and to bundle their clothes and to put them on a pile. Women and children were driven to some building, from which after a while a horrible scream was heard. It lasted just a few minutes and then there was silence. Men were forced to run around the square and when they were barely alive, then they are driven into the chamber, and they are finished off there. The few men selected from the transport were divided into two groups. One group was left to sort the clothes and the second group went to the Toten Lager and they had to take the corpses out with pitchforks from the chambers and throw them into a machine, which plowed the earth...

Number 11

... and the corpses of these human beings were covered there. The corpses were not of each human being separately. There was a mass of all the bodies, one shapeless mass, all stuck together. Babies' corpses crushed into women's corpses; those closer to the middle could be recognized more easily. But this must have been someone very close. There was a lawyer Jachimowicz, who had escaped from the Toten Lager. He was saying that when he was moving the corpses with a pitchfork, he recognized the body of his wife. He escaped, but he lost his mind. The second group sorted the clothes, underwear, coats, money, and jewelry. There were millions and it all went to the German treasury. This is where our Sara perished. In such a bestial way they murdered her. And our beloved father and our best mother—was it their fate to die amidst such torture? Maybe fate was gentle and let them perish there, in Mińsk.

Number 12

I will never know what happened, and no one will know. At that time, I still hoped that maybe someone from among our cousins, the younger ones, was left. Later I found out that Henia and Mojżesz were deported; Fryda was murdered after a while. I don't know what happened with our Fryda, the sweet baby and with Chaim—there was a ghetto there as well. There were deportations from there too. Were they deported or were they killed right there? How much did they suffer? Or maybe they are still alive somewhere, like me. Difficult to believe. About Rachela and Leon and their small son—not a word since the outbreak of the war between Russia and Germany. We don't know whether they fled into Russia or perished. At that time our parents were gone—it was the end of August 1942. That's how I was left alone.

It was me who was mourning, crying bloody tears, all my dear ones; one after another. Fate was so cruel to me that it didn't let me die with my beloved ones; it just took me away from them.

Number 13
Here in Częstochowa, people started to talk about an approaching Aktion, to Treblinka. The boys started to think about possibilities of rescue for me. It was easier for a woman, because it was difficult to distinguish Jewish women from Polish women. Men, even if they didn't look Jewish, they had a mark [circumcision]; any doctor would be able to check. Despite this stigma, those men who didn't look too Jewish took a risk; made false documents, Polish identification papers, and scattered wherever they could. They were mercilessly chased, but still some succeeded in surviving for longer periods of time.

I belong to this category. The boys worked in the German steel mill and tried to convince me that they were protected from deportation, because the Germans needed a workforce. The Germans were taking Polish youths to Germany to use them for forced labor, but here there was a lack of laborers. I didn't believe the fairytales that Jews were needed for work anymore. The boys didn't ask my opinion and arranged for a Polish identity card for me. They paid one thousand zloty for it.

Number 14
They were telling me constantly that in the event of an Aktion, I would undoubtedly be deported. They told me that I am the last and only person in the whole world, whom they have, and if I were taken, they would go too. They were saying that every Jew should try to survive just because Hitler swore that not even one Jew would survive in Europe. Maybe a day of revenge will come and then every Jew will be of importance. They convinced and convinced, but I couldn't imagine how I would be able to put on someone else's skin; how would I be able to pretend? It's been just five weeks since we escaped from the hell of the Warsaw Ghetto. The deportations continued in Warsaw. They already deported half a million Jews to Treblinka, and this was just from Warsaw. Here in Częstochowa we expect an Aktion any day. The nights were impossible to survive. In my nightmares I saw the faces of my beloved, of friends, of acquaintances, of the sweet children. These butchers were taking babies from baby carriages, by their small feet and hitting their heads on a wall. These images were etched into my brain, and they will never pale, not till the day that I die. Every morning I was sure that this is the end,

Number 15

. . . that in a moment they will order us to get out; every noise was a gun crackle. My nerves were giving up. One day, it was Tuesday, after Yom Kippur, September 24, at 5 a.m., gendarmes surrounded the ghetto. We got dressed, I packed a few necessary things, and we walked out into the street. Laborers from the steel mill were getting ready to go to work, but all exits were blocked, and I couldn't get out. I was returning back, resigned—let's just get it over with. The boys wouldn't let me. They found another way out where only a Polish policeman stood guard, without a German gendarme. Piniek said: I don't even want to say goodbye and he pushed me toward the policeman. What did I say and how did I convince him that I am a Polish woman, who was in there by mistake—I have no idea. After a few very long minutes I crossed to the Polish side, and I walked to the train station. The Germans were rounding up Poles for forced labor in Germany, so the station was empty.

Number 16

No one talked to me, and I bought a train ticket for Warsaw without any problem. From this moment I became a Polish woman, Genowefa Zawadzka. The boys and I agreed that I would go to Parczew to their sisters; all was quiet there again. Out of ten thousand Jews officially there were one thousand left but after the hiding Jews emerged from their bunkers, there were two thousand. I arrived in Łuków the same day and I spent the night with some friends of the boys. I took a bus to Parczew. In Łuków I escaped from a group taken for forced labor to Germany, so I couldn't risk taking a train. So many Jews dreamt about the possibility of going to Germany as Poles; even for hard labor, just to survive this horrid war. I spent two weeks in Parczew. At that time, they prepared a ghetto for the remaining Jews, but it was in the air that any day now they will finish off the rest. People concentrated just on food and eating. They wanted to eat as much as possible before dying and to leave as little as possible for the Germans. In every house they were building hiding places—bunkers.

Number 17

If they will not leave even one Jew, they will have to go out from the bunkers, because otherwise they would starve to death. For two weeks we didn't know what was going on in Częstochowa, but the trains with Jews from Częstochowa went to Treblinka via Łuków. After two weeks we received a letter from the boys that they were alive, and they were living in the factory. The same day I left Parczew, and I parted with the boys' sisters forever. A few days after I left, they killed all the Parczew Jews. Rutka with her husband and children and Tyla hid with some peasant. This man took from them ten thousand zloty and denounced them to the Gestapo. Once again, I left five minutes before the fire. If I had stayed a few days more, I would have shared their fate. I traveled to Częstochowa for two days. Germans were rounding up Poles for labor in Germany and of course they were looking for Jews and killed them right away. When I arrived in Częstochowa, the Aktion was still in full swing. There were sixty thousand Jews in Częstochowa. In three weeks, they deported some fifty thousand.

Number 18

The rest were placed in the factories where they worked. Slowly and methodically the Germans searched for hiding Jews and deported them. Piniek and Abe were in the munitions factory together with hundreds of other young Jewish men. Every morning they were taken, lined up in fours, under guard to a similar factory; ten heavily armed Germans and Ukrainians kept guard.

After arriving back in Częstochowa, I had nowhere to go. I was together with another girl who came from Parczew. Before the deportation Aktion in Częstochowa she was in the Gordonia Kvutza (group), and she had a boyfriend there. She didn't know what happened to him, but since all the boys from the Kvutza worked in the same factory as my boys, we were sure that her boyfriend was there too. We couldn't just walk around town— this would be suspicious. She looked quite Semitic. During my journey to Parczew from Częstochowa I met a Pole, and we talked a little. He told me that he worked in the same factory as the boys. Jews and Poles worked together in the Pelcery steel mill.

Number 19

I knew that I would be able to benefit from meeting him and I asked for his address. I had to pass a test for being a Polish woman. I said that I do business and just today, which means on the day when they surrounded the ghetto, I had arrived to get merchandise, but since the ghetto was under siege, I would go back to the Lublin area. It was a believable story. Right after arriving in town, I went to the address this man gave me and I found out that he has a wife and two children. They welcomed us quite nicely. We had a place where we could leave our packages, at least. We found out the route by which the

Jews were taken to work, and we went to await them. Finally, they appeared. I was very emotional, and I hoped to be able to exchange a few words, but this didn't pan out. When I saw the boys, I just walked around as if I'd gone mad, and my friend was searching for her boyfriend. How they looked! They looked like beggars. Piniek walked and tears came down his cheeks. Abe was pale like a corpse; we were just a few steps apart, but it was like an abyss— I was a Polish woman and I walked on the sidewalk—they walked in the middle of the road surrounded by armed guards. They gave me signs with their eyes to go away.

Number 20
... in case they recognized us, but I couldn't care less; I walked, I tripped as if I was blind. I walked with them to the gate of the factory, and I watched them till they disappeared. Dwora didn't see her boyfriend. I wrote a letter to the boys, and I went to this Pole who took my letter to Parczew. He was his foreman. I told him that the parents of these two Yids sent me to find out something about them. I asked him to deliver this letter to them and he agreed. We spent the night in the house of the man we met in the train. He gladly agreed to take us in. The next day again we went to wait for the group returning from work, but the boys were not in the group. I ran to the fore-man, and he told me that yesterday, after they returned from work, German gendarmes arrived and took one hundred and four men, among them my two boys. Most probably they were deported but it was not certain. Now I was all alone, and I didn't know what to do. The same day when we found out about the disaster, Eliezer Geller arrived from Będzin to rescue as many people as possible. They had a large Gordonia Kvutza in Będzin.

Number 21
Będzin was on the territory of the Third Reich, and things were quiet there. Dwora left with him, and I stayed alone. They wanted to take me with them, but I wasn't sure if the boys were really taken, so I wanted to stay in Częstochowa and find out what had really happened. I talked to the people where I had already spent a few nights, asking if I could stay with them and they gladly agreed. The neighbors were whispering that Dwora was Jewish, but after her departure it quietened down. I asked Eliezer to write to me, so I would be at least in touch with one Jew in case I would be in trouble here. After all I was not registered, and my ID is forged. I am lucky that people are limited and not intelligent and others are good and don't ask questions. It's

easy to fool them. For three weeks I paced near different groups of Jews who were walking to and from their place of work. I asked after the boys, but no one knew anything. The Germans allowed six thousand Jews to live in four cramped streets, surrounded by barbed wire with just one exit.

Number 22

Only Jews between the ages of sixteen and thirty-five were allowed to stay; in addition, they left a few dozen children of doctors and policemen. Later there were some more, because they left their hiding places and even those who were hiding in the Polish quarter, returned to the ghetto. After three weeks I found out that my boys had escaped from a transport to Treblinka and for three weeks they stayed hidden in some bunker and now they had returned to the ghetto.

In the first days after the creation of the ghetto, the youth from the Shomer and Gordonia united and created one kibbutz. Piniek and Abe joined them. The day after I found out that they were alive, I told my landlords that I am leaving for a few days, and I entered the ghetto. It wasn't difficult to enter and to leave at that time. When the work groups returned to the ghetto, they were not counted and even when they were leaving it was possible to get out. At the border of the ghetto, they left all the Jews living in a building, because there was a workshop working for the Germans (today it is at the corner of Wilson and Kakielów).

Number 23

Poles lived in this building as well, and it was easy to get in and out. I had to enter the courtyard as a Polish woman, enter a Jewish apartment, put on the armband with the Star of David and become a Jew. When a group of Jewish women crossed the gate and it was accompanied by just a Jewish foreman, it was easy to jump into the group and you were in the ghetto. Later they even used dogs, but it was possible to outsmart them. Every few days I entered the ghetto, where I spent a day or two and then I left. I couldn't stay permanently because I would have to register and go to work. I was already known as a Pole in town; I was registered and if I would go to work with a Jewish group, someone might recognize me. The fact that I was on the Polish side could be beneficial for us. I was able to bring in food and arrange things.

Number 24

Eliezer traveled from Będzin to Częstochowa and to Warsaw—he tried to transfer people and he tried to arrange for convents to accept Jews and Jewish children; it was important to have contacts. Many came to me and wrote to my address. People were not experienced and didn't realize that they needed to be careful; something was bound to happen. The people who lived in the building in which I stayed were from the lowest social group—drunks, thieves, and most of all, anti-Semites. They were prewar nationalists, not the intelligent ones, but the most primitive of people. I lived among them, and I had to live like them and not show how repulsed I was by their conversations. I had to listen to their constant blaming of the Jews. When they remembered that they were Christians and that one is not to kill, etc. they would say: we felt sorry for them as people, but as Jews—we are happy that they are being killed. And I had to keep my mouth shut, grind my teeth, and hear it all. If someone said one positive word about the Jews, he was called a "Jewish henchman," or they started to interrogate them, to see if by any chance this person was a Jew, if he takes their side. I lived among them for two months when the neighbors started. . .

Number 25

. . . to whisper that for sure I am Jewish, as all my visitors looked like Jews. Finally, one of the neighbors told me directly that she would go and denounce me to the Germans. What should I do? If I were to escape that would be like admitting to being Jewish and then I wouldn't be able to stay in Częstochowa at all. No! I decided not to give in. "To the police station? I said—no problem. I am not afraid. If you denounce me, I would go; they would kill me before I would have a chance to explain anything—this is their system. This will be on your conscience. But if I have a chance to explain—they will beat you up." This kind of language they could understand. I knew that if they were to denounce me that would be the end of me. I really didn't want to die on this side alone like a dog. If I am to die, then at least among my own people. I didn't give in to panic. I didn't leave the apartment for six days, expecting the Gestapo to come for me any moment. The slightest noise seemed to me to be the steps of gendarmes. After six days I couldn't take it any longer and I announced that I am going to my parish to bring my baptismal certificate, to make them stop their babbling.

Number 26

I went into the ghetto—it was the end of November. At that time, I had already befriended a Polish family in Częstochowa, who were hiding a Jewish boy. I used to visit them and during these moments I could return to being myself, a Jewish woman. These people were an exception; they risked their own lives to hide a Jew. If they were caught, the penalty was death. On the other hand, if there were no denouncers, so many more Jews would be able to save themselves or be rescued. But these hyenas tracked and nosed after every step such that even if a good Pole wanted to help, the other one wouldn't let him. The Brust family was such an exception. They didn't care if it was a Jew, a Pole, or a Roma ("Gypsy")—what was important was if he was a good person. He was a proletarian, a workman, and a real democrat. His wife—a woman with a heart, but more scared than her husband. No wonder, they have three children and if they were denounced, the whole family would be killed. It's just that he was calm, brave, and most humane. The children: fourteen-year-old Ala; twelve-year-old Henia and ten-year-old Szczepan. Each of the children was brought up without any prejudices; they have it in their blood. One can depend on them as with adults.

Number 27
They hid a Jewish boy in their apartment, in one room, and the children gave up friends so no one would come to visit. When I went to see them for the first time, I was very tense, they could give me up. I had to go, because I had a debt of gratitude toward a girl who brought me news that my boys were alive. She asked me to go and bring a letter to her fiancé, who was hidden by these people. I had to go. I was rewarded generously. I met people who became so much more than just acquaintances in my life.

I stayed in the ghetto until January 4th. We were not part of the kibbutz any longer. We separated into a few groups. I traveled to Warsaw to meet some "Shomer" [organizer] who arranged for a baptismal certificate for me. We didn't have too much money anymore. The boys left about forty thousand zloty and some dollars—all of it was sewn into the lining of a jacket, which they had to abandon in the steel mill, when they were deported. All we had left was what I had.

Number 28
When I escaped the Częstochowa Aktion, I had to pay one thousand zloty for the birth certificate. The boys begged me to go to Parczew to find out what had happened to their sisters. The End.

[*Probably added by Mr. Brust who copied the original*]
"Taken to Germany for forced labor as a Polish woman; worked in agriculture in the vicinity of Hanover."

APPENDIX 2:

A Diary in Note Form

This last section appears to have been written at a different time or as separate diary—it is rather disorganized and random; perhaps Ita was trying to recreate the diary she kept in Warsaw, which she had burned before leaving there.

2.[1]

No one is like they are. After invading a country, they chased and displaced the Jews from one place to another. During these transfer actions there were dozens of victims. Later they formed labor camps for Jews, which were not labor camps but death camps. For three years all men aged sixteen to sixty were in these camps. The rest were packed into a ghetto walled up by a two-meter-high wall. In smaller towns instead of brick walls, they surrounded the ghetto with barbed wire. In these ghettos thousands of Jews died of starvation. Mostly these were people brought in from small towns, who lost all their possessions. Others got rich on their misery. In the end they built a place called Treblinka! Remember Treblinka! This is the place where they murdered the Jews.

3.

It is the original gas chamber invented with such duplicity, where human beings are gassed and burned and turned into ashes. Treblinka is a mass grave of seven million Jews [sic.]. Actually, this is a second location. In the place where the gas chambers were originally, there was such a stench from the gassed bodies that they had to move it. They found a place, where no one lives nearby and that is surrounded by forests. They moved it there, these butchers. And this is Treblinka. There are other gas chambers like that: in Majdanek near Lublin, but smaller in scope and not only for Jews. They started the mass murder of Jews in Poland in the beginning of 1942. First

---

1   This is the numbering as found in the diary.

was Lublin—they did it in such a devious way that no one knew where these people were taken. A few thousand were killed right there.

4.

Two thousand were placed in Majdan near Lublin, and the rest they put into freight trains, like cattle, and took to Treblinka. There all were murdered; my sister Henia with her husband and her one-year-old son were murdered there. Some people ran away to Warsaw or other localities, and they perished there. Of our dearest, the first one to be killed was Sara. The Warsaw Ghetto was being destroyed a few months after Lublin. It started in July 1942. Mińsk Mazowiecki was quiet at that time. Our cousins: Fryda, Henia, Moshe—they were doing well. When the murderous Aktion started in Warsaw, or as it was called "resettlements to the east"—no one realized that Treblinka existed. The elderly were most endangered at first, and we thought about our parents. They lied to us that the young people would not be sent away, because working people...

4. [double numbering]

... would not be deported. We sent a telegram to Mińsk Mazowiecki asking them to take our parents and me. Sara was with Kuba and his parents, and they didn't want to think about leaving. I didn't want to part from my dearest Sara, but it was very difficult to part from our beloved father. I decided to stay with our parents till the end. After all Sara had Kuba. A week after the start of the deportation Aktion in Warsaw, Fryda sent a car from Mińsk to take us. It just so happened that at this very moment I was hidden in some basement at a different location, and I wasn't able to reach home. The German gendarmes armed with machine guns were standing in the street and rounding up people for deportation. When I finally reached home, our parents had already left. The car couldn't wait for me, and they had to go. Sara was the one to take them to the car. I didn't even have a chance to say goodbye. Our dear father had to agree to go. I accepted the situation, and I was very happy when we received a letter from them...

5.

... that they are fine, and everything was quiet there. We had it much worse, and it was becoming more difficult to hide. The German murderers had many henchmen. They organized a special unit to conduct the murder of Jews. They took Ukrainians for this. On the inside they had Jewish accomplices, Jewish police. Right after they created the ghetto, they appointed a Jewish Council and a Jewish police force. These people later brought their own parents, brothers, and sisters for destruction.

I held on to Sara—we had only each other and Kuba. I wished that whatever would happen to them should happen to me. This accursed fate again decided otherwise. They manipulated and distracted us, so we wouldn't figure out what they were doing to us. They deceived us every step of the way. When they announced that only the elderly would be resettled, they gave us hope for survival.

6.

They cheated us by saying that the young people working for them would live and they created workshops. Later they took the employed laborers and made them live in the factories, so Sara had to go with Kuba, and I had to stay with my husband. Later it didn't matter, and the wives were not protected any longer, so the women and children were taken to the trains. There were some seven hundred thousand Jews in the Warsaw Ghetto.[2] Six thousand Jews were deported daily; probably the machines in Treblinka couldn't take more. My dearest Sara went first. The factory where Kuba worked was surrounded and they took Sara. Kuba wanted to go with her, but they brutally pushed him away, just because he wanted to go. They took other men. For three more days I had no idea what had happened, because I couldn't go out.

7.

They caught everyone who was in the street, and the building I was in was safe. The head of the Jewish police lived in this building and other Jewish Gestapo operatives. There were enough traitors among the Jews. For the first four weeks this building was safe.

Before the big Aktion started, two boys from Parczew came to us. Piniek and Abe Fajgenbaum. Mania, you visited them once. They had to flee from the Gestapo, which had taken their father and was after them. They fled to Warsaw. They lived with us till the start of the big Aktion in Warsaw. At the beginning of the mass deportations, we moved in with Sara, because we wanted to be all together. The boys went to live with their cousins Rojza and Chaja from Chełm. I'm sure that you and Justin knew the one who lived in the house I mentioned. My father moved to Warsaw after the Jews of Jeziorna were deported. My father issued a fictional Ktubah for me and the older brother, Piniek.

---

2   The actual number was four hundred and sixty thousand at its highest point in April 1941, see Engelking and Leociak, *The Warsaw Ghetto: A Guide to the Perished City*, 49.

8.

Piniek worked in some workshop. When Sara had to stay with Kuba in his factory, I moved in with the boys and I was safe there. I begged Sara many times to move in with me into this building, because it was a safe place. She didn't want to listen to me. I couldn't enter the factory where Kuba worked. For three days no one said a thing, but after three days I couldn't take it anymore, being without news from her and I made my way to Sara's place. That's when I found out about the tragedy. Kuba didn't even look like a human being. I have no idea how I got back to the boys' place. I think Piniek carried me in, and I was unconscious for twenty-four hours. I am not sure how I didn't go mad. I was alone. I was hurt so deeply that it seemed to me that I would not be able to live with this pain. I didn't even know that Sara had been taken to her death. There were rumors that the trains were carrying people to an unknown locality, where the elderly, sick, children, and the handicapped were killed.

9.

The rumors said that young people had to give up all their possessions and that they were given paper clothing with a number for each of them, and then they were sent to camps for hard labor. This was enough to make you crazy, but it didn't even occur to me that they had murdered Sara. I am not sure what day it was that Sara was taken, but it must have been in the middle of August 1942. I became indifferent as to what would happen to me. I knew that I couldn't reach our parents in Mińsk Mazowiecki. A few days after they took my Sara away, they deported my sister Fryda, with her husband Kogut and their four-year-old son and her husband's whole family—maybe twenty people. Chaim Shloyme Fajgenbaum was already deported as well, and his children were completely lost. Wherever you turned, all you saw was desperation and corpses in the streets. The Kodenczyk family was gone too. Of my entire family, only Kuba was left and my father with his wife, my youngest sister, and two of their youngest sons. They were together with Chaja's husband and her ten-year-old daughter.

10.

Chaja was so lucky that she had died of typhus a few months earlier.

Because Kuba worked in a German factory, at first Sara was protected from deportation. I had a fictitious husband who had a job in one of the workshops, but two weeks after our parents left, the rules changed.

Every factory or workshop had to take in their workers and place them in factory dorms. Sewing workshops, shoemaking workshops, and others;

people were obsessed with thoughts about how to get employment in one of these workshops. They didn't think about resistance and not giving up their parents, their wives, and their children. All that they thought about was a workplace where they would get one hundred fifty grams of bread and one liter of watery soup. Every father wanted to save his child and the young people wanted to save themselves. They all thought that these were deportations for hard labor, and no one knew that it was to death. The Jewish Council assured us that this is a resettlement and that the rumors that the trains take the people to death were a lie. At first, they didn't take everyone—just that the Ukrainians, Germans, and the Jewish police surrounded whole blocks and all the residents had to come out of their apartments. They were forced onto horse-drawn wagons or on foot they were driven to the Umschlagplatz under armed guard. In this square they forced people—two hundred into each train car and hermetically locked the doors. The trains took them away. At that time, they said that all the people were taken to the Pińsk marshlands, but today we know that they took them to Treblinka.

Documents, Photographs, and Artifacts Donated to the USHMM by the Dimant Family

Ita Dimant:

    Acc. Number: 1998.A.0258.2 (Series 2, Box 3) Ita Rozencwajg-Dimant Diary 1943-1945 (Polish)

    Acc. Number: 1998.A.0258.2 (Series 1, Box 1.1-1.2) Wartime correspondence with the Brust family (Polish)

    Acc. Number: 1998.A.0258.2 (Series 2, Box 1.13) The Brust diary undated (Polish)

    Acc. Number: 1998.A.0258.2 (Series 2, Box 2.1) Ita's Memoir 1993 (English)

    Acc. Number: 1998.A.0258.2 (Series 2, Box 2.3) Ita's Memoir 1993 (Hebrew translation)

    Acc. Number: 1998.A.0258.2 (Series 3, Box 2.7) False identification documents for Ita Rozencwajg as Genowefa Zawadska/Sawadska, 1943-1944

    Acc. Number: 1998.A.0258.2 (Series 3, Box 2.9) Photographs, 1932-1971

    Acc. Number: 2016.561.1 False tooth of Ita Dimant that once contained a cyanide capsule

    RG-50.002.0209 Oral History with Ita Dimant

Symcha Dimant:

Acc. Number: **1993.34.1** Striped concentration camp uniform jacket

Acc. Number: **1993.34.6, 7, 8** Buchenwald Standort-Kantine concentration camp scrip, 1 RM

Acc. Number: **2014.461.2** Red and white patch worn by Polish-Jewish Buchenwald inmates

Acc. Number: **2014.461.3** White patch with prisoner number worn by a Polish-Jewish inmate

Acc. Number: **2014.461.4** Yellow warning skull and crossbones pennant from Buchenwald

Acc. Number: **2014.461.5** *Reichsadler* insignia found after the liberation of Buchenwald

USHMMPA no. 95314 Prisoner card for Symcho Dymant at Buchenwald no. 15349

Acc. Number: **1993.34.13** Series 1 Biographical materials of Symcha Dymant 1936-1945, e.g.: Invitation to the wedding of Symcho Dymant and Tonia Wargon, August 23, 1936

Photograph of Symcho and Tonia Dymant, November 17, 1936

Letter written to Karl Wargon in New York, May 21, 1943 (German)

Post-war travel documents issued by the Allied Expeditionary Force, Germany 1945

RG-50.754.0001 Audiotape of Buchenwald survivors' memoirs, 1965

APPENDIX 4:

Miodownik Family Tree

Courtesy of Marian Alster (the son of Rachelka)

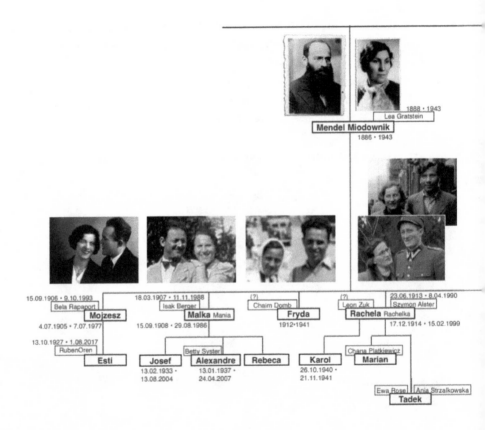

MIODOWNIK

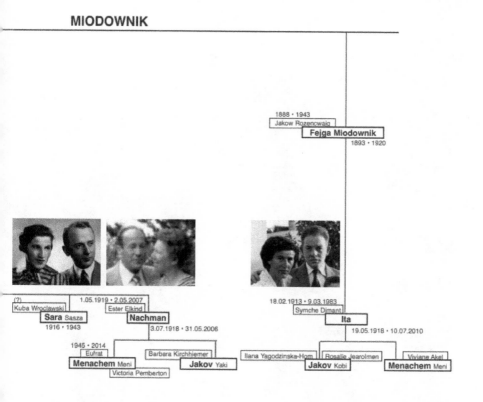

1888 · 1943
Jakow Rozencwajg

Fejga Miodownik
1893 · 1920

(?)
Kuba Wroclawski

1.05.1919 · 2.05.2007
Ester Elkind

18.02.1913 · 9.03.1983
Symche Dimant

Sara Sasza
1916 · 1943

Nachman

Ita

3.07.1918 · 31.05.2006

19.05.1918 · 10.07.2010

1945 · 2014
Eufrat

Barbara Kirchhiemer

Ilana Yagodzinska-Hom

Rosalie Jearolmen

Viviane Akel

Menachem Meni

Jakov Yaki

Jakov Kobi

Menachem Meni

Victoria Pemberton

List of Illustrations

Figure 1. Ita Rozencwajg with her half-brother Shimon, Warsaw, April 1939.
United States Holocaust Memorial Museum (USHMM) Archives, Acc. Number: 1998.A.0258.2 (Series 3, Box 2.9, no. 44), courtesy of Jacob Dimant.

Figure 2. Ita Rozencwajg sits outside in the yard with her uncle Menachem-Mendel Miodownik on a visit to Mińsk Mazowiecki in 1939.
Unites States Holocaust Memorial Museum Photo Archives (USHMMPA), no. 28505, courtesy of Ita Rozencwajg Dimant.

Figure 3. Ita Rozencwajg with Nachman Miodownik walking down a street in Warsaw, 1938.
USHMM Archives, Acc. Number: 1998.A.0258.2 (Series 3, Box 2.9, no. 6), courtesy of Jacob Dimant.

Figure 4. Ita Rozencwajg with her half-sister Henia walking down a street in Warsaw, 1938.
USHMMPA, no. 28507, courtesy of Ita Rozencwajg Dimant.

Figure 5. Sara (Sarenka) Miodownik and her husband Kuba Wrocławski.
USHMM, Acc. Number: 1998.A.0258.2 (Series 3, Box 2.9, no. 50), courtesy of Jacob Dimant.

Figure 6. Group portrait of Jewish preschoolers in the kindergarten established by Ita Rozencwajg in the Warsaw Ghetto.
USHMMPA, no. 28513, courtesy of Ita Rozencwajg Dimant.

Figure 7. Aba (Abe) Fajgenbaum, Parczew, c. 1940.
Photograph courtesy of Sarah Halabe-Levine, his niece.

Figure 8. Pinhas (Piniek) Fajgenbaum, Parczew, c. 1940.
Photograph courtesy of Sarah Halabe-Levine, his niece.

Figure 9. Ita Rozencwajg with her half-sister, Henia, at Henia's wedding in March 1939.
USHMM, Acc. Number: 1998.A.0258.2 (Series 3, Box 2.9, no. 52), courtesy of Jacob Dimant.

Figure 10. Ita Rozencwajg with her niece, Fajgele Erdman, Warsaw Ghetto, 1942.
USHMM, Acc. Number: 1998.A.0258.2 (Series 3, Box 2.9, no. 42), courtesy of Jacob Dimant.

Figure 11. Ita Rozencwajg performs exercises with the children in the kindergarten she established in the Warsaw Ghetto.
USHMMPA, no. 26802, courtesy of Ita Rozencwajg Dimant.

Figure 12. German ID Card for Genowefa Zawadska in Tschenstochau, 1943.
USHMM, Acc. Number: 1998.A.0258.2 (Series 3, Box 2.7, no. 6), courtesy of Jacob Dimant.

Figure 13. Portrait of Polish rescuer Stefan Gromuł holding his infant child in 1943.
USHMMPA, no. 28504, courtesy of Ita Rozencwajg Dimant.

Figure 14. Henryk Brust and his wife Aniela Brust (sitting) with their daughter Ala at a reception in their honor in the Dutch Embassy in Warsaw, 1981.
USHMM, Acc. Number: 1998.A.0258.2 (Series 3, Box 2.9, no. 74), courtesy of Jacob Dimant.

Figure 15. Forged Baptismal Certificate for Genowefa Zawadska, born in Sieradz, 1922.
USHMM, Acc. Number: 1998.A.0258.2 (Series 3, Box 2.7, no. 1), courtesy of Jacob Dimant.

Figure 16. German Work Card for Genowefa Zawadska, 1943-1944 (front).
USHMM, Acc. Number: 1998.A.0258.2 (Series 3, Box 2.7, no. 3), courtesy of Jacob Dimant.

Figure 17. German Work Card for Genowefa Sawadska, 1943-1944 (back).

USHMM, Acc. Number: 1998.A.0258.2 (Series 3, Box 2.7, no. 4), courtesy of Jacob Dimant.

Figure 18. Ita and Symcha Dymant in Israel with their two sons Jacob (right) and Menachem (center), circa 1957.

Photo courtesy of Jacob Dimant.

Figure 19. Symcha Dymant with his first wife, Tonia Wargon, who was murdered in Treblinka with their child. This photo is dated November 17, 1936, shortly after their child, Aaron, was born.

USHMM, Acc. Number: 1993.34.13, courtesy of Jacob Dimant.

Figure 20. Prisoner Card from Buchenwald for Symcho Dymant no. 15349, issued on December 24, 1944. The card notes in red ink that this Jewish prisoner was registered by a Hollerith Machine, which was a primitive computer made for Nazi Germany by IBM. The Nazis used it to keep track of the prisoners in concentration camps.

USHMMPA, no. 95314, courtesy of Jacob Dimant.

Index

Contributors

Ita Dimant (née Rozencwajg) was born in Piaseczno, Poland in 1918. She ran a kindergarten in the Warsaw ghetto, from which escaped in 1942, before being deported to Germany as a forced laborer. After the war she lived in Israel and the United States. The diary records her experiences during the Holocaust.

Martin Dean holds a PhD in History from Cambridge University. He worked previously as a war crimes investigator and is now a historical consultant. He has edited and translated several books and is the author of four monographs, including *Robbing the Jews* (2008), which won a National Jewish Book Award.

Jacob Dimant, Ita and Symcha Dimant's son, holds an MD from Hebrew University in Jerusalem and is a Clinical Professor of Medicine at New York University's Grossman School of Medicine.

Teresa Pollin served for many years as a curator for the United States Holocaust Memorial Museum and is fluent in Polish, English, Yiddish, and Hebrew. She translated the diary using the handwritten Polish originals donated by the Dimant family to the USHMM.

Printed in the USA
CPSIA information can be obtained
at www.ICGtesting.com
JSHW081212280923
49282JS00002B/2